Greek Tragedy and Contemporary Democracy

Greek Tragedy and Contemporary Democracy

Mark Chou

B L O O M S B U R Y
NEW YORK · LONDON · NEW DELHI · SYDNEY

Bloomsbury Academic
An imprint of Bloomsbury Publishing Plc

1385 Broadway	50 Bedford Square
New York	London
NY 10018	WC1B 3DP
USA	UK

www.bloomsbury.com

Bloomsbury is a registered trade mark of Bloomsbury Publishing Plc

First published 2012
Paperback edition first published 2013

Library of Congress Cataloging-in-Publication Data
A catalog record for this book is available from the Library of Congress.

ISBN: HB: 978-1-4411-7188-7
      PB: 978-1-6289-2250-9
      ePDF: 978-1-4411-7830-5
      ePUB: 978-1-4411-9048-2

Typeset by Deanta Global Publishing Services, Chennai, India

Contents

Acknowledgements

Before beginning, a short word of thanks to the handful of individuals whose kindness and encouragement made this work possible. First, I am indebted to Roland Bleiker, a mentor and friend in the truest sense. Second, to the small group of scholars and friends who urged me to go on when all I wanted to do is stop. Here, I'd particularly like to thank Seb Kaempf, Emma Hutchison, Luke Glanville, Katrina Lee-Koo, Michael Ure, Robin Cameron, Tim Aistrope, Heloise Weber, Richard Devetak, and of course Leah Aylward. The names of these individuals may be absent from the pages that follow. But their influence is not.

This book has now gone through more drafts than I can remember. But imperfect as it remains in content and in form, a fault that is mine alone, it is what it is today only because individuals like Stephen Chan, Costas Constantinou, Kim Huynh, and a select anonymous few took the time to give what they could to help me see what I had not seen. I will always be in your debt.

I'd also like to take this opportunity to acknowledge Marie-Claire Antoine, my editor at Continuum, who gladly took this project on; the School of Political Science and International Studies at the University of Queensland and the School of Social and Political Sciences at the University of Melbourne where this project first began and is now drawing to an end; and the McKenzie Postdoctoral Fellowship scheme at the University of Melbourne which gave me the time and space to complete this project.

Finally, none of this could have been possible without my family, who continue to support my study and forgive my long absences away from home, even during the difficult times. The past few years have seen some change in our family. I moved away from Canberra. My Grandma passed away. My Dad single-handedly rebuilt our house (with the help of some lovely but truly dodgy builders), which is now gigantic, before retiring after more than 40 years of work. And then my Mum was diagnosed with cancer. Since then, my Dad and my Sister, who is a credit to our entire family, have sacrificed so much to give her the best care possible. But the best care possible is not always enough in these circumstances, and not a day goes by that they don't fear for the worst. Still, today at least, we're all hopeful for the best. And finally, to Bec, thanks for continuing to go on pho dates with me!

Earlier versions of several chapters within this book were first published elsewhere in other forms and formats: Mark Chou and Roland Bleiker, "The Symbiosis of Democracy and Tragedy: Lost Lessons from Ancient Greece," *Millennium: Journal of International Studies* (Vol. 37, No. 3, 2009): 659–682; Mark Chou, "Democracy in an Age of Tragedy: Democracy, Tragedy and Paradox," *Critical Horizons: A Journal of Philosophy and Social Theory* (Vol. 11, No. 2, 2010): 289–313; Mark Chou, "Postmodern Dramaturgy, Premodern Drama: The Global Resurgence of Greek Tragedy Today," *Journal for Cultural Research* (Vol. 15, No. 2, 2011): 131–152. I thank each publisher for giving me permission to include the content within this book.

Introduction: Democracy and Tragedy

It was a late November evening in 2004 when, at the close of a State Theatre Company of South Australia performance of Euripides' drama *The Trojan Women*, an unexpected cry pierces the theatre's silence. A woman, who had shifted from her seat in the auditorium's lower balcony, suddenly shouts out to the departing crowd that 'this' – referring to Euripides' tragedy about the violent conquest and occupation of a local population by a mighty foreign army – 'is what's happening in Falugia today'. Fingers pointed visibly at the stage, she makes the point to those still seated in the theatre that '[w]e should be ashamed' of what we are doing in Iraq today. 'It's our troops, in Iraq', she continues, 'now, killing women and children'.

Ruth Thompson, a theatre critic who sat through the night's performance, recounts the events that followed.[1] As she recalls, startled or maybe just buoyed by the woman's offhand remarks, 'concurring cries of "Shame! Shame!"' arose throughout the theatre. Soon, more and more people began to speak up, until the theatre filled with their applause and their murmurings 'about our collective responsibility as electors of the current government; as citizens of a country that had sent its troops to an "illegal war"; that we must not passively allow it to continue'. Though there was nothing like a formal resolution to act, and certainly no overt political references made during the performance, a chorus of citizen viewers did arise that night to voice dissatisfaction and dissent. What Thompson remembers quite clearly then was a collective if not democratic spirit emerge; one that, fleeting as it was, caused the vast majority of theatregoers following the night's performance to unite in a collective 'Here, here'.

When Thompson later relayed these events to Rosalba Clemente, the Australian playwright and director who was responsible for producing the Euripidean tragedy, her reaction was surprising in that she did not seem at all surprised. 'Good. Good' was Clemente's response. As Thompson notes, on hearing the democratic tone of the audiences' response to the tragedy, Clemente went on to surmise that 'I feel now that I've done my job'. For her to say these words the implication was almost that, even in a context and for an audience largely removed from the classics of the ancient world, a Greek tragedy like Euripides' *The Trojan Women* might still have the potential to speak politically. Additionally, there may also be something unique to the tragedies of ancient Greece that makes them apt to arouse democratic sensitivities today just as the tragedies of Aeschylus, Sophocles and Euripides had done so during democracy's first high point in ancient Athens some two-and-half millennia ago.

But that, of course, is a minority view. Today, it is almost unheard of in everyday political debates for democracy to be associated with tragedy or for tragedy to stimulate democratic debates. Unlike the ancient Greeks to whom we attribute the birth of Western democracy, we do not turn to their tales of tragedy (even though we may continue to turn readily to their teachings on politics and philosophy) when seeking to revitalize our own democratic politics. That symbiosis, between democracy and tragedy, may have been vital then. Now, in more modern times, choosing to see tragedy as a democratic art form seems nothing short of a political nonsense.

At one level, this is understandable. The world we inhabit, the political challenges we face and the types of institutions we require to ensure the smooth functioning of our increasingly globalized society are vastly different from the demands faced by the ancient Greeks. We think, act and live as humans separated by two-and-a-half millennia of historical development.

Yet, even if we were to take these differences into account, and ignore for one moment the temporal gulf that separates now from then, the allure of Greece still remains audible. Which is why, even today, there are political scientists and international relations scholars who number among those writing about democracy and tragedy – often returning to ancient Greece as they do so.[2] Sophisticated as the scholarship is though, what is habitually missed or missing in this literature is an effort to explicitly revive the intrinsic link that existed between democracy and tragedy. In order to learn something of that link, we are often forced to look further afield, particularly to studies carried out in philology and cultural history.[3] Thus, what this seems to suggest is that, despite the political fascination that Greek democracy and tragedy still hold for us, we are no longer as convinced by the political significance of their symbiosis. One consequence of this separation is that now, when asked the question 'What has Athens to do with Washington?', our answers often tend to be partial and thus incomplete.[4]

Taking the centrality of tragic drama to the development and growth of democracy in both ancient Athens and today seriously, the goal of this book is to offer an answer to the above question that avoids the dual pitfalls of partiality and incompleteness. To do so, it asks a number of critical questions, all of which attempt to get at and unravel one fundamental puzzle, which is: why, given its role in the development of democracy, does tragedy play no part in contemporary discourses and practices of democracy?

Why, in other words, are we no longer interested in finding out what it was about democracy in ancient Athens that encouraged, and even needed, the ascendancy of tragedy? Why is it now considered politically beside the point for our own democratic initiatives to understand how the mass performance of tragic drama represented democratic politics? And why can it appear disingenuous to ask whether tragedy might be a useful source for keeping democracy flexible in today's rapidly changing age of globalization, now that we are faced with urgent struggles for popular rule in places as disparate as Egypt, China, Libya and the United States?

These sorts of questions animate this book, which is but a small contribution to the broader literature seeking to foreground concepts and practices that have been overlooked by today's democratic thinkers and activists. In reviving the long forgotten link between democracy and tragedy, it holds the core conviction that there is a great deal to this ancient symbiosis that can offer highly relevant insights for today's global democratic challenges. In particular, it argues that current efforts to re-envision democracy in global terms and to extend its practices into communities and procedures that have erstwhile resisted democratization can benefit greatly from reading tragedy's so-called multivocal form as a democratic text.

Ensuring the global advancement of democracy at the local, national and international levels is both a gargantuan and unprecedented undertaking. But in the age of globalization, it is also an increasingly necessary undertaking. Today, more and more citizens the world over are affected by forces that lie both beyond their control and beyond their sovereign borders. As David Held once said, the processes of globalization have fundamentally altered how politics is conducted at all levels, from the local and national to the international level.[5] Democracy, long considered the sole preserve of the nation-state, is now failing to keep pace with porous political communities and the ever-expanding intensity of cross-border flows. The monopoly of political power is dispersed and increasingly shared among national governments and an array of sub- and inter-national actors and conglomerates. How a nation-state – and the citizens therein – effectively conducts its domestic affairs and pursues its national interests no longer rests solely on the decisions and aspirations of the political community involved. Localized political, economic and cultural power has become progressively eroded by and dispersed among transnational corporations and organizations. As a result, citizenship, free and fair elections that are held from time to time, as well as the access to official forums of decision making are no longer in themselves sufficient barometers for what constitutes adequate democratic franchise. Because political decisions now have the potential to impact upon individuals and nations far removed from the corridors of powers where those decisions were made, it is crucial for everyday citizens to find a global voice.

Unfortunately, there are few institutions of democracy and no democratic ethos that are really fit to tackle this task. Instead, democratic principles, procedures and institutions remain wedded, almost exclusively, to the nation-state, especially those in the West. The institutions that shape global politics, from international organizations, transnational corporations to NGOs, are neither entirely transparent nor accountable to a truly global democratic constituency. They fail to take into account the realities of those whose perspectives and demands are least frequently heard. And they are incapable of effectively dealing with the fluctuating and unfamiliar aspects of our world. With few specifically tailored ideas and initiatives at our disposal capable of assisting the promotion of democracy in a manner that is reverential to local customs, national interests and international demands, it is little wonder that affairs of the economy and politics, of security and the environment, continue to remain matters largely unreflective of the interests of all but the world's elite.[6]

Spurred on by these global developments, scholars, policymakers and practitioners have begun to debate how best to extend the institutions and procedures of democratic deliberation so that they are better able to do justice to the ever-intersecting local, national and international interests.[7] This is an endeavour which has no concrete guiding precedent. While it may be the case today that democracy at the domestic level has become an established and indispensable governing tool, democracy on a more global scale remains an altogether different affair. This is not just a task that seeks the creation of new institutions and procedures, but it also seeks an effective ethos of democracy with the power to include actors and aspirations both known and unknown in a global environment that is, at the same time, expanding and collapsing in on itself.

Like democracy in classical Greece, therefore, the prospect of a democracy on this global scale is a new and even revolutionary idea. With no prior principles or past practices to guide the creation of a politics of popular participation at the global level, the challenges we face are, in many ways, as novel as those faced by the ancient Athenians when they first engaged in democratic politics. Given this, their experience may be politically incisive because they were the first to found democracy in a political context where no such ideas and practices had previously existed. What can we learn from the ancients and how they grappled with the never before experienced questions associated with 'democratic excess'?[8] By expanding democracy to the courts, festivals, marketplaces and, of course, to the theatre, they soon heard voices beyond the official political purview. Yet, what they recognized as invaluable, praised as incisive and celebrated with all their souls and minds, we in more modern times have seemingly abandoned – even as our own aspirations for more egalitarian, fruitful and inclusive democracies remain and intensify.

Tragedy's multivocal form: The lessons for democracy today

But even if we were to reorient our views, would the peculiar institution of tragic drama really have anything to say to contemporary democratic efforts? This book argues that it does. Tragedy, it will show, has a great deal to say that is politically relevant today. This is so for the simple reason that it captured the ethos of the ancient Greeks' nascent democracy, which was the ethos of the West's very first great democracy. To the Greeks, tragedy dramatized the insight that no single voice or way of life was absolute and wholly true; that even the greatest among them was not all great and all wise. This, among other things, was a democratic reminder that men and women in their hubris will continue to tempt fate and, in so doing, overstep their individual limits.

When Athens first became a democracy, tragedy was quick to guide the newly empowered citizens through their first definitive attempt to found democratic institutions and procedures against a context where no such ideas and practices had previously existed. Faced with a similar predicament, we too might be able to draw on the democratic insights of the Greeks' tragedy in order to come to grips with our own political and cultural transformations, not to mention the cries for more radical and inclusive forms of political participation.

In particular, this book makes the case that the most politically relevant insight of the symbiosis of democracy and tragedy stems from tragedy's so-called multivocal form – that is, the ability of tragedy to bring a variety of otherwise marginalized stories, characters and voices onto the public stage and into democratic debate. Such an insight has the potential to teach contemporary democrats seeking to extend the institutions and procedures of democracy globally, two novel lessons. The first is the understanding that the idea and practice of democracy must never be solely concerned with the institution of order in political life. Tragedy teaches us the lesson that while order is necessary for a stable and productive communal existence, sites of disorder likewise provide insights into dilemmas posed by political instability, inequality, exclusion and flux. A truly democratic order must seek to include and give voice to democratic disorder. The second lesson drawn from tragedy's multivocal form is that both 'factual' and 'fictional' sources of knowledge can be potentially valuable when seeking to negotiate and overcome complex democratic dilemmas. Only by broadening the scope of reality, by resorting to what has been delegitimized as political fictions, can democrats hope to legitimate a variety of otherwise marginalized stories, characters and voices today.

In essence then, the argument put forward in this book is made up of three core tenets. In what remains of this chapter and the chapters that follow, these tenets will be systematically explored and developed.

Underlying premise: Greek tragedy was an intrinsically democratic art form

The first core tenet is that of the underlying premise for returning to Athens, which is based on the claim that tragedy was an intrinsically democratic art form that spoke to democratic concerns unlike any other medium.[9] In the aftermath of the Athenian democratic revolution, tragedy emerged as a fundamental if alternate site of democratic politics.[10] For many, tragedy was the site where both the spirit and the practice of democracy were truly given life.[11] Not only was it more politically inclusive than Athens' democratic Assembly, it also drew more people, attracting crowds of up to 20,000 from all across the ancient world.[12] With business halted, the city would pause to participate in this public event that, for Richard Ned Lebow, 'almost certainly stimulated post-performance discussions among citizens about the issues that it raised on stage.'[13]

In this sense, the institution of tragedy became elevated by democracy to check the democratic forces being unleashed. Through their fictional dramatizations, tragedians were tasked with the job of scrutinizing the interplay between order and disorder, something which became politically important in the aftermath of the democratic revolution. To the Athenians, democracy was not only an 'ad hoc invention' but also an unstable form of governance that destabilized the aristocratic order and opened the door to the previously unknown and unheard.[14] Propelled by a sense of radical independence, it could be said that what distinguished the Athenians' democracy was more, not less, paradox. Democracy, in other words, was premised on the palpable realization that uncertainty and openness are as crucial to communal life as certainty and closure. Indeed, according to Cornelius Castoriadis' reading of classical democracy,

> [i]f a full and certain knowledge (*épisteme*) of the human domain were possible, politics would immediately come to an end, and democracy would be both impossible and absurd: democracy implies that all citizens have the possibility of attaining a correct *doxa* [common belief] and that nobody possesses an *épisteme* of things political.[15]

Thus, by refuting any definitive endpoint or absolute knowledge, democratic politics had as its aim to produce a delicate balance between the aspiration for diversity and the pursuit of absolute knowledge.

The tragic dramas of Aeschylus, Sophocles and Euripides, each in their own ways, dramatized the paradoxical nature of existence that emerged under democracy. As a whole though, their dramatic representations transformed 'political pursuits into a pleasurable sensual experience', making 'the otherwise unbearable bearable and inconceivable conceivable'.[16] The world depicted through tragedy was one of marked heterogeneity and tension, of characters and circumstances enticed by glory and wrought with chaos.[17] Through its diverse cast of characters and the raft of differing ideological beliefs entertained, these dramas revealed to the polis that there is never absolute knowledge or truth in just one voice.[18] The only truth that exists is this: that all things great, risk demise and chance destruction. Even great heroic figures like Antigone, Oedipus or Pelasgus, because of their own wisdom or lack thereof, can come undone. At their lowest, having given of their highest, these individuals all arrive at the realization that the self is never sufficient, that knowledge is at best partial. There is a need for the insight and the aid of others, even if this provides no guarantees. In this new political space, a uniquely open and dramatic forum for public debate was thus generated.[19] Through these tragic plays, old and new voices, even strange and uncomfortable perspectives from outside the Greek world, were given centre stage – encapsulating the unstable but truly democratic spirit.

There was, in this sense, something uniquely democratic about tragedy. At the cusp of the democratic world order, tragedy stepped into the breach, soon developing into an official democratic forum. Playing on Old World tensions in novel ways, tragedians reminded audiences that even the greatest among them was not all great and of how easily the known order of things can come undone. Articulated away from the pressures of everyday existence, where the limitations of reality were suspended, each member of the audience was urged to reflect upon and empathize with each other's imperfections. As these insights reinforced democracy's message, they were inflected back into the polis, seeping into democracy's other institutions and practices as an important check and balance.

Central contention: Greek tragedy's multivocal form dramatized the democratic interplay between order and disorder and reality and fiction

That tragedy could so aptly intervene in democratic politics and highlight concerns overlooked by democrats in reality was due largely to its so-called multivocal form. Specifically, the book contends that it was tragedy's multivocal form – its ability to bring a variety of otherwise marginalized stories, characters and voices onto the public stage and into democratic debate – which reaffirmed a crucial democratic interplay that was implicit in the rise of democracy though not always realized through it thereafter: the insight that order and disorder and reality and fiction are inextricably wedded together.

Coined by the classics scholar Edith Hall, the term 'the multivocal form' denotes Greek tragedy's ambit to dramatize a wide range of stories, characters and voices that may have been, at different points and in different guises, reverberating around the polis.[20] This was done to politicize what official political institutions and statesmen had rendered unpolitical. Despite being lauded in contemporary popular culture as an age of equality and freedom, Athens was probably more often than not a hotbed of xenophobia, patriarchy, imperialism and slavery.[21] For all its advances, democracy had severe limits. Reflective of this was the fact that democracy extended only to the citizen, which at the time did not incorporate women, youths, slaves and foreign residents.[22] Such individuals could not participate, vote or rule in the polis. A crucial function of tragedy was to give voice to these individuals and the issues that mattered most to them. Through its multivocal form, tragedy pierced the glossy surfaces of the Athenians' ordered reality by bringing to stage dissident figures and anathema topics at one of the key political events in democratic Athens. And while social and political inequalities were not always or immediately removed – not by a long shot – more stories, characters and voices did enter democratic politics as a result.

This had the effect of influencing democratic politics in two ways. First, tragedy's multivocal form reaffirmed the democratic interplay between order and disorder through its call to continuously defy every closed system of thought. And this was key because democracy was founded precisely on this crucial interplay. Being the first system of governance that gave the once disenfranchised masses a direct voice in the governing of the city, democracy deployed its institutions and procedures of participation to incite disorder within the polis. But radical as it was, democracy was ultimately no different from any other political system in the sense that the appeal to understand, know and control reality, in short the appeal to give order to reality, can quickly overshadow and even subsume the open search for disorder. And so, particularly when democracy could not reinvigorate closed systems of thought – its own included – tragedy became an institution capable of prompting audiences to stay open both to what was known and to what was unknown. When democratic politics had reached its limits, tragedy's multivocal form went further by bringing disorder into the Athenians' midst through a dramatization of otherwise marginalized stories, characters and voices.

But, tragedy's multivocal form could only do this because it operated in the realm of fiction as well as in the realm of reality. Or more precisely, tragedy drew from reality, often metaphorically, to comment on the limits of political reality without necessarily succumbing to it. Past myths were reinterpreted by tragedians to educate audiences about the new political complexities they were facing. This was the second way that tragedy reinvigorated democracy in Athens: by reminding democrats that legitimate sources of democratic knowledge could be accessed through 'fictional' as well as 'factual' accounts. In a world where nothing seemed certain, where what was known was never fully known for a fact and where what was unknown formed the basis of legitimate political inquiry, the political resources that one had to draw on to understand reality were near limitless. Here, the contemporary dichotomy of reality and fiction, or of politics and imagination, which today we see as natural, had yet to be set down so definitively. The Greeks did not restrict themselves to the use of only rational methods to account for reality as we have been taught to do. On the contrary, they considered fictive sources just as legitimate and expedient as their non-fictional counterparts in the conduct of politics. It was normal – even prudent – to draw from political, philosophical and aesthetic sources in an attempt to resolve democratic dilemmas. Only by doing so could they think through and, where this was insufficient, creatively imagine what they had yet to grasp, what had yet to be discovered. The fictional aspect of tragedy's multivocal form enabled the Greeks to get into the heads of their adversaries, to understand better their own fractured emotions and to create new and more inclusive realities. Such was the 'classical moment' where, for a generation or two, the cultural roots of the West can be located.[23]

Implications for contemporary global democracy: Tragedy's multivocal form offers two crucial democratic lessons

But, as interesting as these ancient insights may be, we need to ask how investigating the democratic nature of tragedy's multivocal form can teach us anything about our own global democratic challenges. What, if anything, can the interplay between order and disorder and reality and fiction add to contemporary efforts seeking to extend and revitalize democracy?

To apprehend why the wisdom of Greece may be of use to us now, it is necessary to first recall what democracy has become today. Today, a dual tendency exists within prevailing democratic discourses, whether aggregative or deliberative, that first uncritically preferences order and rationality and then associates them with democratic politics and good governance. Rational discourse and procedures, it is argued, helps to establish an overarching order within the political realm. Accordingly, current proposals for global democracy – varied and many as they are – tend to share an implicit yet fundamental fixation on rational institutions and procedures and their ability to create a stable democratic order. However, this fixation on order and rational reality can be problematic to the extent that it severely restricts the legitimate means and methods that democrats have at their disposal to bring to light what is currently shrouded and silenced. A democracy that is premised solely on the creation of a rational political order in reality has acute limitations; it is just barely democratic and must be further democratized so as to truly enfranchise a multifarious global citizenry.

Examining tragedy's multivocal form speaks to this democratic predisposition in two ways. First, it reminds contemporary democrats that democracy should not be solely about the institution of order in political life but also about the recognition of disorder. Though it may seem strange, problematizing the dichotomy between order and disorder has explicit democratic benefits. This is particularly so in view of contemporary democracy's obsession with erecting a stable political order.

Unlike the Greeks, we tend to see the relationship between order and disorder 'as a series of exclusive dichotomies'.[24] And this is democratically enervating because order, writes the social and literary critic Katherine Hayles, generally connotes what can 'be classified, analysed, encompassed within rational discourse', whereas disorder is 'allied with chaos' or what 'by definition could not be expressed'.[25] By dispensing with what may seem chaotic or inexpressible in political life solely for what we can classify, analyse and encompass within rational discourse means that we can potentially overlook – for the fact that we cannot see – anything or anyone that threatens to disrupt our ordered realities. This, given our penchant for the latter – that is, our obsession with 'how order can be attained in the human community' – means a democratic deficit will likely ensue as a consequence.[26]

The point that is being made here is not that we must necessarily or always discard order in the search for disorder. After all, without order, neither meaningful human existence nor communal coexistence would be imaginable. Confusion, incomprehension and division would impede understanding, rationality and unity. But, it is precisely because our political obsession with the latter has become so totalizing that it now comes at the expense of all else. Our understanding of political reality too has become so entrenched and defined that it automatically excludes a diverse range of phenomena, experiences and individuals who threaten to undermine our sense of order. We have forgotten how the Greeks approached disorder; a signification that, for them, conjured the void or unknown from which all meaningful orders emerge.[27] Disorder, in this way, is simply what exists before a certain thing or phenomenon has been domesticated through rational faculties, before it has been systematically understood and controlled. In other words, disorder is just another way of denoting the array of otherwise incomprehensible and seemingly threatening entities and objects that we all live among. But, though intimidating, what is always possible in this state of becoming is change. Not only that, but alternatives to pre-existing conceptions can be located and then acted upon. And suppressed perspectives and foreign individuals – those who find themselves marginalized politically – can be heard. And so, in disorder what we uncover is not the absence of order as much as possible or differing notions of order: of what is yet unknown and possibly unknowable. Seen in this light and it becomes easy to fathom why political efforts to engage disorder merely amount to the recognition that in a democracy, what we do not know may be as important as what we do know. Those who have been empowered by political franchise, in short, have as much to say as those who are denied the right to speak and vote. Political efforts to enfranchise them should be key priorities within a democracy.

Such an understanding was what made democracy 'democratic' in the Greek sense: to know everything, everyone and their opposite. The ensuing result was a characteristic that has marked few democracies since: the search for the basic yet fragile equilibrium between what is and what is not.[28] This is something which no democracy should avoid.

But, partly because Greek democracy, as has already been stressed, was far from perfect in reality, tragedy was made to intervene in the polis through its multivocal form. As it did so, the dramatic representations reminded the masses that political instability, inequality, exclusion and flux are not incongruous with but constitutive of a stable and productive communal existence. The lesson in democracy, as such, was this: a democracy must, from time to time, look behind its veils of success and greatness. Drawing from these lessons, the political theorist Peter Euben wants more contemporary democrats to do the same. There is a need, more so than ever, he writes, to re-envision democracy as 'a social process through which fixed identities and naturalized conventions periodically confront their conventional status . . . [Democracy must be] as much a politics of disturbance as a form of government and order'.[29] And so, before any new institution and procedure of global democracy is settled on, and even after it is, we cannot discount the democratic potential of practices that problematize the notion of order through the search for disorder.

The second lesson that tragedy's multivocal form offers to contemporary democrats concerns the democratic benefits of drawing on both factual and fictional sources of knowledge. Only by broadening the boundaries of acceptable theories of knowledge and ways of knowing reality can democracy hope to legitimate a variety of otherwise marginalized stories, characters and voices. In this regard, any efforts to extend democracy must learn to problematize the rigid binary of reality and fiction that pervades contemporary political thought. Legitimating only what is demarcated as real and rational prevents us from seeing, hearing and learning from a vast range of phenomena that lie beyond these barriers. It is as Castoriadis says:

> The modern world presents itself, on the surface, as that which has pushed, and tends to push, rationalization to its limit, and because of this, it allows itself to despise . . . the bizarre customs, inventions and imaginary representations of previous societies. Paradoxically, however, despite or rather due to this extreme "rationalization", the life of the modern world is just as dependent on the imaginary as any archaic or historical culture.[30]

We live, in other words, by our own fictions. Rational realities are erected on fictional grounds. But, because they have been told and retold so habitually and by those who have in the process attained positions of power, they no longer seem imaginary, irrational or fictional. These stories become politically legitimate despite the fact that they were created or selected from a broader range of facts. Reiterating them *ad nauseam*, insisting only on political 'facts', delimits what we can know and who we can hear. Listening repeatedly only to a few select stories and viewing the world through a set of myopic lenses may very well maintain a stable order in reality. Yet, this order has to come eventually at the expense of wonder, diversity and innovation.

Ultimately, the point that is being made here is a simple one. Stories in our present age of globalization need to be as diverse and dynamic as are the flows of people, capital and information in today's world. To see, hear and learn from disorder, politically, means we might have to relearn to see the relationship between reality and fiction as fluid. This is imperative because drawing on fictional sources of insight is part of the process that can, in Kate Grenville's words, generate 'new circuits, new ways of thinking, new tools that the brain can then use for other purposes.'[31] The result, argues Carmel Bird, means that

> [i]n fiction the imagination has the license, perhaps the imperative, to invent, to take things further, to shift time and space and shape and form, in order to construct a new and different world, a different reality, a reality that can open the reader's heart wider and deeper and afford a stronger connection with other people's lives and situations.[32]

By broadening the scope of reality, through resorting to fiction, democrats can conceivably begin to populate the world in which they live and work with a set of never before heard narratives, told by individuals they have only had brief encounters with in the past. Only then can disorder have any chance of impinging on order without destroying what we hold dear to us in reality, both individually and as a community. This is the democratic utility of fiction. And it is as politically important today – perhaps all the more so given that it is no longer considered politically legitimate – as it was in classical Greece.

Analysing the democratic impact of tragedy's multivocal form can therefore push us to appreciate that democracy was not, and should not now be, solely pre-occupied with erecting a rational order – as is the general trend today. The Greeks' democracy concerned itself with instituting equality, justice and individual rights only in part. And while it recognized the indispensable need to establish an order that entrenched procedures of political participation and representation in reality,[33] it also pointed to something deeper, something indispensable both to politics and to life more broadly. They understood, in short, that existence is a composite of both order and disorder and reality and fiction.

Tragedy conveyed this message to the polis for its part through the multi-vocal form. Order, as it enacted, could not and should not always be imposed. Any genuine system of governance should never be premised solely on one idea or ideal to the exclusion of others. Order is necessary, even though it might be the source of oppression. Just as disorder can be destructive, although some-times destruction is precisely what is required to supply new opportunities for change. When audiences learnt to embrace such an open and open-ended attitude, they necessarily came to recognize and explore democratic potential in unlikely places. It is in this respect that they began to draw on both fac-tual and fictional sources of insight in the course of democratic deliberations. Democracy was thus enriched, and the balance between order and disorder better tempered, when its constituents drew on a range of unconventional sources.

A multivocal contribution to contemporary democratic debates

When applied at the broadest level to our own democratic dilemmas, we can perhaps point to several areas where the multivocality of Greek tragedy might advance current thinking. After all, the point made within this book is that even the very specific insights uncovered by the scholars of ancient Greece can possess the capacity to achieve a wider cultural relevancy today – but only if we manage to see the forest from the trees. This analysis, unlike those designed exclusively to return to the antique past, takes the view that there are certain important aspects of that past which when divorced from their strict disciplinary blinkers and scholarly language, can touch on society both in actual and practical ways. And it is these aspects that, from a cultural political perspective, we must do more to focus our energies on.

With this in mind, we can say that a reading of Greek tragedy's multivocal form can add to our repertoire to affirm both the political transformations of the late twentieth and twenty-first centuries as well as the new politics of dissent which has emerged in response.[34] Given the recent reconfigurations in matters of identity, the environment, religious convictions, human migration, legitimate institutions of governance and standards of living, conventional political practices have not always been capable of dealing with the nascent challenges. As a result, political battles not only have had, by necessity, to be waged in the official forums of deliberation and decision making but also have had to be relocated to unconventional arenas and take on alternative forms. And together they have had to represent the messy and chaotic nature of a political reality that, try as we might, is not always containable within formal institutions and procedures, even democratic ones. 'In a society increasingly fragmented by centrifugal displacements of once-centered authority and community', political philosopher Christopher Rocco claims that the 'fierce struggles over local identities . . . pose a new and unruly challenge to the current politics of cultural hegemony'.[35] Today, he continues, this challenge manifests itself as a 'micropolitics of difference based on suppressed, submerged, or other ignored narratives of ethnicity, gender, race, religion, sexuality, class, and other cultural (and subcultural) affiliations'. As was the case with the democratic revolution in ancient Athens, any truly global democracy today must learn to contend with this micropolitics of difference. This book revives and analyses the democratic impact of tragedy in part to do precisely this.

But, this book also makes a more general contribution: to enrich political engagements at all levels through the use of a range of unconventional sources, such as tragedy. By doing so, it hopes to show how new perspectives can emerge in the wake of aesthetic explorations; something which existing democratic efforts have steadfastly eschewed and ridiculed. Inured by entrenched modern conventions that underscore the importance of rational reality and order, few would acknowledge the democratic impact of tragedy. But even today, tragedy continues to offer insights into our own democratic challenges. Indeed, '[i]f tragedy has something to offer readers and spectators in the present' as the classicist Page duBois argues it does, then

> it should be more than nostalgia for the private, individual subject of modernity, cherished or lamented by many readers precisely because it is receding in a world of postmodern globalization. Rather, a reading that sees all the differences in tragedy, slaves and free, men and women, kings, queens, and citizens in action, conflicted, contradictory action, can speak to us now.[36]

Beyond the concerns for individual subjectivity, or so she seems to be saying, tragedy possesses the ability to uncover a myriad of stories, characters and voices that now make up our world of postmodern globalization. This is an explicitly democratic pursuit, one which aims to recover those who have been labelled as irrational or whose voices have been drowned out by the incessant hum of 'transnational corporate power', not to mention those whose vision of reality is antithetical to mainstream political order.[37] This speaks to us now, in the present. As Rocco maintains in his definitive text, *Tragedy and Enlightenment*, a study of democracy and tragedy effectively constitutes a 'struggle over the legacy of the Enlightenment, and so over the very characters and identity of modernity'.[38] It is our political present and future and not so much our political past that concerns this book.

In other words, how we are to reconcile pre-existing national and international institutions of governance with the mounting appeals for a truly transnational democracy – which covers the expanse from the local to the global – remains a topic that is still open to debate. Because of this, the resources we should draw upon to embolden ourselves, as global citizens and leaders, to square what takes place in the corridors of power with the demands and expectations of disempowered indigenous populations the world over, must be equally open and open-ended. They must be imaginative and creative. While liberal, deliberative and cosmopolitan notions of democracy are fundamental, they are not enough. Radical and unconventional forms of democratic participation are also needed.[39] Exploring the democratic potential of tragedy makes a contribution to the latter. It reminds us that facing the global challenges ahead requires a broad-based democratic spirit: a spirit that acknowledges the importance of institutions but, at the same time, self-critically engages its own order and embraces the inevitability of disorder; a spirit that is boldly inquisitive in its search for new realities in unlikely locations. By travelling back to Greece to examine the democratic impact of tragedy's multivocal form, this book seeks to revive this democratic spirit once again for contemporary citizens, scholars and policymakers seeking to revitalize democracy as an idea and a practice with genuine global purchase.

What this book does not do

Written predominantly to speak to contemporary political issues, this book may therefore not do several things which readers would commonly expect a book like this to do. For one, this inquiry is neither historical nor philological in nature. Countless scholars have already explored Greece through these lenses and this book makes no meaningful contribution to these complex debates. Instead, its focus is on democracy in today's rapidly changing age of globalization. Given this, the reading provided here of ancient Greece is selective, perhaps even rudimentary at times. Drawing on texts and contexts will allay these concerns to some extent, although to do so in a manner that satisfies cultural historians is not a task that this book undertakes. At best, it will roughly apply relevant historical lessons to the contemporary political environment and, in the process, synthesize history with politics. Historians have, in various ways, recovered these lessons from antiquity. Having done so, however, few explicitly relate and apply them to the thought and practices prevalent within our own societies. This book's objective is to begin this task.

However, it must be stressed that by applying these historical lessons, this book is not suggesting that we can bring back – or authentically represent – the respective political dynamics. But neither can we get to the root of things, today or in future, without first understanding our traditions. A brief excursion into the antique past is useful given that Greece is where Western democracy emerged.[40] Tradition, in this regard, always intervenes in the present, though it is sometimes hard to see. Its mark remains visible, although inverted, jumbled and scarred by historical development. Seeing things this way tends to undermine the conventional dichotomy that partitions the past from the present from the future.[41] In viewing history fluidly, the book seeks to retell particular stories from democracy's past – especially stories we have tended to forget and, as such, forgotten to tell. This helps to renegotiate and even invigorate the meanings and practical significance of democracy today.

But, at another level, this book will purposely undertake a selective reading of these ancient institutions – despite the resort to both texts and contexts. This is because the aim, after all, is to read democracy through tragedy and, more broadly, to explore their intrinsic links. By doing this, it runs the risk of excluding various other institutions, procedures and practices which were also crucial to the rise of democracy in Athens, such as comedy.[42] While a comprehensive study of the development of democracy must take these factors into account, such a study would be beyond the scope of this book. Its purpose is more modest: to critically analyse how the political ascendancy of tragedy helped reinvigorate democracy during its adolescent years and to extract political insights that might help us extend democracy in the age of globalization.

There is one further disclaimer that should be mentioned at this point, which is that despite the emphasis on the virtues of tragedy's democratic potential, we should not forget that the democracy that tragedy helped shape was the very democracy that bred an environment and a mindset broadly supportive of Athens' imperializing mission. We are, to this end, reminded that tragedy was a medium through which the dichotomy between Greek and barbarian was first defined, though some would say also problematized.[43] Tragedy was considered evidential proof of Athens' superiority and 'cultural prestige', a didactic commodity which could and perhaps should be exported to other city-states in Greece and beyond.[44] Others, like Edward Said, would agree, noting that tragedies like Aeschylus' *Persians* or Euripides' *Bacchae* were all early examples of orientalist texts, where a West was demarcated from an Orient. 'What matters here', according to Said, 'is that Asia speaks through and by virtue of the European imagination, which is depicted as victorious over Asia'.[45] Given this, tragedy did confer to Athens' imperialistic forays into the Greek interior and beyond a distinct sense of virtuosity and right. Athens, in this reading of tragedy and democracy, liberates and then educates the East and offers to it a rationalism which is 'undermined by Eastern excesses, those mysteriously attractive opposites to what seem to be normal values'.[46] Such a view, which these commentators argue is endemic to Greek tragedy, explains why it cannot be divorced from democracy's less savory aspects.

We cannot, as such, in retelling democracy's story ignore the entrenched links between democracy, tragedy and empire. Instead, we must, according to the political thinker John Keane, acknowledge the 'link between hubris and democracy', which is to say, the role that tragedy played in a polis that 'would make arrogant mistakes, such as acting cruelly against enemy cities, just for the hell of it'.[47] The now infamous Athenian expedition to the Spartan colony of Melos in 416/415 BC stands as a reminder that democracy was both just and supremely unjust, peaceful on the home front and yet blood thirsty abroad, democratic and still avowedly dictatorial, all at the same time. The tale of the defeat, slaughter and enslavement of the Melians by the Athenians would later be dramatically weaved into the story of mourning, loss and excess in Euripides' *The Trojan Women*, the very same story which Rosalba Clemente brought to that South Australian stage in our own time. Though well known, this is only one of the many episodes where we are reminded that '[t]he rule of democracy was sealed, in cruelty and blood'.[48]

Attempts to revive and rekindle the democratic impact of tragedy today, particularly as a corrective to our own faltering efforts to extend democracy globally, should at least note that tragedy's history was not one-dimensional. This book does so by acknowledging the utility of democracy and tragedy's counterstory. It acknowledges that tragedy reflected and reiterated many of the undersides of democracy. But, it is also important to emphasize that tragedy was both a symptom and panacea of democracy's woes. And while it would be disingenuous to dissociate the democratic impact of tragedy from Athens' imperialistic tendencies, it would be equally flawed to ignore the democratic innovations and correctives implicit in the tragic art form. In short, we should neither oversimplify the actual influence and import that tragedy had in the ancient polis nor misconstrue its democratic potential in our own age of globalization.

Structure of this book

The next chapter begins this task, showing that democracy and tragedy were intrinsically linked during the time of the Athenian city-state. The rise of democracy encouraged citizens to collectively question and subvert traditional hierarchies, institutions and systems of knowledge in the creation of new and more inclusive ones. Tragedy's political ascendancy should be read in this light: as a dramatic institution elevated by democracy to check democracy. Through tragedy, audiences were reminded of their flawed existence, that even the greatest among them was not all great, and how, ultimately, the known order of things remains susceptible to the chaotic unknowns that lurk just beneath the surface. Articulated dramatically, these insights reinforced and reinvigorated democracy's message both at the personal levels of psyche and emotion and at the collective level, seeping into democracy's other institutions and practices.

Chapter 2 continues in a similar vein, but it does so by making the more specific point that it was tragedy's multivocal form which allowed the art form to
speak democratically. Tragedy's multivocal form brought a variety of otherwise
marginalized stories, characters and voices onto the public stage and into democratic debate. In doing this, it captured the delicate democratic balance between
order and disorder, on the one hand, and reality and fiction, on the other hand.
But the question that this chapter poses is whether and in what way might tragedy's multivocal form inspire democratic sensitivities today? This, in some ways,
being the more pressing question, demands an answer that permits contemporary audiences to appropriate what was democratic about tragedy's multivocal
form without being too mired down by a rigid or conventional approach to the
classics. With this in mind, the chapter's goal is to draw broadly from tragedy's
multivocal form so as to design a framework which can enable us to read tragedy as a democratic text for today. This is a politically valuable undertaking,
as the chapter will demonstrate, since reading tragedy's multivocal form as a
democratic text may better locate us to think through some of the more trenchant and vexing global challenges confronting democracy today – in critical,
unorthodox and imaginative ways.

Chapter 3 marks the beginning of the empirical phase of the book. In this
and the subsequent two chapters, the book sets out to examine the historical and
theoretical claims it has made. To do so, it turns its focus to one tragedy in particular: Aeschylus' *Suppliants*, a drama which for many commentators continues
to be a uniquely democratic tragedy. Long considered to be our earliest extant
Greek tragedy, it is also the only tragedy that explicitly makes reference to the
democratic Assembly and to citizens who voted to receive foreign refugees into
their city-state. As a result, it provides us with an unrivaled look at how tragic
drama intervened in democratic politics at that time and the types of political
lessons that tragedy might have offered. It is true that we may not be able to
draw direct parallels with our own democratic customs and events, but the ethos
exuded through this play has a great deal to offer us today. Accordingly, in lieu
of providing a superficial reading of this tragedy, the book plans to offer a systematic reading that analyses it in both its original form and in a form adapted
explicitly for the twenty-first century.

In Chapter 3, the objective is to briefly introduce Aeschylus and, in particular,
his tragedy about ancient supplication. Written intentionally for a non-specialist
audience, the chapter provides an overview of Aeschylus' tragedy that situates it
against the politics of its day and engaging with the turbulent politics of the days

to come. Aeschylus' 'dramatic art', we are reminded by Franz Stoessl, 'was subject to the struggle of political forces and was itself part of this struggle'.[49] They are, as Cynthia Farrar writes, important 'interpretations of both freedom and order and suggest that only democratic politics can reconcile them'.[50] Through Aeschylus, in other words, we can glimpse both the potential and the pitfalls of democracy in fifth-century Athens.

Having drawn together this broad sketch, the book's fourth chapter narrows the focus and reads the multivocal form of Aeschylus' *Suppliants* to piece together a more detailed portrait of the democratic politics of the mid-fifth century BC. As democracy in Athens headed into one of its most trying periods, the reading shows that Aeschylus used his tragedy to paint a picture of how democracy should be. *Suppliants* represented a political image of everything that Athens' democracy of the mid-fifth century was not. It gave pride of place to a band of foreign and tempestuous women. It humbled otherwise great statesmen. And it reminded the audiences in Athens that a democracy should endure intrusions of diversity, even if it destabilizes domestic and international affairs. Through these otherwise marginalized stories, characters and voices, democratic Athens, along with its political pettiness, aristocratic nostalgia and aggressive foreign policy, was put on stage for all to see.

However, this book's claim is that the democratic insights of Aeschylus' drama are not limited solely to the antique past. Though they are no longer considered a legitimate form of political discourse, they may still be able to provide cutting commentary on our own democratic aspirations. Chapter 5 examines this claim through a reading of Charles L. Mee's play *Big Love*, a renowned contemporary adaptation of Aeschylus' *Suppliants*. It argues that far from being politically irrelevant, Mee's play actually recasts Aeschylus' drama for today. Mee's plays, in his own words, 'are broken, jagged, filled with sharp edges, filled with things that take sudden turns, career into each other, smash up, veer off in sickening turns'.[51] What, if anything, does this have to do with contemporary theories and practices of democracy? Ostensibly nothing, as even a quick glance at Mee's *Big Love*, for instance, shows up the play as outwardly frivolous and abstract. But take another look and it is clear to see that his Aeschylean adaptation provides an unconventional commentary on contemporary liberal democracy and consumer capitalism. Beneath its folly, hilarity and gratuitousness, the play discloses the links between democracy and a historical violence which at once marks and is shrouded by our civilizational constructs. In *Big Love*, we are reminded of how violence, despotism and exploitation remain a means to a democratic end – a fact which continues to haunt many of our proposals to promote democracy the world over.

The book's final chapter draws this reading to a close by pointing to two overarching lessons that tragedy's multivocal form can impart on global democratic politics in the twenty-first century. The first is the understanding that the idea and practice of democracy should not be solely concerned about the institution of order in political life, but also about the place of disorder. In other words, while order is necessary for a stable and productive communal existence, sites of disorder too provide insights into dilemmas posed by political instability, inequality, exclusion and flux. Unlike prominent conceptions of democracy today, it aims to show how a truly democratic order must seek to include and give voice to democratic disorder. The second lesson highlighted is the need to democratically legitimize both factual and fictional sources of knowledge. Only by broadening the scope of reality, through resorting to fiction, can democrats hope to legitimate a variety of otherwise marginalized stories, characters and voices in our own democratic deliberation. This is what tragedies, ancient and modern, are apt to do: to revitalize democracy in its multivocal form.

1

Democracy and Tragedy in Ancient Athens

The birth of the West's first great democracy in ancient Athens coincided with the political ascendancy of tragic drama. For those who know anything of democracy today, this would no doubt seem a strange proposition. To think: the origins of our democracy are somehow linked to this peculiar art form which conveyed the antithesis of progress and individual agency. Be that as it may, to the Athenians that first invented democracy and staged tragedy, the relationship shared by these two institutions was inimitable and central to fifth-century Greek existence.

Why was this so? What was it about democracy in ancient Athens that encouraged, and even needed, the ascendancy of tragedy? Why and how did the mass performance of tragic drama play so central a role in the democratic polis?

Drawing in large part on the work of Cornelius Castoriadis, the twentieth-century philosopher of autonomy whose account most succinctly identified the fundamental links shared between democracy and tragedy in ancient Athens, this chapter will demonstrate that both democracy and tragedy, individually and as a symbiosis, evoked and were evocative of a similar world view. For democracy, this world view, as Castoriadis puts it, was captured by the push for self-institution and self-limitation.[1] For us to understand what these dual concepts mean today, it is important that we first realize something fundamental about democracy in the Athenian sense. Unlike the way it is customarily perceived and practiced today, the West's first great democracy did not emerge as a ready-made or stable set of institutions and customs. It did not pertain solely to the notion that franchise and rational deliberation would eventually yield progress. This perhaps is to state the obvious; though there remains a sizeable community of democrats who continue to view democracy in almost ahistorical terms, choosing instead to believe that democracy is, as it has always been, a vehicle to ferry human beings towards greater political enlightenment.

Yet, such an approach simply will not do if we are to understand democracy in the Athenian sense. In order to be able to do this, we are required to suspend the familiar set of ideas we associate with democracy today for a practice and mentality which, in antiquity, was known equally for its promise as well as its utter destructiveness.[2] Being radical, it was also dangerous, volatile and inequitable. Achievements aside, democracy was far from perfect. Political consciousness and participation, the expansion of equality and citizenry rights, as well as the increasing ability to reconcile oneself with others all flourished together, being, in many cases, inseparable from the horrors of imperialism, slavery, patriarchy and exclusion. But this was precisely democracy's aim: to create and then destroy, expand and then retreat, to self-institute and then self-limit. By doing so, democracy symbolized the beautiful yet ominous equilibrium between that which *was* and that which *was not* in the world of ancient Greece. For Castoriadis, this is why Greek, especially Athenian, democracy was so unique and intriguing.[3]

Tragedy featured in this scheme of things because it dramatized a world view that emphasized the intrinsic homelessness of the human condition in a world that could not always be known or predictable.[4] The existential truth that tragedy exposed, in Castoriadis' words, was the understanding that our 'Being is Chaos'.[5] In this way, because what comprises us can also be what unravels and confounds us, the newly democratized polity viewed tragedy as a personal source of democratic inspiration. The dramas staged by the tragedians encapsulated the democratic spirit to the extent that it called on all, in Charles Segal's words, to be open to the 'disintegration of the cosmic, social, or psychological order without losing all sense of coherence'.[6] Thus, it was not long before tragedy found itself elevated by democracy to check the fateful rise – and decline – of democracy. Drawing from and exuding to the democratic polis, tragedy reminded the Athenians that no single voice or way of life was absolute or wholly true. Truth, instead, resides in the cacophony of voices, the composite of all life. Highlighted through these dramas were the differing, contradictory and competing actors, perspectives and choices that populated and made meaningful their democracy.[7] As an institution of civic life, tragedy gave back to democracy what democracy had first given Athens: the fleeting awareness that the pursuit of totality has its limits; indeed, that the very core of existence is limited.

This chapter engages with these ancient institutions at length. To do so, it will rely loosely on the methods pioneered by the so-called Paris School of cultural history. According to this approach, what is crucial when trying to understand ancient institutions and practices are their history and being. For our purposes, this means that we must view democracy and tragedy from two seemingly incongruous planes of analysis if we are to understand them today: historiography and ontology. Nothing less, according to Christian Descamps, can adequately account for ancient Greece. As he writes,

> To study Greece, in fact, is always to rediscover a sort of aporia. On the one hand, there is the Greek language, the famous term "Being," and, on the other hand – though all this is connected – one witnesses the birth of the organization of the City, a type of practical reflection.[8]

Reflecting on 'being' and 'the organization of the City', specifically, requires undertaking two interrelated tasks.

The first task is to approach texts – about democracy and tragedy – in relation to their historical contexts. This means that when interpreting democracy and tragedy, it is essential to be mindful of the social, political, economic and cultural milieu in Athens that germinated the institutions and practices under examination. Josiah Ober reminds us that historical texts are really symbol systems whose meanings do not exist in a vacuum,[9] and, as such, they cannot be interpreted or understood this way. Texts are representative of their environment and they form part of a whole. For Stephen Greenblatt, that whole can encompass, for instance, the broader genre or discipline which embodies the texts, the grounds for its creation, practice and performance, as well as the responses of the participants involved.[10] In their attempt to read *Athenian Drama in Its Social Context*, John Winkler and Froma Zeitlin demonstrate just what this method involves. Interpreting a Greek tragedy today, they argue, requires that a reader concentrates not only on the script but also on the 'extratextual aspects', violating traditional philological methodologies in the process.[11] Such an approach is more holistic since it must 'look behind the masks and under the costumes and peer out into the audience, and investigate the various elements that went into a finished performance'. It should also consider 'what happened before and after the plays and take notice of other locations in ancient Athens, like the Assembly and the law courts, where para-dramatical social events took place'.[12] What is important about this approach is its rejection of accounts that claim to be objective and ahistorical in its reading of a text. And it certainly rejects that '"the text is the thing!" and the only thing'.[13] Instead, understanding a text is to attempt to understand the webs of power that gave it specific meaning and significance, and these always have their sociopolitical reference points.[14] Likewise, for us to understand the symbiosis of democracy and tragedy today, we must engage equally in a range of different practices spread across a range of different disciplines, for example, history, literary criticism, politics, art, philosophy, anthropology and economics.

The second task also approaches texts in terms of their context, but this time it understands context to incorporate ontological contexts.[15] These, according to Jean-Pierre Vernant, comprise categories of thought and reasoning, values and beliefs, as well as the various means through which sense and sensibilities are given form.[16] Together, they constitute what it is 'to be': what type of human being and humanity is made possible under these conditions, offering motives and reasons for the actions they undertook. Only by analysing context this way, can we read democracy in light of tragedy and vice versa, which is what they demand of interpreters today.

But, before this chapter begins its analysis, two brief disclaimers need emphasizing. The first concerns the exceptions to the symbiosis of democracy and tragedy. Given tragedy's reputation, the reality is that it soon spread to city-states throughout Greece and beyond – irrespective of whether that city-state was democratic or not.[17] Additionally, the continued survival and revivals of tragedy throughout subsequent centuries, for the most part, have occurred within societies which were vehemently anti-democratic. Even Friedrich Nietzsche, one of the more ardent contemporary supporters of tragedy, alluded to the disparity between democracy and tragedy.[18] In addition, there is the critique that the use of democratic ideology to interpret tragedy, and vice versa, can produce any number of results and unnecessary biases.[19] These qualifications are important and need highlighting. But they should not detract from the point that the institutions of democracy and tragedy 'shared time, space and spirit'.[20] Today, it is this spirit that is worth exploring, particularly as the virtue of democracy has become near universal and its meaning rigid and indisputable.

The second caveat comes in the form of a rider. Despite the admission that democracy was not perfect – being a system based on inequalities and exclusions itself – we must acknowledge that tragedy too had limits. Both institutions faced very real obstacles in reality, which denied them attaining their full potential. Democracy sustained a city-state, in part, because it was sustained by a slave economy that denied women, foreigners and youths their political rights. And tragedy, even though it dramatized democracy's pitfalls and double standards, did not always have a tangible or immediate political impact. This is evidenced by the persistence of democratically induced slavery, patriarchy, xenophobia and aggression. Moreover, as the next chapter will touch upon, tragedy would itself be ridiculed by particular factions for imbuing inappropriate emotional responses in its audiences, ones adverse to a stable political order. A romanticization of ancient Greece is often easy to propound, even if the consequences of doing so, as Costas Constantinou reminds us, can be dire.[21] The hope is that this book will avoid the worst of these dangers while still being able to draw applicable insights from Athenian democracy and tragedy for today. Doing so means that, at times, it necessarily skews the analysis to the benefits produced through these institutions, these being the traits it hopes to emphasize and learn from.

Divided into two sections, the chapter introduces Athenian democracy and tragedy in such a way as to illuminate their overlaps. In the first section, it articulates democracy – the socio-historical milieu in which it emerged, the idea, the institutions and the practices – as an existential paradox premised on both self-institution and self-limitation. This is what rendered the polis susceptible to tragedy. The second section offers an account of tragedy and explains why it became such a crucial democratic institution in Athens. Here, Castoriadis' articulation that tragedy dramatizes our Being as Chaos will be particularly instructive for understanding tragedy's ability to speak to the Athenians' efforts at self-institution and self-limitation.

Democracy as self-institution and self-limitation in ancient Athens

But first, the objective is to highlight some of the key socio-historical, institutional and existential shifts that underpinned the rise of democracy in Athens. Doing so will help us understand what it was about democracy that encouraged, even needed, the ascendancy of tragedy.

Of course, the tenor that this account will take is not to document every social, political and philosophical component of Athenian democracy, not that this is even strictly possible. Its goal, rather, is to paint a portrait of democracy that is broad of brush so as not to detract from the real task: to problematize the modern mindset that perceives democracy as a wholly structured, predictable and even inevitable phenomenon. Indeed, by underscoring the often violent struggles and tensions, the continuous creation and re-creation and the severe relapses and intrinsic flaws, it will reveal how Athenian democracy represented an endless process whereby convention was pitted against innovation, hierarchy against equality, violence against peace and one voice against the many.[22]

The result sees a story whereby democracy was more or less, in Farrar's words, 'cobbled together' over a period of several centuries.[23] Though it is commonly agreed that the reforms of Cleisthenes in 508/507 BC signified the key ideological and institutional shift towards democracy,[24] the question of democracy's birth is a topic that arouses more debate than one would expect. For some, democracy's emergence can be dated as far back as the establishment of Solon's constitution in 594/593 BC[25] or, for others, as far forward as the restored democracy of 403/402 BC.[26] We need to be concerned with this ambiguity, and with these particular individuals and events, only to the extent that they illustrate something of the organic and erratic development of democracy in Athens, a phenomenon that took various forms and transpired over an expansive period of nearly three centuries.

During this epoch though, it is fair to say that the Athenian landscape underwent tremendous changes in almost every respect. For one, we see in this period an increase in both the centrality and occurrence of trade, warfare and imperialism in the Athenian way of life. Additionally, several significant democratically inspired redivisions of Athens' social classes also took place. Given this, it was not long before new ambitions and fields of activity arose to accommodate the nascent forms of knowledge and political expectations that had germinated.

But why did this happen? And how did it happen? What were the historical and social triggers for the emergence of the democratic spirit? To answer these questions, a brief account of some key paradigmatic shifts experienced in and around Athens may help shed some light.

Given that the total sum of these shifts would themselves fill the pages of many books over, we obviously cannot go into exact historical accounts. Rather, all that we can do is offer some rough political background to the rise of democracy. For this reason, maybe only three shifts really warrant a mention in this context. The first is the fusion of families, clans and tribes, which occurred throughout Attica from around 1050 to 750 BC.[27] These changes were crucial because they symbolized the antecedents of what would later be known as the polis. Though initially created for the purposes of acquiring greater security and stability, these groupings soon became much more. Indeed, as the size, number and complexity of poleis grew, life within these social units was slowly transformed into something else; the pursuit of victory, beauty and excellence being foremost among them. As an enduring tribute to Greek civilization, the polis would grow to become a largely non-bureaucratic form of society that cherished aesthetic pursuits and agonistic competition. It would prove central to the Greeks' way of life in the coming centuries, especially life under democracy.

A second notable event in this story charts the moves towards greater equality in Athens, particularly as a result of the reforms instituted by Solon and then Cleisthenes. While the finer institutional details will be discussed later, it is important to flag now that the movement towards democracy in Athens was not neat, but triggered in large part by mass discontent.[28] The reforms of Solon and Cleisthenes, two of Athens' foremost statesmen, appeared against historical periods of pervasive indebtedness, enslavement, dictatorship and civil strife, when a wealthy aristocratic class was splintered from the lowly peasant classes.[29] In its place, Solon and Cleisthenes sought to reorganize society by clearing debt, protecting individual freedoms, disrupting traditional class allegiance and structures and, perhaps most importantly, by shattering the autocratic monopoly on office-holding. Neither schemes were perfect. Both were met with violent resistance and tyrannical rule. And yet, for all that was wrong and for all that still needed improving, these reforms embedded an irrepressible kernel of equality within the social consciousness of the Athenians. Indeed, due in large part to these reforms, one's status soon became decreasingly dependent on birth and class and more on individual capacity and persistence. In saying this though, we can too easily exaggerate these developments, which did not extend to improving the social standing of women, slaves, youths and the foreign residents of Athens.[30]

But still, they did begin to move the political consciousness of the masses, and this constitutes the third key shift. Made clear through the defining battles of the Persian Wars at Marathon and Salamis was the realization that the Athenian *hoplites* (citizen-soldiers) and *thetes* (free men not of the landed class), men who comprised mainly the middle and lower classes, would be at the forefront of any greatness which the Athenians laid claim to. Both victories, which had been purchased with the sacrifices and ingenuity of the Athenian masses, meant that they could henceforth regard themselves as fundamental to the newfound security, notoriety and advancement of their polis.[31] Through these military triumphs, the fruits of Solon's and Cleisthenes' efforts could finally be said to have materialized.

However, it is crucial to point out that these innovations in social structure, equality and mass political awareness also triggered their share of instability, relapses and reprisals. From individual families, clans and tribes emerged poleis composed of varying families, clans and tribes; from the rule of elites, we read of their overthrow and the institution of greater equality which followed and finally, drawing from the heroic figures of the Greek myths for inspiration and daring, the *hoplites* and *thetes* demonstrated what the masses were capable of, if given the opportunity. Yet, as destabilizing as these shifts were, such was the ferment from which democracy would eventually emerge.

As such, the point that we should take away is that without these paradigmatic shifts, democracy might not have sprouted when and where it did. This, however, is not to say that any of these shifts, whether by themselves or in toto, were in fact directly responsible for the establishment of democracy in Athens. They were not. To draw such a conclusion would simply be taking the inference too far. A more accurate assessment would need to temper its interpretation of the facts. It might stress that, for example, while these shifts did not in and of themselves immediately trigger democratization, they would have nonetheless triggered an outflow of other initiatives and activities more apposite to the emergence of democracy.

This is how we can approach a number of innovative institutions and procedures that sprouted up in the aftermath of these various paradigmatic shifts: as mechanisms created to accommodate and reinforce these socio-historical shifts. Together, the function they performed was vital for Athens' burgeoning democracy, being the first institutions and procedures to channel popular will into something that would eventually resemble popular rule.

This began, in many ways, with Solon and his constitutional reforms to alter the existing customs that had governed Athenian political participation and office-holding. By first dividing the Athenian citizenry into four wealth-based classes and then by redefining political franchise, his constitution established the foundation upon which Athens' democracy would be built. Specifically, what Solon did was to restrict the eligibility for participation in the *Areopagus* (Aristocratic Council) to Athens' richest class, whereas participation in the *Boule* (the Council) was limited to its second and third classes, while the *Ekklesia* (the Assembly) and courts became the preserve of Athens' lowest class.[32] It is true that such a division can hardly be considered democratic by today's standards. Yet, as a first step, the democratic significance of these institutional reforms cannot be understated. And in any case, as the push for democracy became stronger, these institutions naturally underwent tremendous transformations, ranging from the *Boule's* expansion and the increasing significance of the *Ekklesia* to the eventual abolition of the aristocratic *Areopagus*.

Thus, despite its modest beginnings, it was the *Ekklesia* that would come to initiate policy and make decisions with an authority that was total at the height of democracy's prominence. As the people's assembly, it can be loosely likened to modern-day lower houses of parliament. All enrolled Athenian citizens over the age of 18 were permitted to attend and address the *Ekklesia* on all matters from taxation, the declaration of war, the signing of treaties, to issues of public works.[33] This, of course, did not always translate into overwhelming public attendance, even though numbers ranging from 5,000 to 13,000 citizens were not uncommon.[34] Despite this, and despite the fact that the majority of attendees would not have spoken, the size, openness and sheer unpredictability of such an assembly would have ensured a greater number of voices and issues being publicized in Athens than any time before.

The *Boule*, on the other hand, worked independently of the *Ekklesia* to check the *Ekklesia*. A representative council of citizens, the *Boule* was initially made up of 400 citizens following Solon's social redivision, although that figure was later extended to 500 citizens after Cleisthenes' division of Attica.[35] Comparable to modern-day upper houses, the *Boule* guided and prepared the work done in the *Ekklesia*, although it could not itself initiate new policies and laws for enactment. Also, like the upper houses of contemporary democracies, the *Boule* was more proportionally representative than the *Ekklesia*, as *Bouleutai* (councilors) were chosen by lot to equally represent all the tribes of Attica.[36] On top of this, prospective *Bouleutai* had to be over the age of 30 and could only ever serve two one-year terms. This ensured that the *Boule* would, in theory, be more experienced and learned than its counterpart. It was envisaged as a safeguard placed on an *Ekklesia* prone to naivety, manipulation and excess.

For a long time, both the *Ekklesia* and *Boule* were subject to the rule of the *Areopagus*, an institution composed solely of aristocrats.[37] As the oldest permanent institution in the Athenian polis, the existence of the *Areopagus* remained a vestige of Athens' aristocratic past, even as its powers were progressively delimited under democracy. That said, it was not until the reforms of Ephialtes in 462/461 BC that the *Areopagus* had all its functions, bar the jurisdiction to try homicide cases, transferred to the *Ekklesia*, *Boule* and popular courts.[38] These courts, composed of everyday citizen-jurors, heard and determined matters of law brought before it by other citizens.[39]

Cumulatively, what these institutions did was to disperse power and affect a spike in political volatility and the politicization of issues which had previously lain dormant within the Athenian polis. No longer was one's life to be dictated from above. Nor was power to be conceived solely as an unimpeachable good possessed only by an elite few. Instead, democratic life demanded of its citizens a mentality and agenda that would celebrate, question and reform the very freedoms and responsibilities that they now possessed. The product was often messy, uncertain, conceited and even disastrous. In the face of this, all that the democrats could do was to continue to draw from an array of sources so that they might be better prepared to express and understand the nascent anxieties which had begun to taunt their lives. Institutions like the *Ekklesia*, *Boule* and popular courts were indispensable to this end.

Just as indispensable to the democratic effort were a number of key procedures that were put in place to ensure that power would never become concentrated in the hands of a minority and to encourage citizens to remain politically active. There is any number of procedural innovations which can be drawn together with the onset of democracy in Athens. But again, the point to remember is that this overview is not to catalogue all institutions and procedures as much as to offer a sample of how these various mechanisms played their part in inspiring and extending democratic practice.

In this way, a good illustrative example we can turn to is the procedural shift which was set up to alter the method by which the *Boule* was comprised; a procedure which came about through Cleisthenes' redivision of Attica. Even more radical than Solon's wealth-based division, Cleisthenes' design to create 10 new tribes (*phylai*) disrupted and ultimately destroyed traditional loyalties and monopolies of power. In their stead, these new tribes – which were composed of three intermediate political units (*trittyes*), each made up of smaller, local communities (*demes*) – fused the local with the central in a fashion that united elites with non-elites, rural with urban and local governments with the central government.[40] By undermining the old order, this redivision founded a new order that was chaotic at heart. Procedurally, each of these 10 tribes was then required to supply 50 *Bouleutai* to make up the *Boule* or the Council of 500.[41] The initial rationale and eventual impact of these arrangements was to rupture established social cleavages, and their corresponding inequalities, in the formation of new, diverse communities. From slaves, foreigners, women and men to those of former-aristocratic heritage, democratic Athens was therefore, within certain limits, becoming more a fusion that melded unity with a sense of bedlam.[42] Somewhat emblematic of this is the procedure by which the *Boule* was compiled.

But, so important was this interplay between structure and disarray to democratic life that it permeated a number of other procedures. A particularly good case in point here is the procedure known as ostracism. Quite simply, ostracism was a yearly procedure which allowed citizens to vote to expel one citizen from the city who, during the course of that year, had become too arrogant, domineering or antagonistic to the order of mass rule.[43] Unlike the procedure of pre-democratic exile, which was more akin to violent overthrow, ostracism was a regulated democratic procedure that sanctioned dangerous individuals, individuals whose opinions so contravened popular sentiment as to threaten communal existence. For their transgressions, a 10-year expulsion from the city-state would be enforced. But once served, these individuals would be permitted to re-enter the city, freed of any stigma and with all their possessions intact. While the symbolism of this procedure will be taken up more fully in a later chapter, it is worth noting how ostracism encouraged citizens to think seriously about their freedoms – their own and that of others – as well as the consequences of their actions.

The point that is therefore being made through these rather random examples is this: together, these institutions and procedures reflected both the changing nature of citizenship and the citizenry. Moreover, they acknowledged the irrefutable connections that each citizen had with their social environment – with each other, with those who were not citizens and with those who suffered and perished so that they could live the lives they did. '[I]ndividuals have worth just for being individuals' was the new democratic plea.[44] And because this was so, a myriad of previously silent voices and unseen entities started to appear publically, each vying for recognition in their own right. The process that this instigated, while not always successful or stable, was continuous.[45] Beyond or intrinsic to having one's say and being equal, this was the power (*kratos*) that the people (*demos*) possessed under democracy (*demokratia*).[46]

Democracy read this way becomes somewhat different from how we commonly understand it today. Rather than just being about a form of governance that seeks to establish a stable order grounded in proportional representation, periodic elections and the rule of law, the Athenians understood democracy to mean a struggle that pits the need for order with the open search for disorder. With the movement towards greater equality in Athens, previously untouched and untouchable traditions came under scrutiny. In other words, as democracy took a firmer foothold in Athens' political imaginary, the way life had been became ever more destabilized, juxtaposed now with what life could be.

This is why Castoriadis quips that the age of democracy would soon be known as one of the less stable and indeed more radical periods in Athenian history.[47] The fine balance between order and disorder that democracy required its citizens to maintain, in their own lives and in the life of the community, meant that social norms had to be at once respected and questioned. That this was possible implied that, around the time of the democratic revolution, the Athenian polis had already set about to displace at least certain entrenched traditions of thought and being, which were previously considered beyond questioning. And while it would be incorrect to characterize what occurred as a complete politico-intellectual revolution, it is true to say that after the reforms of Solon and Cleisthenes, Athenian governance, politics and life had turned a corner.

Indeed, with the revolution that swept erstwhile subjects into power, quickened by the intensifying presence of inequality, exploitation and brutality, mass resentment soon instigated a search for real and viable alternatives. From the violent ruptures of the status quo emerged an almost foreign measure of freedom, equality and choice, which rocked the once stable, known and knowable world.[48] It was an unsettling time, as accepted customs and practices were dismantled and remade. This is why many scholars believe that when democracy finally materialized, it broke 'into reality in a way that [was] beyond containment within any closed system of thought'.[49]

Disorder, in other words, was at the heart of the democratic endeavour. There was unrest, instability and sometimes even anarchy as the polis struggled to come to grips with what had been suppressed for so long. But to some extent, the Greeks had always been a civilization mindful of the fact that there is chaos at the core of all existence.[50] It was just that the open search for and recognition of chaos had been politically delegitimized under the dictatorships of Athens' past. By contrast, what distinguished democracy from these previous forms of governance was precisely its ability to politicize the presence of chaos. Democracy made the entire polis aware that just behind their civilizational constructs and, in particular, their way of life, lay the unknown and a sense of nothingness. It was this subterranean landscape, where their most unspeakable fears and animosities presided, that the institutions and procedures of democracy would progressively disclose to the polis.

To this end, it might be said that democracy emerged as both a way of life and a form of governance that enabled its citizens to appreciate just how the certainties of their lives were susceptible to the menace of the unknown, and that this was not something to fear or suppress. The reason for this was because human life, knowledge and civilization – that is, our existential order – spring from, incorporate into and must ultimately succumb to chaos. Put another way, democracy helped the Greeks to understand that order – or the world they had created, whose mysteries they have slowly unraveled and replaced with knowledge and understanding – will never shroud the chaos from which all things emanate, try as it might. The seemingly implacable order that exudes from human life, knowledge and civilization is fleeting, not to mention imperfect. By recovering chaos, democracy actively sought out, if it only tacitly acknowledged, the limits and flaws within any way of life – particularly one's own. And this, the democrats believed, was what allowed them to take pleasure in the tragedy of existence; the impetus to think and act freely, to accept one's shortfalls and the need to look to others in a world blemished by hardship and death. Chaos implores human beings to revel in and then relinquish the gift of life, which is only a rare and fleeting negation of mortality.

Regrettably, at the height of existence, the spectre of chaos can become concealed, quickly forgotten or considered as threatening. That is to say, at the height of existence, questioning, paradox and openness – the means by which we slowly begin to appreciate the place and power of chaos – can take on pejorative connotations. Yet, questioning, paradox and openness were precisely what the democratic movement found wanting, though utterly necessary, within the order of aristocratic Athens. Democratic institutions, equality among citizens and the ability to voice one's predicament and be heard were entrenched within the polis so as to foreground difference or that which exceeded the parameters of order in Athens. Yet, instead of seeking out just order or chaos to the exclusion of the other, democracy reconciled them. Order and chaos came to function as a paradoxical unison; a constant and dynamic dialogue between that which *was* and that which *was not* in the world of ancient Greece. In this way, the object of democracy was to empower the self as well as others, the polis and all that was beyond it, that which was familiar and that which was alien, or that which exists in our world as with the world *itself*.

Here again, the writings of Castoriadis can help to shed light on this democratic interplay between order and disorder. As he argues in 'The Greek Polis and the Creation of Democracy', his most influential essay on the links between democracy and tragedy, the presence of chaos would mean that a certain and ultimate system of knowledge could never do if the Athenians were to fully engage the world in which they lived.[51] Rather, more creative, inclusive and reflexive modes of thought and action had to be instituted, as Castoriadis believed, given that life was a paradoxical mix of order and chaos, existence and nothingness, self and other. For him at least, this was what (pre-Socratic) notions of philosophy and politics captured. And, it was what democracy was created to capture.

For all these reasons, Castoriadis held the view that Athenian democracy had to be grounded in what he calls the project of autonomy,[52] something he defines as 'the reflective questioning of socially instituted representations, including those instituted with the help of philosophical reflection'.[53] Democracy in Athens was, therefore, not chiefly about the demarcation of universally applicable principles. Democratic thought did not presuppose a stagnant, knowable world that could be definitely theorized once and for all. Nor did it insinuate, on the other hand, that nothing was knowable or constant. Instead, it realized that all things sat uneasily, reflexively between these two poles of existence, like existence itself.

As Castoriadis goes on to affirm, this conception of democracy is the sum of a perpetual tussle between the forces of self-institution and self-limitation. As a brand of politics, it obliges its constituents to appreciate that their existence – all that is known and meaningful to them – is the result of creation or institution, which itself presupposes two things.

First, it recognizes that 'the collectivity . . . can only exist as instituted', to use Castoriadis' words.[54] This means that for human lives and civilization to flourish, to be meaningful and productive, certain concrete structures and systems of knowledge must be established. In other words, we need to fashion an order from manifest chaos, existence from nothingness and meaning from apparent meaninglessness. We need, argues Castoriadis, the 'validity and legitimacy of rules and representations just because they happen to be there [such as those dictated to us by an] external authority (even, and especially, "divine"), of any extrasocial source of truth and justice'.[55] We need institution. Democracy gave the people, or its citizens to be more precise, the explicit right of institution, individually and as a polis. It gave them the right of self-institution. Each citizen, as such, was granted the power to fashion and maintain a way of life that would be meaningful to them. To help them imagine new futures and to cope with what they had imagined, a range of sources, including fictional ones like tragedy, became essential to politics. Reaching back into the mythic past, these democrats likened their own daring to the great heroes of the Homeric epics. Conceptualizations of reality became fluidly fused with fictional tales and characters from Athens' past. But intrinsic to this right was the concomitant responsibility: to 'live with and even respect the voices' of those one opposed and was opposed by.[56] This was democratic self-institution.[57]

Second, by recognizing that the collectivity exists only because of self-institution is also to recognize, and perhaps even recover, the chaos, nothingness and meaninglessness which gave rise to order, existence and meaning in the first place. As such, the collectivity had to be called upon to confront 'its instituting character explicitly, and [question] itself and its own activities'.[58] It had to, as part of its self-institution, always be mindful of and ready for self-limitation. One's need of and right to self-institution intrinsically subjects oneself to the grips of self-limitation.

The unenviable reconciliation between these two diametrically opposed ends, which alone seek to capture existence but together enable humans to exist, was a democratic one. Self-institution must incorporate and is as necessary for existence as self-limitation. To have one and not the other ensures life as an unbearable burden, a farce and the antithesis of democracy.

This, in sum, was what the socio-historical, institutional and existential underpinnings of Athenian democracy instituted: a novel or previously impossible solidarity between what was and what could be.[59] By questioning the polis and the self of Athenian civilization, democracy reminded the Athenians that 'all citizens have the possibility of attaining a correct *doxa* [opinion] and that nobody possesses an *épisteme* [certain knowledge] of all things political'.[60] On all fronts, this encouraged greater daring and arrogance, even violence – only to be matched with a corresponding level of humility and openness. In this duel between order and chaos, extremity was met with balance, involvement with detachment, the concrete with the reflective and peace with violence; all of which was captured by Pericles when he declared, 'for everything that grows great also decays'.[61]

This was the paradoxical lesson at democracy's heart: 'What includes excludes'.[62] For while the citizens of Athens increasingly saw themselves as equally important parts of a whole, this 'whole' also sustained the monsters of imperialism, war and slavery, not to mention the political exclusion of women, foreigners and children. Democracy, in a very real and undeniable sense, sustained itself on a slave economy and the political exclusion of women and barbarians. Not only that, but democracy did not always function in practice the way it was conceived to do. The everyday pressures, biases and trivialities associated with politicking regularly consumed the idea and practice of democracy in Athens. It was imperfect and, if we use today's standards to assess it, hardly democratic at all. Yet, this was all part and parcel of the Athenians' first effort to found democracy against a backdrop of domination, hierarchy, exclusion and injustice. For all its manifest advances, the West's first great democracy cannot be divorced from these less savory realities.[63]

But that, as this section has demonstrated, was an inevitable part of democracy's attempt to balance self-institution with self-limitation. Its failures, varied and many, also gave rise to the understanding that any opening would itself induce another, more entrenched closure that might be equally unjust and violent.[64] Any order must necessarily recognize its limits: what lies beyond and sustains it. For this reason, the process of self-institution and self-limitation must be continuous, just as the tussle between order and chaos is continuous. Today, if we remember just one thing about the Athenians' democracy, it should be this.

Being as chaos: Tragedy's democratic intervention

The upshot of a political project so radical and unstable was threefold at least. The first was the extremely delicate and volatile nature of democracy. Here was a nascent system of governance that not only benefited from but also actually depended upon the active participation of all its citizens. Yet, used to a lifetime of dictatorship, this was an enormous challenge with countless risks for an uninitiated and inexperienced citizenry. How would the people exercise their power? And what could inspire and teach them to do so? Added to this was a second concern: democracy was a regime that encouraged creation along with destruction, inclusion with exclusion and civilization with violence. Democracy was unpredictable for the very reason that the world it sought to capture was unpredictable, and paradoxical too. To capture it successfully would require new techniques and greater daring. And so the third upshot: the democratic forces unleashed both required and inspired more resourceful ways of thinking and acting – which, as the Athenians found out, could not be limited simply to what took place in the *Ekklesia*, *Boule* or the popular courts. This explains why the democratic revolution coincided with a cultural one, wherein philosophy, politics and artistic expression fused organically to give expression to the new uncertainty.[65]

Indeed, with Cleisthenes' reforms, a new philosophically informed 'aestheticization' became necessary to nourish and inform the political sphere.[66] What was now needed and pursued were other, more nuanced ways of disclosing and coping with the new sense of existence. No longer were dogma and unthinking traditionalism to be esteemed, but an innovative irreverence that would be content only when the answers provided sparked new questions, which demanded answering. This was an artistic–intellectual endeavour that would continually open and transform the Greek world. Athens, being the centre of this world, was both the progeny and progenitor of this continuous state of flux.

Tragedy was a direct corollary of these artistic–intellectual endeavours.[67] Even more than that, tragedy was shaped into a political institution of sorts under democracy so as to check the democratic forces being unleashed. Unlike in more contemporary times, the performance of tragedy in Athens was not primarily a matter of entertainment. It was, instead, an important site of democratic politics. So popular was tragedy that over 1,000 plays were produced in Athens in the fifth century alone.[68] Today, we only possess a minute fraction of them, occupying a time frame from 472 BC (Aeschylus' *Persians*) to 402 BC (Sophocles' *Oedipus at Colonos*). Specifically, six plays from Aeschylus, seven plays from Sophocles and nineteen plays from Euripides survive.[69]

As the city's official storytellers and political philosophers, these tragedians educated theatre audiences on questions of morality, politics, philosophy and the arts. But beyond that, they represented issues on morality, politics and philosophy differently – that is to say, artistically. Quite simply, these dramatists took the stories, characters and ideas of their ancestors and recreated them for their contemporaries. The people heeded these tragedies as they would the teachings of the city's statesmen or philosophers. What this indicates is that '[t]he ancient Greeks theorized in theater as much as they dramatized theory in the Platonic cave'.[70] All of it, as Constantinou continues, formed part of 'the ambit of the affairs of the polis'. The democrats were drawn to this medium, this fictional art form, which also became a political art form that was valued for the way that it weaved between reality and fiction and back again. It became a unique form of political discourse.

Most commonly structured around divisions between law and nature, mortal and divine, male and female, family and state, the inside and outside, tragedy comprised fictional plots that dramatized the logic and framework of heroic personas met with insurmountable dilemmas.[71] Heroes tended to be venerable though not necessarily loveable, intelligent without being completely wise and independent while still inexorably subject to the whim of nature.[72] Because of this, their downfall, the kernel from which these tragedies typically germinate, evoked a sense of empathy and irony, and perhaps even inevitability. As figures that aspire for the best only to be rewarded with the worst, tragedy unveiled 'that efforts to limit suffering through the accumulation of knowledge or power might invite more suffering'.[73] Yet, this is the paradoxical logic which pervades the world. And having seen and exposed it, tragedy pled with human beings to be mindful of the structures they erect and reside in, to know that they do not always know and to remain ready and able to adapt.

One's refusal or inability, but sometimes even one's ability, to do so explains why the essence of tragic drama was imbued with insurmountable conflicts or *agons*. Representing the duel between two or more competing ends, all with an equally rightful claim, the *agon* presented to tragic heroes the choice between *compromise*, something which in time would betray their deepest aspirations even as it keeps them alive, or *realization*, whose pursuit will bring with it greatness but at the highest price. The *agon* permits no middle ground. It says to the '[t]he soul' that she 'must, in her housekeeping, waste to save, and what she wastes is initially as costly, as precious, as desirable as what she keeps'.[74]

By staging the outbreak and resolution of these existential crises, the dramas of Aeschylus, Sophocles and Euripides, therefore, had the effect of reminding audiences that life is ephemeral, the result of which can trigger a search for certainty and even immortality – fixations which are impossible to divorce from one's own arrogance, folly and downfall. Yet, in hinging open the underbelly of order, in unsettling the dominant myths and orthodoxies that, for some, have sustained life so well, tragedy also underlined how pain and destruction are an inevitable part of life. Living with a fuller appreciation of this can never be easy. But to live any other way is merely to live by a delusion.

For our purposes then, the important thing is that tragedy, by exposing the delusions that all humans live by, somehow also echoed the sentiment and ethos that democracy had begun to convey within the Athenian polis. How it came to do this, to speak democratically in other words, is really the fundamental question. And it is a question that cannot be answered satisfactorily, at least in the way which this book seeks to do, without first answering the other fundamental question, which is: why and how did the practice of tragedy develop?

Questions regarding the origins and development of tragedy have long plagued scholars fascinated by the classical world. Despite this, the answers they have come up with have not so much been conclusive explanations as suggestive theories. And what they have suggested by and large seems to go something like this.

Long before tragedy came to be associated with familiar names like Aeschylus, Sophocles and Euripides, we are given to understand that tragedy had less to do with drama as we know it than it did with a 'goat' or 'goat song'.[75] Though no doubt odd, since extant tragedies have practically nothing to do with goats or rituals involving goats, this lineage can be traced back to the notion of the Dionysian and its artistic embodiment in the half-man, half-beast satyr. Essentially, as the theory goes, tragedy's origins are either linked to or inspired by a primal life force that precedes and terrorizes any life form constructed by humankind. This is a life force that conjures in us sentiments of excess, mysticism, fusion and the sublime – ultimately leading to the dissolution of our subjectivity and even our existence.[76] Yet, beyond the pretence that life is important or that our constructed realities are enduring, this was not, in essence, a horrifying revelation. Instead, what horror and pain it disclosed was done so in the presence of a nascent wonder and joy that could be just as overwhelming. This was the Dionysian state embodied in the satyr and the *satyrikon* (or dithyramb). As the epitome of Dionysian revelry, the satyr was the primordial (goat-like) being who personified this truth and rawness.[77] It understood the need for civilization, but also saw in it a futile quest for unobtainable permanence. Wedged between these two conflicting worlds, and tormented by anguish, the satyr, nonetheless, could find reassurance in a chaotic sense of bliss. The dithyramb–*satyrikon* became the purest expression of this. Through the satyrs' revelry, a heady mix of madness, intoxication, self-abandonment, pain and their opposites were given a release.[78]

But this, of course, was only the origins from which tragic drama would emerge. The development of tragedy as a form of drama would be another matter altogether. Indeed, though the dithyramb–*satyrikon* had rightly captured life's tragedy, it did not translate it into theatrical drama. That crucial step came with the Revolution of Arion who, in 600 BC, incorporated the dithyramb into the chorus, a lyric dance that used music to accompany and coordinate speech and imitative gesture.[79] In laymen's terms, what Arion did was to introduce structure and rigidity to the unadulterated dance of the satyrs. Its importance for us lies not in the technicalities but the amalgamation of three opposing life forces: discipline with abandon, intellect with emotion and the stationary with the dynamic, for instance.[80] In doing this, Arion did more than structure Dionysian expression; he introduced the Apollonian forces of order, rationality and certainty to offset an otherwise chaotic existence.[81] As Nietzsche would later write, the implications of this union had profound effects, not least for the birth of tragedy in fifth-century Athens.[82]

But, we should not make the mistake from this overly simplified account that the tragedy which emerged was somehow monolithic in form and content. It was not. As a form of drama, tragedy would undergo numerous vital changes and reflect variously the broader sociopolitical shifts of the day. For instance, Patricia Easterling makes the point that Aeschylean tragedy is commonly assumed to be the most primitive of all extant tragedies, while Sophoclean tragedy is somehow representative of the art form's pinnacle, and Euripidean tragedy, by contrast, marks the drama's decline.[83] Indeed, with Euripides' introduction of the *deus ex machina* or 'the god of machines', some commentators have argued that audiences were denied the ability to suffer and experience the joys that come through suffering. Instead, they, like Euripides himself, were starved of the opportunity for reconciliation through tragedy and, in turn, they eventually lost faith in tragedy as a social and political institution. Others, like William Ridgeway, would contest this view. For Ridgeway, it was not Euripides' tragedies that were infused with rationalism and optimism, but Aeschylus'. It was Aeschylus, as Ridgeway writes, who 'had the sublime confidence that by rightly employing their reason men could avoid catastrophe'.[84] To this end, there is no actual evidence that Euripides was under Socrates' spell, as some believe he was, and we should not so easily conclude that his dramatic productions moved tragedy closer to philosophy. 'While the superabundance of dialectical fireworks in some Euripidean tragedies dissipates out tragic emotions', Ridgeway draws the conclusion that 'it usually illustrates the futility of reason, its inability to prevent tragedy'. This demonstrates the variations in tragedy and the various ways we can interpret both the tragedies and the tragedians who created them. While some would argue that Aeschylus' and Sophocles' productions represent the purest examples of tragedy, others believe that the more subversive and indeed more tragic dramas came from Euripides.

These caveats aside, though, the overall point to recall here is that tragedy was really more than just drama. That is to say, drama's importance was not just dramatic. It conveyed a crucial existential message, one which had undergone a continuous process of disclosure and concealment. Tragedy dramatized that process; the subsequent developments in actors, action and plot being slotted in for 'dramatic effect'. This explains why, for Peter Euben, drama was so central to the Greek way of life.[85]

More specifically, this begins to explain why tragic drama would become so central to the democratic way of life. True, tragedy was chiefly a dramatic art form. Yet, as should already be clear, Greek drama was, in many ways, 'inseparable from the ancient Greek political process', given that, for Constantinou, it was 'a medium of critique and self-reflectiveness'.[86] This is no less the case for tragic drama which, despite its pre-democratic origins,[87] really only began its true ascendancy with the rise of democracy.[88] Such was tragedy's democratic impact that many even identify it as the site where both the spirit and practice of democracy were truly given life.[89]

Specifically, as Christian Meier contends, tragedy was as necessary to the Athenians during this time of great upheaval as their Assembly, Council and other democratic institutions.[90] It was a political medium that gave expression to both order and chaos. It debunked the absolute certainty and life force that had sustained the aristocratic world without debunking the certainty and life force needed to sustain the Greek world.[91] And it inflected the problems caused by the escalating numbers of political actors; the dispersal of power and responsibilities; the rise of novel and abstract ideas; the lack of time-honoured state apparatus and the pervasiveness of human arrogance and violence into something that prompted and challenged the Athenians to act, without leaving them overwhelmed or indignant. Because of this, Stephen Chan has said that 'it was not in the Athenian *agora*, the public debates, that concepts of justice were determined, but in the Athenian theatre'.[92] Through the creation of a valued institutional space, the Athenians were taught to reflect on themselves and the world they lived in. By detaching themselves from reality – using fiction to address issues too difficult to express in reality – they were emotionally strengthened to re-engage their reality with a greater level of commitment. In short, through telling stories – dramatizing them for all to see – order can be given to phenomena which would otherwise have seemed chaotic.

And so, dramatized in a stylized fashion, tragedy represented a world of marked heterogeneity and tension, of characters and circumstances enticed by glory and wrought with chaos. In these portrayals of existence, it was possible to see not only a myriad of individuals, even those marginalized in everyday Athenian society, but also the ideological status quo and desires which undergirded and challenged the evolving polis. Dissonance, therefore, was crucial to tragedy. And this is why tragedy was so crucial to democracy.

In fact, the very same dissonance which democracy had slowly begun to unveil struck at the very heart of the tragic festivals of the City Dionysia and Lenaia, which took place in Athens each year. During these festivals, which were akin to national days of celebration, Athens opened her doors to the Greek world and paid homage to all that was great and enviable about the city-state.[93] Featured in this Panhellenic festival were ceremonial rituals and displays, all of which were aimed at demonstrating just how financially wealthy, politically ascendant and militarily powerful the city was.[94] This spectacle was further intensified by the spatial arrangement of the audience.[95] Seated together in one theatre were block after block of citizens, statesmen, soldiers, foreign dignitaries and even women and slaves. The product was the creation of a unique citizen body and civic gaze. In various ways, this assembly, which often drew as many as 20,000 spectators,[96] reminded each individual of the importance of past and future military sacrifice, of the polis as a benevolent carer and educator and, most of all, that order must be maintained for the good of all.[97] These, of course, were the explicit aspirations of the Athenian state too, which was tasked with the responsibility of organizing these festivals.[98] It was the city's duty to coordinate, fund and select the poets, plays and eventual victors of these festivals. Poets and arbiters alike would therefore have had to been conscious of the plays' literary, philosophical as well as its political tone. For all these reasons, Simon Goldhill concludes that '[e]ach of these ceremonials in different ways promotes and projects an idea and ideal of citizen participation in the state and an image of the power of the polis of Athens. It uses the civic occasion to glorify the polis'.[99]

But, polis glorification was never the sole purpose of the festivals of the Dionysia and Lenaia. In fact, set against the grain of the festivals' Athenocentrism was always a more Panhellenic and politically subversive thrust.[100] Being festivals of Panhellenic significance, the Athenocentrism exuded was met, received and problematized by a heterogeneous response. Opening her doors to the Greek world meant Athens also had to open her soul to influences previously foreign, invisible or feared. In such an environment, Athenians would no doubt have confronted issues and peoples not known or not wanted. And this openness also permeated domestic structures too. It is widely acknowledged that, during these festivals, a public place was reserved for the city's women, children, slaves and foreigners, individuals who normally had no political standing.[101] Whether or not they attended en masse is contested. But the frank authorization of their presence indicates an extreme deviation from the norm which Athenian civilization had erected. Within this state of inversion, citizens, foreigners and private individuals revelled as one under the figurehead of Dionysus, the god of intoxication and the 'every man'.[102] A dichotomy, as such, was 'set up between the structured and stable picture of Athenian citizens in their rows of civic order, in a setting imbued with the strength and stability of Athenian legitimacy in Greece, and the tenuous, unpredictable, unstable nature of life'.[103]

This dissonance, crucial to democratic politics, was also evident within the tragic dramas themselves. On the one hand, as both Edith Hall and Michael Zelanak have noted, tragedy frequently celebrated the greatness of Athens.[104]

Whether through its dramatization of great heroes or its endorsement of Athenian identity vis-à-vis barbarian identities, a definite arrogance and xenophobia perforated these dramas. All that was heroic, wise and great, the tragedies proclaimed, pointed to Athens. Even dramatizations of controversies and transgressions against the Athenian polis were but evidence of what the Athenian psyche and system could accommodate. Yet, as would typically be the case in tragic plots, the disarray and dissidence would ultimately be met with a satisfactory end, which would only further valorize the Athenian way of life.

Even so, tragedy characteristically lent itself to a variety of sometimes contradictory interpretations, some of which were not always complementary of Athens or its way of life.[105] Depending on the social and political backdrop in which the drama was performed, tragedy could just as easily champion, question or even subvert the democratic polis. Frictions or *agons* were created to draw out, among other things, the relationships between democracy, patriotism, xenophobia and empire. Because of this, tragedy often drew attention to the heroism of marginal figures and the issues which occupied their existence. From women, children and slaves to foreigners, tragic plots delved into taboo themes revolving around the family, sexual deviancy, murder, greed, the horrors of war and the unsustainability of Athens' political order.

First staged in 458 BC, during a time when political infighting and factionalism had nearly torn Athens apart, Aeschylus' *Eumenides* gives us an example of just how a tragedy could dramatize and even heal the rifts which threatened to split the society in two. As the last instalment in the *Oresteia* trilogy, *Eumenides* sits at the end of a series where from familial turmoil Aeschylus goes on to dramatize the inability of murder and revenge to ever bring justice about. In this third play, having taken his revenge on Clytemnestra his mother, Orestes is finally made to stand before the *Areopagus* to learn his fate. What is interesting about this is that only three years prior to the trilogy's premiere, in 462/461 BC, the actual *Areopagus* had just been disbanded, with its powers transferred in full to the more democratic *Ekklesia*. The event, which was the source of much infighting and bloodshed in Athens, eventually cost the life of Ephialtes, who was murdered by his political adversaries for spearheading the democratic reform.[106] Though the democrats of Athens were on the precipice of winning a key political victory, it was true that the city was teetering on the brink of civil war, hampered by widespread violence, animosity and revenge. These were the very themes that found their way into the three tragedies which make up Aeschylus' *Oresteia*.

Proceeding in three steps, the trilogy is a cycle that begins with murder, goes on to revenge and ends with justice. From a wife who murders her husband to a son who takes revenge on his mother, it ends with his trial before the *Areopagus* in Athens. While the play is profusely imbued with mythical significations, its plot line effectively revolves around the fate and ultimate acquittal of the son, Orestes, at the hands of the Athenian jurors. It is the collective responsibility of the Athenian people, in other words, to mete out justice. Having transferred the *Areopagus'* power to the collectivity, Aeschylus does two things. First, he transfers authority from the minority to the majority. Second, he marks a metaphorical shift away from the system of revenge and violence, prevalent in the earlier instalments of the trilogy, towards a regime based on a justice that represents and is decided upon by the entire citizen body.[107] This echoed the events that had rocked Athens not so long ago and, in its own way, called upon the Athenians to refrain from revenge and violence. Rather, like its Athenian jurors, *Eumenides* petitioned the citizens of Athens to confront the uncertain times and the difficult questions they gave rise to together, through peaceful and open means. It is in this way that tragedies like Aeschylus' *Eumenides* affirmed and then problematized the pride of Athens in a manner that was overtly political.

Tragedy, as such, was a site of paradox, pursuant to the 'god of paradox', Dionysus, under whose name these plays were performed.[108] As the god of theatre, Paul Monaghan argues that Dionysus embodied a dissonance that was fundamental to tragic drama: 'a tension between things, between script and actor, present and not present, real and not real, performance and audience'.[109] Moreover, it is in the 'interplay between norm and transgression' where, for Goldhill, our 'understanding of the tragic moment will lie'.[110]

To begin to draw all this together, we turn one last time to the theorizations of Castoriadis, who sums up what tragedy disclosed through the simple dictum that our 'Being is Chaos'.[111] Whether considered from an institutional or an ontological perspective, what tragedy does, in essence, is to recall us to the fact that Being will always be returned to Chaos. This, in short, is the post-foundational certitude embedded within tragedy.

Synonymous with the order that is produced through human life, knowledge and civilization, tragedy can therefore help us to understand our Being as Chaos in two important ways. The first way is through human hubris or excessive individuation. In popular conceptions, as Nathalie Karagiannis notes, the Greek view of hubris sees humankind consumed in a self-deluded attempt to transcend our very humanness, to defy all that prevents us mortals from attaining immortality.[112] Hubris, as such, insinuates that there are limits which are known to humankind and that we, nevertheless, attempt to transgress to further our own Being. Yet, in Castoriadis' account, hubris is perhaps more a corollary of the fact that human beings do not know, and may never know, their own limits.[113] The crucial marker which states that human beings have gone too far, that they have become inhuman, is nowhere to be found, perhaps until too late. All that we can do is to keep striving, all the while knowing that there are limits. This is why Chaos, for Castoriadis, 'is presented as Chaos *in* man, that is, as his *hubris*'.[114] Human beings, by the very fact that we exist, embody hubris precisely because our existence is premised on the continuous effort to defy the unknown and unknowable.

But, hubris as Chaos only embodies Chaos in life. Chaos in death, or death itself, is what actually poses the greatest threat to Being. While we may all want to believe otherwise, death constitutes the greatest unknown in life. In and through its constant reminders of human mortality, tragic plays therefore exuded this second manifestation of Chaos in Being, which can be understood through the wisdom of Silenus, who declared that '[t]he very best thing is utterly beyond your reach not to have been born, not to *be*, to be *nothing*. However, the second best thing for you is: to die soon'.[115]

Read this way and what we can hold to be certain and true becomes not the life, knowledge and civilization that we have constructed and profited from. This is because inherent to its truth is always another, more enduring certitude, one which has no positive foundation.[116] Through these fictional depictions, where heroes fall and society's outcasts rise, tragic drama thus 'gave its audience a semi-vicarious experience of the fluidity and unpredictability of life where the membrane surrounding the civilised order is seen to be thin and porous'.[117] Beyond the theatricality of the drama, tragedy theorized into Athenian praxis the need to confront and negate the very civic and religious order needed to sustain life so as to grasp its true signification and the darkness that human beings refuse to be blinded by.[118] Only by doing this, can we even glimpse the fragile – and at times dark – nature of existence.

Applied to politics, it becomes easy to see why tragedy was able to echo some of the more existential sentiments that democracy had begun to raise within the Athenian polis. This is particularly so if we turn to another illustrative example, this time Sophocles' well-known tragedy *Antigone*, for illumination.[119] First staged in Athens around 442 BC, Sophocles' tragedy was set against a backdrop of both Athenian greatness and decadence.[120] Pericles, the great democratic ruler of Athens, had only just initiated policies which sought to elevate political allegiance to the state above all else, including those owed to other individuals and to one's own family. All citizens were bound by this decree: bound to serve and follow the polis first and foremost. Against these political developments, Sophocles thrust the figure of Antigone onto the city's stage, perhaps as a deft critique of the newly emerging order within Periclean Athens.

Set in mythic Thebes, *Antigone* revolved around the question of political supremacy. Unable to share and resolve their equal claims to the Theban throne, Sophocles has Antigone's brothers – Eteocles and Polyneices – meet sword with sword in a deadly battle that ultimately leads to their deaths. Wishing to restore order, their uncle Creon, as the new king, quickly decrees that Eteocles, the brother who remained loyal to Thebes, will be buried with full honours. The traitor Polyneices, on the other hand, will lie unburied, unmourned and unforgiven.

A city, Creon rationalizes, cannot survive without order. If Thebes is not to descend further into chaos, it must firmly entrench order and reprimand those who would rob it of order. The memory of Polyneices, through Creon's decree, would serve as a reminder of this. For Antigone, though, Creon's decree does not carry the weight of law. Order is not man's to have, in her reasoning, least of all when it impugns the designs of the gods. Order at Polyneices' expense is no just order at all.

For the audiences in Athens, this performance – replete with political allusions – would quite possibly have invigorated intense reflection and interested debate. In the first instance, some may well have drawn analogies between the rising prominence of Pericles in Athens with the prominence of Creon in Thebes. Others may have glimpsed the insidious nature of order when it is thrust arbitrarily upon a society. For Antigone, his niece, Haemon, his son, Eurydice, his wife and even for Creon himself, the order embodied by Creon's decree was to be the very order that would destroy them. In other words, the institution of his Being, seen as necessary in his eyes, would be what causes his eventual demise. Deaf to the pleas of Antigone, and in fact to the whole of Thebes, Creon blindly, confidently goes it alone. His tragedy, or so Sophocles appears to intimate, is his inability to hear others. When Haemon bids Creon 'not to be wise alone', herein, Castoriadis believes, are democracy's precepts laid bare.[121]

This is why tragedy so poignantly echoed the democratic ambition to balance self-institution with self-limitation: because it reiterated through a dramatic medium the democratic point that any conception of order necessarily shrouds though ultimately succumbs to chaos. That, thanks to tragedy, was something the ancient Greeks learnt to appreciate at the peak of their creativeness, a peak which gave rise to the prominence of tragic art within the newly democratized polis of Athens.[122]

And so , 'Athenian tragedy's claim to having been a truly democratic art-form' was, as Edith Hall argues, 'paradoxically, far greater than the claim to democracy of the Athenian state itself'.[123] By ensconcing a diverse collectivity of individuals into one forum, citizens, dignitaries, soldiers, women and slaves found themselves better equipped to acknowledge, critique and reconcile a greater range of possibilities in life. They became more aware, if not more able, to reconcile themselves with others. Doing so helped to avert the extremes of both radical homogeneity and heterogeneity for something more precarious and contingent.[124] Despite his overt antipathy to liberal democracy, Nietzsche, nevertheless, believed that tragedy could compel its audiences to participate 'in other souls' and to 'look at the world through many eyes'.[125]

This had obvious practical implications. For one, tragedy provided an opportunity for the polis to reflect, away from the pressures of everyday politics and existence, on aspects of communal life that were pressing and, because they were pressing, could not always be freely discussed in reality. The decisions made and the paths taken were juxtaposed – using fictional means – with those that were not made and not taken. An aesthetic experience of this kind had the potential to effect 'positive empowerment and emancipation, liberating sensuousness from the tyranny of reason, releasing libidinal energies and turning "labor" into "play", making life lighter and civilization less repressive'.[126] At the same time, it also courted a deeper engagement, one which inevitably folded back onto itself. By playing on emotional, rational and physical faculties alike, tragedy depicted individual life as that moment of glory we all long for and yet never quite manage to grasp on to for long or in any meaningful way. Life's transience and the incapacity of human beings were manifested in terms of what we try so hard to evade, suppress and demonize. At its most explicit, this was the world of Athens: the women, children, slaves and foreigners who embodied a chaotic diversity that exceeded even the openness of democracy. And though no empirical evidence avails to suggest that tragedy had a direct political impact, its political contribution cannot be so easily discounted. Rather, '[i]n just that noisy dialogism, in its disagreements, verbal contests, dismayed reactions, doubts, and second thoughts, Athenian tragedy largely reflect[ed] the discursive civic context in which it flourished'.[127] It exorcized the travails of Athens onstage so that Athenians could better live – with demons and all – off stage. Through entertaining fiction, Athens was made more able to live with the diverse realities that exist in fact.

Is this is not politics? And democratic politics at that? The process whereby an individual comes to appreciate themselves as a social being, with rights and responsibilities pertaining to that condition, is precisely the point where politics is needed as a tool of mediation. Likewise, the point when a collective begins to live in anticipation of what one another, indeed all others, might have to say about existence, even if it is said against them, is when democratic politics becomes an ontological base. For this reason, democratic politics is always more, and requires more, than just what political tools make possible. Beneath the laws, institutions and structures of Athens' democratic state, this 'moment of anti-politics' was fundamentally what tragedy alluded to.[128] This was the moment – which remains forever present – that first inspired politics but which politics cannot always adequately give expression to. The restorative capacity of tragedy seized on this and, in so doing, 'not only relieved the Greeks of the tensions and agony of political life, but reminded them that politics could not absorb the diversity of life'.[129] In the plots, characters and language of the Greeks' tragedies, these were the sensitivities that found their way, after the festivals of the Dionysia and Lenaia, back into the political realities that democracy had begun to construct in Athens.

A Multivocal Democracy: The Democratic Impact of Tragedy's Multivocal Form in Ancient Athens and Today

Being a by-product of a diverse and often volatile polis still coming to grips with recent sociopolitical changes, tragedy was soon tasked with the job of dramatizing both the potential and pitfalls of Athens' democracy. When all seemed new and hopeful, even when they seemed glib and set to lapse, the dramas of Aeschylus, Sophocles and Euripides were a source of relief and release for the citizens of Athens. Because of this, tragedy could rightly claim to be a uniquely democratic medium, one perhaps able to offer something that Athens' bourgeoning Assembly, Council and various other institutions of democracy were not able to.

Having already provided a broad overview of democracy and tragedy in Chapter 1, this chapter now turns its attention specifically to the democratic impact of tragedy. Just how did this peculiar art form comment on democracy and the new challenges it raised for the very same citizens who had gathered in their tens of thousands to see the plays at the Festivals of the Dionysia and Lenaia? And what lessons might we be able to draw from tragedy, distant as we are from the time and mindset of the Greek city-state, to revitalize our own practices of democracy today?

There are, of course, no definitive answers to these questions. And it is not the book's intention to provide them. Rather, in a less rigid and certainly less conventional fashion, it aims to put forward an answer that looks straight at the form and content of Greek tragedy. This it does by examining the so-called multivocal form of Greek tragedy and its ability to bring a variety of otherwise marginalized stories, characters and voices onto the public stage and into democratic debate.

Simply put, tragedy was a democratic institution because it reiterated, through multivocal form, democracy's key message: that self-institution (or Being) must

be and ultimately will be subjected to self-limitation (or Chaos). By populating
their dramas with a diverse cast of actors and their not always salutary actions,
the tragedians thus used drama to help the Greeks reflect on their own existence.
As if sat before the reflective glow of a mirror pointed directly at them, what the
audiences frequently saw was a polis that had, for too long, been drunk on the
grandeur of its own achievements. They were reminded of the fact that whatever
greatness they had claimed as their own would never be dissociated from the
horrors of empire, warfare, slavery and exploitation that, together, comprised
the democratic way of life.

And so, even though borrowed from the classics scholar Edith Hall, the term
the 'multivocal form' will be used here to refer more broadly to tragedy's democratic ability to publicize multiple realities, actors and actions in a way that
challenged the existing Athenian order.[1] Through the use of diverse plots, characters and languages, the tragedians therefore sought to capture an expansive
spectrum of narratives, individuals and issues drawn from and recreated for
the democratic polis. This, in short, is the characteristic of tragedy that most
explicitly politicized what democracy had rendered unpolitical. Popularized in
contemporary popular culture as an age of equality and freedom, we sometimes
forget that the peak of democracy also bred xenophobia, patriarchy, violence
and slavery, both in Athens and her many colonial outposts. Many individuals could not participate, vote or rule in the polis. Democracy, in this respect,
was often its own worst enemy. Understanding this, the tragedians used the
multivocal form to represent and incorporate marginalized figures as well as
those issues which were too taboo to be debated via formal democratic processes. And while social and political inequalities were not always or immediately removed, tragedy did help to foreground the existence of hitherto silenced
and unseen figures.

When it did this, tragic drama had the potential to do something remarkable.
First, the effect of bringing a variety of otherwise marginalized stories, characters and voices onto the public stage and into democratic debate would have
reminded the gathered audiences of what can be broadly described as the interplay between order and disorder. As Chapter 1 showed, central to the democratic push towards self-institution and self-limitation was the recognition that
chaos perpetually lurks behind the order erected by humankind. In its own way,
this was a theme central within the tragic corpus too: the need to entrench an
enduring order while being taunted by the presence of chaos. But this recognition – that one's fate lies firmly in the grasp of chaos – would have had the effect,

perhaps, of also foregrounding the lives and struggles of individuals who had been routinely discriminated against in Athens.

That both tragedian and their audiences could do this though suggested their collective willingness to suspend their own reality in an effort to imagine other realities or the realities of others. This is how tragedy's multivocal form would have spoken to democratic concerns in a second way. Itself a fictional source inspired from mythical tales, tragedy was emblematic of the need to question and extend reality. And it did this by resorting, paradoxically, to 'fictional' accounts. By moving swiftly between the realm of reality and fiction and back again, tragedians found themselves with the unexpected power to critique reality and foreground what might have been possible had citizens and statesmen acted differently from the way they did in reality. When interned by an unyielding political landscape that increasingly forecloses one's freedom to imagine new realities, alternate sources of knowledge may therefore provide unforeseen insights. They can even help in our effort to better envision and cope with disorder. That was what tragedy's multivocal form did in Athens.

It needs to be stressed that while the actual impact of its doing so may have been hard to quantify, it would have arguably disclosed a side of democracy that was not always visible through democratic deliberations alone. More precisely, the plots, characters and language that tragedy brought to bear highlighted those things which were visible and pertinent to everyday democratic life in light of what was democratically less visible and pivotal. Through fictional representations of unexpected characters, through dramatic lyrics and dance and through the performance of stylized plots and the retelling of myths (otherwise neglected) truths about democracy were entertained. This was why tragedy's multivocal form was so penetrating: because it blended reality and fiction to bring out democracy's paradox. It showed to the entire population that chaos lurked just beneath the order they had erected. This is what tragedies were apt to do: to revitalize democracy in its multivocal form.

In what follows, this chapter explores the democratic impact of tragedy's multivocal form in three steps. First, it sets out to define and outline the key characteristics of tragedy's multivocal form. Here, a working definition of the multivocal form will be provided that draws out the democratic impact of the fictional plots, characters and language of these tragic dramas. In particular, it will emphasize the multiple and often contradictory sets of stories, characters and voices which tragedies brought to the public stage and into democratic debate. The argument is that, this was what enabled tragedy to reiterate the crucial democratic interplay between order and disorder and reality and fiction. The chapter then turns its attention to the political implications that this cultural artifact may have for contemporary practices of democracy. However, in doing this, we are required to do two things. The first is to provide a broad political account of how the symbiosis of democracy and tragedy came to an end in classical Greece, as well as to flag the prospect for its continued relevance today. The second is to create an analytical framework of sorts, drawing from the key characteristics of tragedy's multivocal form, that can allow us to read tragedy as a democratic text today. Though no longer something that is in vogue, the chapter will show that reading these multivocal dramas as democratic texts can place us, as it did the Greeks, in a better position to speak about and confront the promises and pitfalls of our own contemporary democratic challenges.

The democratic impact of tragedy's multivocal form in Athens

First, it is necessary to clarify how this book will define tragedy's multivocal form. As a starting point, it may be worth reminding ourselves that in fifth-century Athens, tragedy was 'a unique invention, a scary gift given to the Greeks because the ethical revolution and the freedoms of experimental democracy converged here, allowing the outrageous to be said'.[2] Tragedy asked poets, actors and spectators alike that they not suppress 'the paradoxical tendencies of Greek culture' but, instead, to 'question and exceed such boundaries in the name of the diversity of life'.[3] Tragedy – its production, performance and reception – became a forum to test Athenian democracy, to stretch it to its limits: to see what democracy could and could not tolerate, what could and could not be tolerated by its citizens. Through dramatic plots, characters and language, Athens could see itself reflected. But that reflection rarely corresponded with how it chose to perceive itself – as it ought to be. Rather, what glared back, through the tragedies staged at the Dionysia and the Lenaia, was Athens as it actually was – in its multivocal form.[4]

By bringing a variety of otherwise marginalized stories, characters and voices onto the public stage and into democratic debate, tragedy's multivocal form therefore reflected Athens as it really was. Which, as we sometimes forget, was a city-state rife with slaveholding, patriarchy, xenophobia, pettiness, hypocrisy and warmongering. Despite its many advances, Athens was no utopia. Within certain parameters, democracy had unquestionably carved out new rights, institutions and possibilities. Outside these parameters, however, things were less certain.

The realities of everyday life, complex and amorphous as they were, could not always be incorporated into the public life of democratic Athens. What needed to be said could not always be said free of risk. Often, what needed to be done could not be done without threat of reprisal. Because of this, democratic debates and institutions did not go nearly far enough. They may have broken new ground. But they did not necessarily always fulfill their radical promise thereafter.

For these reasons, tragedy's multivocal form effectively took on a democratic tone when it illuminated Athens as it really was. In these dramas, it was possible to see not just a myriad of individuals but also the issues and ideas that marked out their different worlds.[5] By demonstrating to the polis that only through a polyphony of voices can truth and understanding be acquired, it was an institution that generated a political space dependent upon open and dramatic debate.[6] As such, through these tragic plays, old and new voices, even strange and uncomfortable perspectives from outside the Greek world, were given centre stage – encapsulating the unstable but truly democratic spirit.

But, at a more precise level, the reason why tragedy's multivocal form was 'multivocal' was because it represented the sum of its parts, its parts comprising the elements of the tragic plot, characters and language. But, it was also multivocal to the extent that each part – the plot, the characters and the language of tragic drama – was characteristically multidimensional, enabling tragedians to make politically experimental and even politically incorrect claims in dramatic ways. This is why the focus here is on otherwise marginalized stories, characters and voices: to permit us a glimpse of how tragedy addressed the inequalities of democratic Athens' slave economy, its wars of imperialism and the tempestuousness and avarice of its political bureaucracy.[7]

Tragic plots

Though they cannot be so reduced, it is not wrong to say that tragic plots habitually brought into relief those aspects of Greek society that had become sidelined or cordoned off from political debate. As a defining feature of both the tragic genre and, most specifically, its multivocal form, Aristotle went so far as to stress that more than any other aspect of tragedy it is the plot that sets the art form apart. The rationale he offers for his verdict is based on the fact that tragic plots are 'complete, whole and of magnitude'.[8] They are representations, commonly based around a reversal of fortune and the recognition of one's fatal flaw, that strive to increase or enlarge reality. Unlike episodic scenarios that do not follow the laws of probability and necessity, tragic plots avoid the flaws of those dramatic representations which do not possess a beginning, a middle and an end.[9] Such is the majesty of their structure that, for Aristotle, 'even without see-ing it performed, the person who hears the events that occur experiences horror and pity at what comes about'.[10]

It is hard to disagree with Aristotle – for this is what customarily defines a tragic plot. But, what can be said about Aristotle's account is that it is based primarily on a formalist reading of the elements that make up a tragic plot. For him, the political dimensions that these plot lines would have had at the peak of their popularity in fifth-century Athens are perhaps not so important. As such, if what interests us about tragic plots is more the latter than the former, then we may need to look further afield.

Importantly, it is crucial that we do look further afield because tragic plots quite commonly had a distinctive social and political component about them. Given that they were typically enacted around some insurmountable crisis or conflict, they had the effect of capturing competing values and dueling wills which were momentous enough to shake the foundations of society. As Hall writes, these were stories that would frequently 'enact the outbreak and resolu-tion of a crisis caused by imminent or actual death, adultery, exile, pleas for asylum, war, or the infringement of what Antigone calls the "unwritten and unshakable laws" of the gods'.[11] This is why Jean-Pierre Vernant argues that tragic plots thrust individuals – both the characters on stage and even the audiences off it – into a vortex of moral choice.[12] It was precisely this vortex that engen-dered in the audience a heightened sensitivity towards the world's heterogeneity. Audiences were quickly reminded that, though dominant, theirs was not the only world view within the polis. And having revealed this social and political multiplicity, tragic plots would go on to demonstrate the 'tragic' consequences of those who hubristically rejected the claims of others.

This being the case, classics scholar Page duBois believes that the 'oxymoron, the incompatible' was always latent within tragic plots, meaning that 'the pre-scriptions and oppositions of political discourse' were never far away.[13] Tragedy, in other words, disrupted the order of the polis by bringing 'the spectator to a moment of recognition that exceeds the homogenous civic community, to an acknowledgement of his or her place among humankind, as mortal'.[14] It brought the spectator to the peak of their limits, which is another way of saying that trag-edy brought the spectator to the point of self-limitation.

To this end, a key capacity of tragic plots was their inherent capacity to link individual actions with the broader social, political and existential milieu. Even though these actions would inevitably involve only specific individuals at a particular time and place, the lessons and themes generated would implicate society as a whole. Such plots nurtured connections and associations between individuals, their actions and the consequences that ensued from them. They revealed the differing ethical commitments, personal rationales and structural limitations present in any crisis or conflict. As Paul Woodruff puts it, 'since a good plot presents actions to us, and actions flow from choice, we should expect a good plot to show us the kind of situations in which choices are made'.[15] Such situations, along with the choices and actions they generate, are the stuff from which tragic plots emerge.

Tragic characters

What differentiates the characters that one typically finds within tragedy from characters in other forms of drama is that they seem to be good, admirable figures – not individuals prone to depravity – which for Aristotle is a defining feature of tragic characters.[16] Given this, he is not altogether concerned about the fact that characters within tragedy are commonly made to embody the moral crisis dramatized through the plots. Nor is he particularly taken by the diverse range of individuals, ranging from kings and queens to slaves and servants, who are regularly drawn together to make up the cast. The political bearing that such characterizations would have had in reality was not Aristotle's primary concern because, according to duBois, 'Aristotle's is not the attitude of a democratic citizen of Athens toward tragedy as a ritual and political institution of democracy'.[17] Consequently, the actual political connotations of a barbarian or a slave interacting with a king, as in Aeschylus' *Oresteia* or Euripides' *Andromache*, for example, would have only been second-order concerns. Yet, for us, it is precisely the political consequences of such taboo interactions that are of interest here.

Drawn from Athens' mythical past so as to capture its present, it is interesting to note that tragic characters were, as described by Michael Chayut, often 'multidimensional, sublime, profoundly complex, whole — all character traits without which no tragic fall could have been possible'.[18] Even more relevant for present purposes are the 'zones of interaction' generated by the tragedian to allow characters, both individuals and groups, with different backgrounds and clashing perspectives to come into direct contact with each other.[19] Think here of Athenians interacting with foreigners, adults with youths, males with females, the free with the enslaved and all with all. But frequently, it was not interaction so much as inversion which the tragedians made their characters undergo. Marginal figures, to this end, would almost be forced to take centre stage while, at the same time, the prominent heroes are subjected to befall a ghastly change of circumstance. Nothing then about these characters or what happens to them is really clear. Nothing about their predicament is ever predictable, even though the sense of dread prevails. Constituted by others, these characters therefore reveal that individuals, though inevitably of a particular ethnicity, class and gender, are never just that. They are incomplete in and of themselves, that is, until they are completed by others: by their ethnicities, class and gender. In this way, what tragic characters make possible, both then and now, is an 'exploration of the Self *through* the Other', a central democratic aspiration.[20]

But, there is a further symbolic component that would have had political connotations as well: the characters' use of masks within the tragic performance. Though largely symbolic, especially for us today, the donning of masks meant that the identity of the actor was fused with the identity of the character being played.[21] Technicalities aside, what is important for present purposes is how opposing identities could have been said to merge without clashing and obliterating the other. By doing so, the actor, a Greek male, complicated his identity – for himself and for those observing the tragedy – as he transposed into characters that were often marginalized within Athens.

But, identities would have merged also for the viewing audience as they came to identify themselves with the characters on stage. Specifically, as Alvin Gouldner claims, tragic choruses offered a form of release from the rational, instrumental and subdued self valued within certain quarters of Greek society.[22] The choruses, in particular, embodied or represented individuals that Athens had forgotten, repressed or exploited in reality: the weak, old, servile and fallen. Through them, audiences could see something of those lives which were often quite foreign to their own. And it was the same for those who were actually weak, old, servile and fallen, as they saw the turn of fate, the downward spiral, for the strong and heroic. The point here was that through the fictional characters of tragic drama, individual audience members were provoked to see themselves from the perspectives of others, to invert their reality through the reality of someone else and to confront that inversion even with its manifest sense of discomfort.[23] It was through transformations like these that authorized the 'freedom of others' points of view [to] reveal themselves'.[24]

Tragic language

In this respect, the third component of the multivocal form, the language of tragedy, became particularly poignant given its ability to express the 'many-voicedness' of the polis.[25] Considered by many scholars as 'a democratic property owned collectively by all who use it', tragic language offered 'individuals whose ethnicity, gender, or status would absolutely debar them from public debate in democratic Athens [the opportunity to] address the massed Athenian citizenry'.[26] This was perhaps the multivocal form at its most literal and democratic: the many united to voice their difference. The cacophony of voices that rang out in the theatre, we can only imagine, must have disrupted the celebratory tone and the 'affective communion' of the festivals of the Dionysia and Lenaia.[27]

Yet, the value of the language within these dramas was not purely a matter of form or content alone. Tragic language was powerful precisely because it represented a convergence of both. The impact of the language, as such, was as much dependent on the point as on how that point was conveyed. Nowhere was this more apparent than in the dichotomy between heroic dialogue and choral lyric.[28] The hero/protagonist and the anonymous chorus were two contrasting categories of form and content – or rather form *as* content – in these tragic dramas. The content or purpose of heroic prose was made to recapture the glories of Athens' mythic past. The way it did so was through rational dialectic. As an example of logical and deductive reason, heroic prose pitted protagonists together who would each approach the crisis at hand from differing perspectives. By doing so, it provided audience members within the theatre with a model of how they themselves should debate when addressing the *Ekklesia*, the *Boule* and the courts.

Tragic choruses, on the other hand, sought to capture Athens as a collectivity. They represented an alternate experience to that of the hero.[29] Often amorphous entities played by some 15 actors, the choruses conveyed a disparate assortment of fears, hopes and opinions. They symbolized collective sentiment, minority opinion and forgotten voices. As a consequence, the message expressed by the chorus was rarely ever set, but rather oscillated as the tragedy progressed; as a counterweight to the heroes' perspectives. Without any simple or clear message, rather a representation of diverse and chaotic emotions, tragedy instituted choral lyric and dance to express what could not be easily and definitively captured in prose. It expressed what logical reasoning could not.

Yet, now as then, it is not always easy to hear and understand what we have become deaf to. And so, if the audiences heard anything at all, it sometimes seemed indiscernible or, worse still, inane. To untrained ears, this is what choral lyric can sound like. The anxiety and uncertainty of it could make those restrained by heroic prose uneasy even if that was what it was precisely intended to do in Athens. The form of choral lyric was its content. Its beauty came close to terrifying, and this was precisely its message. By contrast, heroic dialogue was composed of prose, which was measured, elegant and possessed a timeless feel. Publically, this was the language which that Athens prided itself on. Taking the characters 'at their word' therefore meant taking them seriously.[30] This, above all else, meant that audiences had to learn to regard – and not discard – the worlds that had given voice to these words.

When read together then, what conclusion can we draw about tragedy's multivocal form? What overall political effect, if any, can we say that it had? Obviously, any answer that is provided to this question will to some extent be conjectural in nature and, if not that, certainly biased, depending on one's reading. The answer provided here is no different.

Looking predominantly at the democratic potential and impact of tragedy, we can perhaps say that tragedy's multivocal form did one of two things to critique and help rectify the day-to-day problems of democratic politics in Athens. First, it dramatized before the gathered audiences the democratic insight that disorder exists at the heart of all orders. This, in effect, reiterated the message that chaos lurks just beyond the civilizational constructs created by humankind, something which a democracy should increasingly uncover through the processes of self-limitation. The second point that was conveyed through tragedy's multivocal form concerned the legitimacy of those sources of knowledge which helped to broaden factual understandings of political reality. When faced with intractable political obstacles, new ways of thinking may well provide a better grasp of reality. And that, as the tragedies of Aeschylus, Sophocles and Euripides demonstrated, could often be located in the least expected and most unconventional of places.

As a construct that had been conceived to defy every closed system of thought, it was a central tenet of democracy to continuously seek to uncover the chaos which had been shrouded by the polis.[31] Perceived as the space 'in which the world takes shape', chaos was effectively where the Greeks looked to for inspiration and renewal of what currently existed.[32] It was also where they were most likely to unearth the hidden hypocrisies and brutalisms enacted by their own civilization. In this sense, chaos denoted all that the Greeks considered uncertain, different, abhorrent and unknown. It captured what could not be easily understood or quantified. But, far from being overwhelmed by what caused them apprehension and indignity, the Greeks had a complicated relationship with chaos, viewing it as something that could not, in essence, be shunned from their existential landscape. Chaos was central to the order of everyday existence. It complicated everyday existence, opening it up to a broader range of stories, characters and voices than had legitimately existed under aristocratic rule. Together, order and chaos brought a unity to the Greek world.[33] In the realm of politics, achieving this unity became the task of the West's first great democracy: 'the unity of humanity within a wider unity, bound together by reason; a unity, however, which is not homogeneous, but complex, comprehending within itself the different sexes, classes, and races'.[34]

Unfortunately, as with any political assemblage, democracy did not always reach this ideal. When this occurred, tragedy entered the political arena to publicize what democracy had failed to. In its dramatizations, tragedy gave back to Athens the democratic awareness that order depends upon disorder. Tragedy, in the words of Paul Monaghan, made people aware that

> [a]t any unexpected moment, the pores of the known universe might suddenly open wide and our orderly world, or at least our sense of an orderly world, may be disastrously ruptured by the intrusion of destructive or bestial or divine forces from beyond or indeed from within.[35]

In this sense, tragedy acted in concert with democracy, quickly becoming an officially sanctioned democratic forum.[36] Where democracy excluded, enslaved and abused, tragedy did its best to alert audiences to the hidden perils of doing so.

To this end, the crucial lesson that tragedy's multivocal form imparted to the democrats went something along these lines: 'The only purification lies in denying and excluding nothing, in thus accepting the mystery of existence, the limitations of man, in short the order where men know without knowing'.[37] Beyond exposing the perceived injustices of autocracy and the openness of democratic institutions, tragedy also wrestled from the individual and the polis their claims to absolute truth, sovereignty and permanence. No single individual, institution or way of life can accommodate and explain all existence. Meaningful existence rests as much on a solid and knowable order as it does on the unsettling presence of chaos. When heroic figures and sage individuals befell a ghastly change of circumstance, though they had striven to do their best, audiences were reminded of the unsettling presence of the chaos that wrenches from us our claims to knowledge, permanence and security. Far from leaving audiences indignant or powerless though, tragedy made them more open to those forces they were unable to control and grasp. Tragedy – through its diverse plots, characters and language – asked each individual to seek out marginalized stories, individuals and voices so that they might be better placed to minimize or, rather, embrace the menace of chaos.

But, to do this in a world where nothing was absolutely certain or known completely for a fact meant that the political resources that the Greeks had to draw upon were near limitless. To truly grasp chaos, rational accounts of reality only had limited use. Because what exists beyond the realm of the known did not always accord neatly with the demarcations established through pre-existing theories of knowledge, fictive sources became as legitimate and expedient as their non-fictional counterparts in the conduct of politics. It was normal – even prudent – to draw from a range of political, philosophical and aesthetic sources in an attempt to resolve democratic dilemmas.

This explains why tragedy's multivocal form had such an impact on democratic politics. In a world where what was considered real had yet to be meaningfully separated from what was merely myth, Edith Hamilton maintains that the 'imagination was vividly alive and not checked by reason'.[38] In matters of life, the creations of poetry and drama complemented scientific observation and quantification. Fiction was not distinct from but actually gave rise to reality. It helped fashion 'a humanized world', and freed humans 'from the paralysing fear of an omnipotent Unknown'.[39] Knowing as much as modern schoolchildren might know about the universe, the ancient Greeks drew from what they could to give order to their world. '[A]rt and conduct alike proceeded from the same imperative impulse, to create a harmony or order', which G. Lowes Dickinson reiterates was central to the creation of unity.[40]

In the realm of politics, political fictions had a direct impact on the creation of political order in reality. Fiction was like the 'other' to what we understand as history, politics, philosophy and science today.[41] It captured what these pursuits could not. Because of this, artistic drives were 'pervasively integrated into all aspects of life and was perceived to be of fundamental significance. Art told the archaic Greeks who they were and how it was best for them to act'.[42] Unlike today, art was far from incidental to national ethics, politics and thought. It was, instead, what gave rise to them: the energy that allowed these Greeks to institute life, knowledge and civilization. The product was the foundation of a new order and reality.[43] Accordingly, 'art [was] not expression of what was there before, waiting to be expressed, but discovery of what was not there until it was discovered; it is creation'.[44] Yet, being the imprecise science it was, it inevitably meant that Greek narratives had to, as Alastair Blanshard notes, 'dance to a different tune, one that prefers to couple rise with fall, success with disaster, pleasure with pain, and sanity with madness'.[45] And one might add self-institution with self-limitation in the realm of democratic politics. Drawing on fiction gave these Greeks the veracity to face the consequences of these fluctuations and paradoxes in reality.

Practically, tragedy's multivocal form interweaved reality and fiction in a very particular way. Using the available evidence, contemporary scholars suggest that tragedy rarely entered politics in an explicitly prejudicial or polemic manner.[46] (Except, perhaps, for Aeschylus' *Persians*, which is the only extant play that explicitly dramatized an actual historical event.) What we know of tragedy suggests that they were commonly devoid of explicit references or biases towards specific events, figures, decisions and opinions – which is not to say that they did not comment on them. Instead, they were more metaphoric, constantly blurring the boundaries between reality and fiction.

Through techniques of zooming and distancing, Christiane Sourvinou-Inwood argues that tragedy brought mythical figures and tales, set in faraway lands, into the world of democratic Athens.[47] And this was what brought Athens and the Athenians into a world other than the one they lived. With the use of distancing techniques, tragedians publicized what would otherwise have been left unsaid, even unthought, precisely because the political climate rendered certain things unspeakable and unthinkable. This is the virtue of distancing – the resort to fictional myths, figures and exotic lands. But by dramatizing them in Athens, and during an occasion of immense political significance, they were made to zoom into political reality; the allusions in some cases being too palpable to ignore.

And so, that order and disorder and reality and fiction fused in ways that impacted directly on Athenian society meant that tragedy was not primarily 'literary or aesthetic but social and political'.[48] It was a political institution set up alongside the Assembly, Council and courts.[49] Even Aristotle acknowledges this, saying, '[t]he earlier [tragic] poets made their characters talk "politically"'.[50] To be sure, however, the point made here is not that drama was more political than artistic. Rather, it merely reiterates the logic of the day, which was that poetry and thought, fact and myth, emotion and reason, art and politics all mattered in reality.[51] Consequently, tragedy was not politically peripheral but, in the words of Paul Cartledge, 'an active ingredient, and a major one, of the political foreground, featuring into the everyday consciousness and even the nocturnal dreams of the Athenian citizen'.[52]

Through tragedy's multivocal form, the Athenians were enabled to see how their lives, knowledge and civilization could not be meaningfully separated from those elements which had sustained them in reality: the slaves in the city, the women at home, the colonies and colonized both near and afar, just to name the obvious few. But that was just depicting existence as it actually was – a hubristic life taunted by unknowns and the onset of death, a knowledge that erected certainty and boundaries so that the uncertain and unknowable could be tamed or otherwise subjugated, a civilization that flourished often by means of exploitation, warfare and violence. None of this, at one level, was startling. Yet, because we humans too often shun who we are or have become, a mirror is needed to reflect these flaws as our flaws. Through its multivocal form, tragedy was that mirror, offering to the Athenians this rare glimpse of themselves.

Tragedy's political decline

We know that this is no longer the case today; the world which perceived tragedy's multivocal form as a legitimate democratic discourse is one that seems very foreign to our own. But why, precisely, is it that something so central to the development of democracy, which is still very much in vogue, is no longer seen as a politically relevant resource capable of commenting on the state of contemporary democratic configurations? Why do we not invoke tragedy as a mirror that can reflect ourselves – in our multivocal form?

A distinguishing feature of the world of Athens of the sixth and fifth centuries BC was the absence of many of the dichotomies and boundaries that we have, in more modern epochs, come to regard as essential and even natural.[53] 'Harmony, in a word', as Lowes Dickinson once said, 'was the end they [the Greeks] pursued, harmony of the soul with the body and of the body with its environment'.[54] But lacking the dichotomies and boundaries that partitioned order from disorder and reality from fiction, the times, though harmonious, were not always stable. Order existed only at the behest of disorder, and life was a fragile affair. Unlike now, subjectivity then was never considered a given.[55] This, the Greeks attributed to the capriciousness of their gods and to fate. However, in actuality, it had more to do with the fact that there remained so many unknowns in their world, a world which had only been partially grasped and domesticated. Theirs, as Richard Tarnas puts it, was 'an outflung world bright with color and drama', one that 'was both ordered and mythic'.[56] With no distinctions between the human and natural worlds, where even the immediate future remained mysterious, reality, therefore, unfolded somewhat like 'a drama in which each thing played its part'.[57]

Because of all these factors, Giacomo Gambino believes that Greek civilization can only be summed up as a 'collective enterprise' wherein poets, statesmen and philosophers all engaged in the creation of the whole – that whole being the order and the reality in which the people of the day would live out their daily existence.[58] The norm before the so-called division of forms of knowledge and reflection in disciplines and canons meant that political matters could not be meaningfully disconnected from pursuits in philosophy and the arts.[59] Sensual faculties legitimately supplemented rational ones, and vice versa, in political deliberations.[60] This, for example, implied that tragic theatre frequently 'introduced, in stylised form, the politics of myth, as well as the limits of politics'; the suggestion being that '[t]he plays were as important as philosophy and public debate'.[61] Through the stories, characters and voices that tragedy dramatized, democrats were reminded that if any one thing was at fault, it was the 'universality' accorded to notions like reason and justice in Athens.[62] This was the wisdom at the heart of tragedy's multivocal form: that nothing was universal just as no single form is eternal. Everything, as Camus once quipped of tragedy, is right and necessary within limits.[63] Beyond that, there is much we do not know. There is, in short, disorder. This was the order tragedy erected in reality.

As expected, the fragility, the sense of powerlessness and the utterly unpredictable nature of flux that was part and parcel of this world became a heavy burden for some to bear. That burden, they reasoned, was further accentuated because institutions such as tragedy continuously erected a heterogeneous political reality, celebrating in some ways a 'darkened picture of a lived world' where nothing was stable or actually known in fact.[64]

A departure was needed. And in Greece, that came with the rise of rationalism. According to the philosopher Wendy Hamblet, rationalism was valued because it was perceived as a way of leading 'thought to a certainty beyond the disturbing flux of fleshly and death-ridden existence and the whimsical omnipotence of the gods'.[65] As she continues, '[t]hrough rational and logical discourse, reason seeks the knowable in fixed forms and structures and attempts an escape from the despair of the tragic'. In this way, the desire for fixed forms and logical systems of knowledge that supposedly only rationalism could procure thus indicates what was thought of as undesirable: the disturbing flux and despair of the tragic. Instead of the multivocal form of tragedy, rationalism soon emerged as the overarching, unitary form of political discourse.

The origins of this departure can be traced back to the early sixth century BC and the Ionian city of Miletus.[66] Led by proto-philosophers like Thales, Anaximander and Anaximenes, it was held that the fictional world of myth populated by gods and predetermined by fate was ill-conceived. Rather, as they deduced, there had to be a foundational order to all things. Key to their break with tradition was their use of prose and systematic observation of physical phenomena, not poetry or fiction, to understand the true underlying characteristics of both the human and natural worlds. In the place of dramatic imagery and poetic songs, new ways of thinking inevitably brought about new ways of being. In this regard, even as far back as the sixth century BC, as Eugenio Benitez states, 'philosophers were the great de-mystifiers of things'.[67]

And so, slowly from the world of myth emerged a world increasingly driven by philosophical inquiry.[68] The result would prove disastrous for the symbiosis of democracy and tragedy. With regard to democracy, the trend became increasingly about educating citizens to question and live philosophically so that they could minimize the hazards of flux.[69] This led to an increase in the rhetorical capacity of citizens, whose consciousness began to shift from the collectivity to the rational self. Abstraction, deliberation and aggregation became the highest political tools and objectives.[70] And human beings, not gods, became the measure of all things. As this occurred, the myths and gods, which had previously given life meaning, were gradually rebuked and discredited as mere fiction.

Rationalism's key objective was to replace the disorder that had lurked beneath mythic order with something more real and more ordered. This, which Plato later attributed to Socrates, would only materialize when humankind deploys dialectical reasoning to expose the archetypes, the true Forms or Ideas, which embody the absolute essence of any one thing.[71] Reasoning of this kind can only be realized if it takes place at the level of the mind's eye, not at the level of everyday lived experience. At that level, beyond all conjecture, illusion and uncertainty, the universe's core order can become visible. These are the universals that dictate the rhythms and patterns of both the human and natural worlds – universals previously only speculated at with the help of fictional creations in the form of myths and gods. But thanks to Socrates and Plato, 'the Greek search for clarity, order, and meaning in the manifold of human experience had come full circle'.[72]

These transformations represented no less than an epochal crossroad. With myth deposed, the political legitimacy of tragedy's multivocal form was at stake. For some two-and-a-half centuries following Homer, Greek civilization had been mythic.[73] Myth or fiction, for these Greeks, captured the world of potential: of other realities that existed beyond the dominant reality. By exploring what may happen and in giving expression to the yet undiscovered, mythic expressions attempted to supplement existence with becoming and creation.[74] Poets were interpreters of life and the great works of poetry became revered moral and political treatises.[75] Democrats depended on tragedies and tragedians entered political debates in an explicit manner. Yet, after Socrates 'called down philosophy from the skies', the corruption of the mythic world began.[76] Henceforth, '[k]nowledge of man and knowledge of self become the chief tasks of reflection, just as knowledge of nature becomes the business of research. Reality is no longer something that is simply given'.[77] That was the beginnings of what we can call the Greek Enlightenment.

In light of this, democracy was increasingly discarded for a more sanitized, stable and technocratic brand of politics or, as it is better known, political philosophy. Pressed by the new demands asked of it by the Peloponnesian War, Athenian democracy slowly unraveled during the course of the fifth century BC. The twists and turns that stemmed from the mistakes and miscalculations of war – mistakes and miscalculations that had been democratically endorsed – rocked the confidence of many Athenians while it simply outraged others. Suffering from a lack of effective leadership and control, Athens fell prey, time after time, to 'class conflict, individualism, and a spirit of criticism which replaced the earlier creative effort'.[78] In such an environment, wisdom and virtue were at a premium. By that time, democratic thinking and institutions had descended into what for many was mob rule or, as Plato would have it, 'the anarchy of mere opinion'.[79] Given that it legitimated direct rule by all men and not just by the best or best-educated men, this was seen as inevitable.[80] In this way, democracy posed only as a threat to order; threatening to fragment political unity even further.

The task now was to teach the citizens to distinguish between true wisdom and mere irrationalities.[81] This was no easy charge and could not be filled from any quarter. Only rationalism would do. Left to its own devices, democratic politics was too unpredictable, and whatever progress it brokered could be easily undone. After all, as Paul Fairfield has quipped, democracy is hardly a guarantor of reasoned deliberation and action.[82] Mass rule, in this sense, oftentimes appeared no different from mass deception, domination, incompetence, prejudice, hysteria, cynicism, posturing, blind faith and gossip. For Plato, at least, these were the root of all the evils which had ravaged Athenian society.

And so , by as early as 403 BC, the Athenians began to conceive of the polis anew. Previously, as Constantinou makes clear, 'the polis was in its essence a divided one', and the city in which democracy flourished was considered a 'polyphonic space that bred disunion'.[83] But increasingly this conception of the polis was discredited, branded as 'destructive factionalism and insurrection'. Thanks to Plato's intervention, the polis became idealized 'as a harmonious whole that had universal and permanent interests'.

Tragedy and tragedians were not immune to these shifts. Indeed, it is widely agreed that the later tragedies of Sophocles and Euripides reflected the broader societal moves towards absolute truth aided by dialectical reasoning.[84] This argument is a well-canvassed one and need not be rehearsed at length. Simply put, tragedy became increasingly susceptible to what Nietzsche referred to as 'aesthetic Socratism', an approach which believes in correcting the world through knowledge, in life led by science.[85] The result, if one agrees with Nietzsche's diagnosis, was that soon '[e]verything [had to become] conscious in order to be beautiful'.[86]

Despite these changes, tragedy nevertheless declined in public importance and became detached from serious politics. 'Rather than having committed suicide', as Neal Curtis points out, it was more the case that 'tragedy [was] incrementally disabled and marginalized'.[87] The reasons for this are varied, but three are particularly relevant. The first had to do with the simple fact that as democracy changed – and was then superseded by the political philosophy espoused by Plato – the poetic wisdom of tragedy began to speak less to democracy, indeed, to politics more generally.[88] Politics was now secularized, less mythical and, because of this, articulated through prose genres. Nothing that tragedy did mattered, given that political wisdom no longer came from the world of myth and poetic creations. It came, instead, from philosophy. The second related reason for tragedy's decline had to do with the gradual political marginalization of dramatists. As the polis changed, dramatists found themselves slowly relieved of their role as the city's political educators and thinkers.[89] Resigned to their political insignificance, they began to create theatre that dramatized the travails of the private life. Politically ignored, they turned their attentions elsewhere. And so, the final reason for the political decline of tragedy in the polis: the purported advancements of rationalism. Basically, the existential reality that tragedy had dramatized as insurmountable was slowly proven to be easily surmountable if rationality was applied. Furthermore, it might even be easily preventable, if guided by the right frame of mind.[90] Particularly at blame was tragedy's multivocal form, which gave credence to the whole spectrum of evils in the diverse plots, characters and languages that it would allow to grace the tragic stage.

These sentiments were most explicitly relayed by Plato in Book Seven of his *Laws*.[91] In this dialogue, Plato holds that the philosophers themselves now 'aspire to be poets/makers of the finest and best tragedy [and that their] whole state/ constitution is constructed as a representation of the finest and best life'.[92] Effectively, Plato is saying here that philosophers now do for the city what tragedians had done in times past, which is to preserve the 'finest and best life'. Rationalism does for the city what poetry did once upon a time. With this, the city is made to live under a new order and reality. As for the old order and reality, it had to be denied access into his city, the public sphere of the polis, where affairs of state take place.

And so, as democracy changed and declined in political importance, so tragedy became more an artistic and cultural phenomenon. As a corollary of the political ascendancy of rationalism, the democratic impact of tragedy's multivocal form found itself slowly delegitimized. The work of art – of which tragedy was a key example – was now simply a matter of aesthetics, which as taste was now deemed inferior to the realm of the political. Whereas tragedy's multivocal form epitomized the collective enterprise of poetry, politics and philosophy, the rise of rationalism would only recognize formal reason. In the end, when the interplay between order and disorder and reality and fiction gave way to a new order and reality, the path that both democracy and tragedy had shared began to diverge.

Reviving the democratic impact of tragedy's multivocal form today

This goes some way to explaining why when people began to speak again about democracy, as they did during the period classified as the European Enlightenment, tragedy was no longer of any consequence. By then, tragedy had primarily become a form of dramatic entertainment and not something that was sufficiently rational or fit for the political arena.

Particularly from the time of the eighteenth century on, when Enlightenment thinkers in Europe began to revalue the say of scientific endeavours in human affairs, the blueprint laid by Plato stuck; apt to remain in the minds of anyone who would favour order and fact over disorder and fiction without really quite knowing why. After all, this Enlightenment was, as Richard Tarnas says, 'the inheritor of the basic Platonic belief in the rational intelligibility of the world order, and in the essential nobility of the human quest to discover that order'.[93] In our own generation, what Plato said now almost goes without saying. We are, as Isaiah Berlin's quote goes to show, no less concerned with efforts to 'tidy up the world, to create some kind of rational order, in which tragedy, vice and stupidity, which have caused so much destruction in the past, can at last be avoided by the use of . . . universally intelligible reason'.[94]

Today, we are more likely to recall George Steiner's famous diagnosis, thinking '[i]t is virtually indecent to envisage high tragedy engaging recent and current events as Greek tragedy engaged the Persian Wars or the massacre at Miletus. We distrust the truths of eloquence'.[95] The echoes of Steiner's sentiment, who in turn echoes Plato, are well felt in contemporary politics. Take, for example, the borrowed words that Hillary Clinton chose to attack her Democratic rival, Barack Obama, with during the 2008 U.S. presidential primary campaign: 'You campaign in poetry, but you govern in prose'.[96] Poetry, in other words, sways the emotions; prose cultivates the intellect and is the stuff of serious politics.

In order to cultivate intellect and locate political truth in our own age, we now do as John Locke once said we must, which was to refuse 'all the artificial and figurative application of words eloquence hath invented' because they 'are for nothing else but to insinuate wrong ideas, move the passions, then thereby mislead the judgment'.[97] In a similar vein, Immanuel Kant is attributed with the warning that 'the art of persuasion, i.e. of deceiving by a beautiful show (*ars oratoria*)', is harmful to reasoned judgement and individual freedom.[98] It must not therefore 'be recommended either for the law courts or for the pulpit'.

The implication is that questions and practices of politics, serious as they are, can now only be conducted via rational dialectic, observation and deduction. Politics as a science requires a clear mind, and government itself should be governed by non-arbitrary laws of order and logic.[99]

There is no place for entertainment, illusion or pleasure in these matters. But, by so 'reducing the world to a single, meaningless form, by equating truth with formal reason', Morton Schoolman makes the crucial point that politics increasingly begins to eschew a reality 'composed of a diversity of differences that prefigure aesthetic receptivity'.[100] There is no place for tragedy – neither the art form nor the way of life – in such a milieu. Tragedy teaches people to live by a fusion of their various faculties and depicts a world through its multivocal form as an entity that is not fully known or knowable, where fate remains the single, greatest determinant. No overarching order or knowable reality exists in this world. What this means is that tragedy must necessarily be separated from pursuits that take place in the law courts and in the pulpit – in the running and ruling of the city. It has to, if politics is to have a chance of becoming enlightened.

But, is there really no limit to the supposed universality of intelligible reason? And is there no space in our own day for the type of democratic insights which tragedy's multivocal form provided in ancient Athens?

The answer, in both cases, is no – not in ancient Greece and not today. In fact, it is too often overlooked that at the peak of the Greek Enlightenment, represented by Socratic and Platonic thought, an unusual reversion to the state of myth occurred. As Euben indicates, there is a paradox that can be located in Plato's *Republic* which, despite its overwhelming resort to dialectic reasoning, inevitably deployed poetic devices, such as allegory, imagery and metaphor.[101] It is not always easy to understand Plato's intentions, given that he 'uses many literary techniques that were used in different kinds of writing in his day, including those of tragedy, to make his points'.[102] Scholars have explained this contradiction in one of two ways: first, that Plato only used poetry to talk about the mythic past and, second, that it was done to communicate with those who had no philosophical training.[103]

There is, however, another way of looking at it. To do so requires us to scrutinize what transpired when the promises of rationalism reached their limits at the peak of the Greek Enlightenment. When this occurred, both Socrates and Plato found themselves thrust back into the darkened world of myth which both had hoped to escape. The pinnacle of their rationalistic achievements, in this sense, brought with it a terrifying and unanticipated revelation: that irrationalism is the inevitable by-product of rationalism.

At the height of rationalism, the threat of irrationalism is at its greatest. To confront this threat, and face the indefinite, other resources are required. Indeed, as the man who single-handedly shifted the course of Western civilization discovered at death's gate, only a reversion to what his philosophy had systematically repressed would do: art and myth.[104] Likewise, in Plato, philosophical rationalism was never fully detached from myth. As Hamblet identifies, when Plato reached the limits of rationalism, his dialogues reverted to myth.[105] But, his myths were not of the world as it is: in its multivocal form, where rationalism is just one of many forms needed to understand and make the world. Instead, Platonic myths aspired to an ideal state, a just realm where the death of his teacher, Socrates, would have never transpired. Tragically, as the death of Socrates showed, Plato's 'republic' was neither part of nor meant for reality – and perhaps this is something that Plato realized all too well.[106] This may be why he resorted to myth or fiction. But neither were his 'laws' for that matter, which had to be conveyed by way of noble lies. Thus, as Hamblet explains,

> it must be said in regard to Platonic myth that – despite a valiant effort at puri-
> fying the old myths and replacing them with less dangerous content, despite
> the reconfiguration of the gods and the openings pried in fate to make room
> for ethical choice – ultimately the most dangerous element of myth remain.
> The imagery of the "falleness" of humankind – the inevitable downward spiral
> of all things mortal and bodily and the tragedy of man's silly concern for self-
> knowledge in the futility of the efforts of the best of us – is carried along in the
> new imagery and infects the entire project.[107]

In Plato, as in any search for a single order and genuine reality, we are confronted with the irreducible complexities of the human being and of lived experience that cannot be condensed to any single order or reality.

Tragedy's multivocal form most explicitly reminds us that order and reality are inevitably more complicated than they may appear. When the Athenians elevated tragedy to check the newly established democratic order, it was done so in recognition of their own frailties and the complexities of their world, which democracy had asked each citizen to confront anew. 'In tragedies', Dennis Schmidt writes, 'we are reminded that we live in a world larger than that of our own making or control, and yet a world to which we are answerable'.[108] Such an understanding dispels the notion that we can, or are even able to, deploy reason to erect a definitive order in reality. Rather, all that we can do is be mindful that, though necessary, our order and reality remain answerable to what exceeds them. This is as true today as it was in Socrates' and Plato's day.

And so, though tragedy may not according to Alex Danchev be 'what it used to be', it nevertheless remains a theme of enduring significance.[109] Indeed, despite repeated proclamations that we are living in an age of unparalleled progress, equality and freedom, a palpable sense of dread and doubt prevails. We are, at a communal level, no less afraid of death and false expectations, no less immune to those limits that we typically ignore until too late and certainly no less in need of the simplicity and sincerity that have been jettisoned by some of our most cherished cultural norms.[110] After two world wars, the gulag, a seemingly endless Cold War, the natural disasters of the twentieth and twenty-first centuries, which now seem so destructive simply because we no longer appreciate how truly vulnerable we are, after September 11, the 'War on Terror' and now taunted by financial and environmental instability – we begrudgingly acknowledge that we might share more than just a heritage with the ancient Greeks. Though separated by millennia of change, our conditions are not always so different. We are rational, sovereign agents often left with little or no choice; swept up by diverse, overwhelming socioeconomic forces, which in previous times were epitomized by the gods and by fate.[111]

Furthermore, these realities are, in many instances, intrinsically symptomatic of contemporary democratic society. As Rita Felski writes, '[d]emocracy, after all, does not guarantee happiness, but promises at best the pursuit of happiness, a pursuit that can all too easily result in disastrous judgements, Faustian overreaching, or the agony of being torn apart by conflicting desires or values'.[112] The (im)possibility of having it all, mixed with the (false) promises of a progressive teleology, are very much democratic double binds which have led many individuals to question the totality proclaimed by the self, the state and even the world as we perceive it.[113] The ancient Greeks knew this. They used their tragedy – among other things – to remind themselves that this was so.

What do we use? Or, to put this more bluntly, might we use tragedy to engage democratic politics today?

These are important questions because tragedy, both its form and content, still speaks to and for those who cannot speak for themselves even in the twentieth and twenty-first centuries. This is especially so if we read tragedy through its multivocal form. As Hall notes with reference to the famous playwright Peter Sellars, 'tragedy can offer a venue for saying the otherwise unsayable, to represent the unrepresentable'.[114] As drama, it has been habitually invoked and interpreted in a political light. At a deeper level, a resort to tragedy has often meant a resort to what has been lost or suppressed by Platonic political philosophy. That is to say, a resort to tragedy is what can reinvigorate 'the memory of revolt and otherness that', as Constantinou writes, 'is the condition of our (and any) state of being'.[115] The understanding that nothing is closed or stable but, rather, subject to constant change and encroachment by others is both a tragic and a democratic predicament. If that is the case, then tragedy may still be capable of providing arresting democratic insights, at the very least an alternative democratic form, precisely because it is removed from now conventional political debates and democratic customs. Being exempt from the limitations of political reality, it can encompass more than would be otherwise politically expedient to do. Whether cast in dramatic form or as a category of thought, the tragic sense of life continues to haunt the daily experiences of many.

And so, even though tragedy has become separated from what we now regard as legitimate political discourse, there may still be much we could learn about democratic politics and the nature of democracy if we were to revive and read them in that light. To help us along this path, the final portion of this chapter will now offer an analytical framework of sorts, one which draws its inspiration from the key characteristics of tragedy's multivocal form to help us today to read tragedy as a democratic text. Such a framework will enable us to draw democratic insights from tragedies – both ancient and modern – in two interrelated ways. The first is to enable us to analyse the multivocal forms of tragedy today. And the second is to use that analysis as the basis for an alternate source of democratic insight. Recovering aspects of democracy which have become lost or dissociated from contemporary democratic discourses, through resorting to tragedy's multivocal form, may potentially facilitate our efforts to revitalize democracy in our current age of globalization.

Given its purpose then, the framework asks contemporary readers and audiences of tragedy several leading questions so as to draw their minds broadly to the type of democratic concerns that tragedy was apt to dramatize in antiquity. As a framework that strives to gauge the democratic impact of tragedy today, it is not as concerned with the overly technical, linguistic and dramatic conventions that normally inform such analyses. Instead, it points to four broad-based components evident in the preceding analysis of tragedy's multivocal form, each then divided into two subcomponents:

1. Plot: What is the play about?
    i.   Does it enact a real crisis or conflict, which invokes a duel between values, wills and circumstances serious enough to shake the foundations of society? What are they?
    ii. Does the plot dramatize the world's complexity and foster an understanding that our world view, though dominant, is not the only or even the best world view?

2. Characters: Who are the characters?
    i.   Are the characters real, that is to say, are they 'multidimensional, sub-lime, profoundly complex, whole — all character traits without which no tragic fall could have been possible'?[116]
    ii. Are there 'zones of interaction' where central, familiar and adorned figures interact and trade places with marginal, strange and despised figures?[117] Does this help foster an 'exploration of the Self *through* the Other'?[118]
3. Language: Who speaks and how?
    i.   Is there a 'many-voicedness'? Does the language allow for or provoke the 'freedom of others' points of view to . . . reveal themselves'?[119]
    ii. Does rational discourse coincide with non-rational voice? Does the non-rational – poetry-lyric, music, dance, silence, for example – communicate anything that rational discourse cannot always express?
4. Overall: Does the multivocal form bring a variety of otherwise marginal-ized stories, characters and voices onto the public stage and into democratic debate?
    i.   Does the multivocal form dramatize the interplay between order and disorder?
    ii. Does the multivocal form dramatize the interplay between reality and fiction?

Put in purposely simple and open-ended terms, with all technical language and disciplinary baggage removed, this framework is prescriptive only to the extent that it asks leading questions. How one chooses to answer them, or indeed to supplement them with one's own questions, is left entirely up to individual pref-erence. Because of this, the framework acts more as a loose guide with the aim of training our eyes and ears to approach tragedy not merely as the antiquated art form or form of high entertainment it has become but, rather, as a political resource or, more specifically, as a democratic text which can be read alongside the more traditional and commonly accepted canons of democracy.

But this, of course, is an extremely difficult, not to mention a somewhat odd undertaking. As such, to ensure that we move in the right direction, it is useful to keep an additional set of four factors in mind when analysing tragedy today.

The first factor is the need to acknowledge that when reading (and this obvi-ously includes viewing for our purposes) any text or fragment of language, a large number of possible interpretations exists.[120] Whether understood as a translation, adaptation or performance of a tragedy, the same applies. For some, the number of possible interpretations is near limitless 'because the text is open to infinity'.[121] Each time we read, view and analyse a text, we increase the number of feasible interpretations and generate new texts. The result: we create new meanings.

As a consequence, the second stipulation is that when reading a text, the aim is not to reduce or refine the text to its essence, to provide definitive answers and destroy multiple perspectives. Instead, what we are striving for is to open the text up: to conceive of it 'as a polysemic space where the paths of several possible meanings intersect'.[122] Interpreters do not remain, as conventional wisdom states, external to a work that is closed and finite.[123] Exteriority is a myth. We enter the text and the text becomes a crucial part of our reality. Denying exteriority, as Roland Barthes reminds us, does not necessarily compel us to then deny those interpretations which claim to be objective and ahistorical. We can use them as our base and include them as one of many possible interpretations. In this regard, interpretations produced through the canonical sciences, like philology, can and should be employed, albeit partially, freely and relatively.[124] This is why this framework can so freely draw on certain characteristics of the multivocal form of tragedy.

Third, it is helpful to remember that the act of reading a text is one that intervenes directly into the social environments and realities which are represented within that text.[125] But doing so also provides the very tools and practices needed to reconstruct the social environments and realities that we live in. To appreciate the 'textuality' of our world is to appreciate the constructed, fictive nature of our reality: that how reality is represented through our predominant social and political texts affects how it is perceived in 'fact'.[126] Consequently, a particular way of representing social relations, political power, violence and justice, for example, will impact how these phenomena are conceived and manifest in future. A particular notion of democracy – as conveyed by the ancient Athenians through their tragedies – may help rectify deficiencies in our own practices of democracy today. Reading certain texts, and reading them in a particular way, is imperative as it situates us in the world we aspire to create. Such texts present the very tools and practices – the very language and discourse – that can bring these aspirations to fruition. Read enough times by enough people, such texts then become legitimate, prudent and common sense. The political and the aesthetic can blend. Fiction enters the realm of reality and becomes instructive of it.

Because of this, the fourth point to remember is that reading tragedies today can be a necessarily political and even democratic act if that is the brand of democracy we hope to inspire. Though not wishing to deny other interpretations, the purpose of the following analysis is to use the framework established here to read tragedies explicitly as democratic texts. DuBois reminds us that too frequently in the contemporary age, tragedy has been reduced solely to the great man or woman, the tragic hero, as the apotheosis of the modern sovereign subject.[127] When this is done, tragedy loses its democratic potential. Indeed, what makes tragedy so evocative – and so democratic – are particularly those times 'when that subject has been called into question by a variety of kinds of fragmentation, dislocation, and difference'.[128] Reviving this aspect of tragedy means that 'a much richer and more diverse set of bodies and questions than Aristotle and modernity bequeath to us' can once again be entertained. Tragedy, in other words, can once again begin to stage a uniquely democratic cast. This is the interpretation that this framework hopes to highlight and revive. Moreover, the point is to learn to read tragedies democratically once again and not solely as an artistic, fictional artifact of history. As Daniel Mendelsohn writes,

> [W]e must be careful, when evaluating and interpreting the works [of Athenian tragedy], of our own tendency to see drama in purely personal terms, as a vehicle for psychological investigations. If anything, Athenian tragedy seems to have been useful as an artistic means of exploring concerns that, to us, seem to be unlikely candidates for an evening of thrilling drama: the nature of the state, the difficult relationship – always of concern in a democracy – between remarkable men (tragedy's "heroes") and the collective citizen body.[129]

This is how the ancient Athenians likely perceived tragedy, which explains why it became such a valued political institution. If this interpretation were to become legitimate today, what we would effectively be doing is to perceive tragedy as if it were no different from any other great democratic text. And that, in turn, would impinge on how we come to interpret democratic texts more generally, given that a text 'is necessarily read in relationship to [other texts]'.[130] The goal of this project then is to read tragedies democratically, so that we can draw on them as legitimate sources of democratic insight. That is how this book will read the tragedies that follow; a crucial move if the proposed framework is to have its desired political effect.

Dramatizing Democracy: Introducing Aeschylus' *Suppliants*

In his 1941 book, *Aeschylus and Athens*, George Derwent Thomson made the claim that 'Greek tragedy was one of the distinctive functions of Athenian democracy', a claim that this book has also been making.[1] But so far, that claim has only been made abstractly and with broad brushstrokes. To make it concretely, that is, to explore the democratic potential of a specific tragedy in a specific time and place, a particular tragedian and a particular tragedy is needed.

Taking our cue from Thomson, the tragedian and tragedy which this book will focus on is Aeschylus and his drama *Suppliants*. The choice of Aeschylus may seem a puzzling one, particularly if we believe the argument that his tragedies were not representative of the art form's high point. Yet, that argument is not merely subjective. More importantly for what we are aiming to do, it also fails to account for the crucial fact that Aeschylus is the only tragedian we have record of that lived through and championed the democratization of Athens during its initial stages. Aeschylus, according to Thomson, 'was a democrat who fought as well as wrote'.[2] Having taken part in the defining battles at Marathon and Salamis in the fifth century, Aeschylus quickly became a renowned democratic authority in a city that had only decades earlier become the birthplace of Western democracy. It was this topic – the birth of democracy – that inspired his art. And it was his art that helped entrench the political significance of tragedy during the fifth century BC. Drawing creatively and fluidly from the politics of his day, perhaps more so than any subsequent tragedian, Aeschylus sought to engage with the tumultuous politics of the days to come. Indeed, as Farrar writes, '[t]he plays of Aeschylus offer interpretations of both freedom and order and suggest that only democratic politics can reconcile them'.[3] His 'dramatic art', Stoessl continues, 'was subject to the struggle of political forces and was itself a part of this struggle'.[4] Coming to grips with the shift from traditional tribal units to a democratic city-state was the 'fundamental question which engrossed him all his life' and this, for Thomson, is what 'invests his art with a permanent historical importance'.[5] He is, as such, not just the first of the great tragedians whose work survives to this day. He was also, by all accounts, a fierce and active democrat who lived and worked through Athens' greatest period of democratization. As Aeschylus is the only tragedian we have access to who experienced the democratic revolution first-hand, he therefore makes for a particularly fascinating case study.

However, the equally important question is what gives his *Suppliants* special significance over any of his other tragedies? Certainly, it is not a historical drama, at least not in the way that Aeschylus' *Persians* was. In other words, it was not a precise or patent dramatization of past events and figures. And compared to the plays of his *Oresteia* trilogy, it can hardly be considered political at all. Even though it does pose several questions relevant both to ancient city-state and contemporary nation-states, it is not a sound tragedy. Two out of the three dramas that make up the *Danaid* trilogy have since been lost. In other words, the only surviving play is *Suppliants*. But having said that, this Greek tragedy, which was long considered to be our earliest extant tragedy, remains the only tragic drama that explicitly makes reference to the gathering of citizens at a democratic Assembly. Called together to decide the fate of a band of foreign refugees, the citizens in this mythical democracy put their democratic resolve to the test and, in the process, risk war with a mighty foreign army. For this reason, *Suppliants* provides us today with an idea of how democracy might have worked to assuage these concerns then. Additionally, a number of commentators believe that this Aeschylean tragedy would have provided its ancient audiences with food for thought, given its allusions to the chain of events that were pushing Athens towards greater equality and openness during the mid-fifth century. Perhaps something of a democratic memento when it was first performed in ancient Athens, it is therefore interesting to ask how can we learn to read this tragedy – and others like it – as a democratic text today?

Because Aeschylus' tragedies represent the reconciliation 'between theory and practice, between poetry and life', it is easy and possibly correct to interpret him and his dramatic texts as having nothing to offer contemporary audiences.[6] While some conventional scholars of antiquity may be gladdened to hear this, relegating Aeschylus effectively 'to the basement of the museum' would, as Thomas Rosenmeyer writes, equally betray his true worth.[7] And so, though we may want to avoid reading him as we would just another contemporary playwright, it does not follow that we should not try to read the tragedies of Aeschylus fluidly and as a source of inspiration for the tragedies that we confront in our own times. Despite speaking to his own audiences and the social environment which he was familiar with, the insights he provides into the nature of the human soul and human communities are not without bearing in our own day. Being mindful of the social and political dimensions of Aeschylean tragedy does not so much consign his work to the antique past as help us to better envisage the links between now and then.

This chapter, which acts as a sort of segue between the theoretical and empirical parts of the book, therefore offers a very brief introduction to Aeschylus and, in particular, his tragedy about ancient supplication. To do so, it will first sketch a rough portrait of the life of this ancient tragedian, of which the definitive facts are little known. However vague they may be, there is enough to draw the conclusion that Aeschylus was a key Athenian democrat who, along with more notable statesmen, opposed conservative efforts to return Athens to its former authoritarian state only decades after it had become a democracy. The chapter then summarizes the core tenets of Aeschylus' tragedies, with particular reference to its political dimensions, before making its case for analysing the tragedy that will consume the following two chapters: Aeschylus' *Suppliants*. Of course, in line with the spirit with which this book has approached the topic of democracy and tragedy in ancient Athens more broadly, this inquiry is not tailored for a specialist audience. Written rather for a broader audience, one interested in learning what the classics of Greece may have to impart to our own political circumstances, this chapter will not so much appeal to classical scholars as to scholars of contemporary political and social theory.

Aeschylus, the democrat

This being so, it is perhaps necessary to begin with two questions. First, who was Aeschylus? And second, why are his tragedies particularly worthy of our attention now? These questions are not the easiest to provide clear-cut answers to, least of all because what is known about Aeschylus the man is subject to dispute and differences of opinions. Additionally, most of the plays he penned during his lifetime have subsequently been lost. When it comes to the life of this ancient tragedian, Robert Holmes Beck aptly sums it up: '[t]here is a kernel of fact and quite a lot of conjecture'.[8] Given this, it is intriguing that his opus, or the little that is left of it, continues to rank among the most influential works of the Western political and dramatic canon.

Though there is always a cloud of doubt, there are some things we can say for sure about Aeschylus' life and most of this comes to us from the anonymously penned, *Life*.[9] From this and later sources, mostly recorded or fabricated after his death, we know that Aeschylus was born in 525/524 BC to a family of aristocratic heritage in Eleusis, a town situated some 14 miles north-west of Athens.[10] Son to Euphorion and brother to Cynegeirus and Ameinias, Aeschylus apparently knew from an early age that he would one day compose tragedy. There is one story in particular that is often told, which recalls a dream that Aeschylus had as a youth.[11] In this account, the teenage Aeschylus has fallen asleep while standing guard in a countryside vineyard. Perhaps fittingly, Dionysus appears before the young man in a dream. As he stands over Aeschylus, or so the story goes, the god of intoxication compels him to compose tragedy. Not wanting to disappoint the god that had instructed him so vividly, when Aeschylus awakes, he does precisely what had been asked of him. To Dionysus' credit, he was not wrong and the art form of tragedy came almost naturally to Aeschylus from that time forth. Regardless of the veracity of this version of events, which certain scholars have questioned, it provides a rare anecdotal insight into why Aeschylus began producing tragedies. But, were we to err closer to the side of caution, then this account must be relegated to the one more commonly agreed upon. According to that account, which we find in *Life*, it is simply recorded that Aeschylus 'began tragedies as a young man'.[12] Though much less illuminating, it is arguably all that we can accurately say about Aeschylus in this regard.

Also as a young man, there is convincing evidence which shows that Aeschylus took part in the two defining battles Athens fought as a burgeoning democracy: the battles at Marathon and Salamis in 490 and 480 BC, respectively.[13] 'They say', so goes a line in *Life*, 'that he took part in the battle of Marathon with his brother Cynegeirus, and in the sea fight at Salamis with Ameinias the youngest of his brothers, and in the land battle at Plataea'.[14] The significance of these battles with respect to Athens' democracy is something already touched upon in previous chapters. It is enough, therefore, to note that Aeschylus took part in them, that his wartime experiences fed into his later dramatic representations of war, most notably in his tragedy about the fall of the *Persians*, and that 'this act of citizenship was the most considerable event of his life'.[15]

The other notable fact that is frequently cited when recounting Aeschylus' life is the two trips he made to Sicily.[16] The first expedition took place after the successful premiere of *Persians* in Athens in 472 BC, when he was invited by Hiero I of Syracuse. Perhaps encouraged by what he had witnessed during this first visit, or disheartened by the events taking place in Athens, we read that Aeschylus then made a second expedition to the island, this time to the city of Gela, most probably around or after the first staging of the *Oresteia* in Athens in 458 BC. There is a great deal of speculation as to what he did while abroad. Who he visited, what plays, if any, he produced while abroad and whether he intended to return to Athens – these are the questions frequently posed though very infrequently answered with any certainty. All we know is that Aeschylus never did return to Athens. After only two, possibly three years away from the city in which he had achieved his fame, Aeschylus died in 456/455 BC in Sicily. The story that commonly accompanies his demise is not without its comic dimensions. Mistaken for a large stone, Aeschylus was said to have been killed when an eagle, hoping to crack the exterior shell of a tortoise it had been carrying, dropped the animal from a great height directly onto the bald scalp of the aging playwright.

Unfortunately, with the technique of biography yet to be invented, this is as much as we really know about Aeschylus' life, and even then there is some speculation as to the precise facts involved. Obviously, scholars of cultural history and the classics can say a great deal more with a greater degree of accuracy. From a philological perspective, the present account has been neither sufficiently exact nor detailed; a point that this chapter concedes. But presenting a painstakingly precise record of Aeschylus' personal history will not, by itself, produce insights into the real question that this inquiry is interested in, which like Stoessl asks: 'was Aeschylus a man who thought in political forms and who wanted to express his political convictions in his poetry?'[17]

More specifically, the question that will be explored here in greater detail is whether Aeschylus was a democrat? To attempt to answer this question, we need to go beyond the hard facts that are available about Aeschylus' personal history, where a level of conjecture will inevitably cloud our judgement, and look at the social and political developments taking place in and around Athens during his lifetime.

Certainly, if we focus solely on Aeschylus' heritage and his youthful days in Athens – during which time the tyrant Pisistratus and his sons ruled over the city – we can only conclude that he lived among the leisured classes.[18] Taken on its own, however, this says very little about Aeschylus' political leanings. He was, after all, only a child during this time. But what can be given greater credence are the events that unfolded during Aeschylus' mid-to-late teens when, in 510 BC, the rule of Hippias, the son of Pisistratus, came to an abrupt end as he and his clan were expelled from Athens. From that time until the violent revolution that swept through the city three years later, Athens would see herself transformed from a dictatorship into a democracy. In the much-altered social and political landscape that resulted, the young Aeschylus would have had his perception of the world and his place within it equally altered. Thanks to the reforms of Cleisthenes, as John Herington writes, '[a]ll citizens of Athens were now to be equal before the law, and all were empowered to participate, at least in some degree, in the government of the community'.[19] These events would, no doubt, have played on the young tragedian's mind. All of a sudden, or so it would have appeared, things largely unchanged since the dawning of the long-ago Bronze Age began to change and then disappear. Aeschylus lived through these momentous shifts and, as Herington goes on to point out, it became a core function of his later dramatic energies to grapple with 'the sudden impetus toward a new way of life and thought' that 'sprang not from abroad but from within themselves'.[20]

Moreover, if we recall that Aeschylus perceived his contribution to the Persian Wars as his single greatest act of citizenship, then we might have cause to think that these wars, fought in defence against Persia's advances, affected him as intimately as they would have affected other citizens in Athens. Why or how these wars were fought is not immediately important, except for the fact that they went on to instigate a more self-assured, optimistic and egalitarian democratic order in Athens.[21] Having fought in these battles, and later documented them for his Athenian compatriots, he would not have been immune to the effects that a victory such as this would have had on the body politic. Spurred on by the popularity of the Cleisthenic reforms in the immediate decades after the democratic revolution, Athens' victory against an opponent of greater military might gave an early indication of what the citizens of a democracy were capable of. For Marsh McCall then, '[t]he first two generations of Athenian democracy record a glorious era for her citizenry: Marathon, Salamis, Plataea, the growth of an empire. Aeschylus experienced it all, and it was the core of his being'.[22] As a citizen, a soldier and later as a tragedian, these events would have done a great deal to consolidate the importance of democracy in his eyes.

Indeed, as numerous scholars of the classics and cultural history have identified, Aeschylus did eventually become closely associated with the movement to develop and expand democracy in Athens. He was not just another citizen or just any citizen, but an integral fifth-century political thinker, writes Stoessl.[23] For Alan Sommerstein, he was 'a politically committed dramatist and a supporter successively of Themistocles, Ephialtes and Pericles'.[24] Though only the last of these three names may have any resonance with the contemporary reader, all three figures were, in fact, indispensable in the push for greater democratization in fifth-century Athens. Themistocles, a figure who will make a reappearance in the next chapter, came to prominence as the man responsible for expanding Athens' navy, a strategy without which Athens could not have become the naval power it did. Always the staunch democrat, Themistocles subsequently devoted his political energies to warning his fellow citizens against the impending threats that confronted democratic governance in Athens. And though we cannot reduce his efforts to any single cause or policy, what he is often best remembered for is his ardent opposition against a resurging and authoritarian Sparta after the Persian Wars. For his efforts though, he was ultimately ostracized by his political adversaries from Athens. As Thomson documents:

> Themistokles perceived that, in the new situation, the danger threatening Athenian democracy was not the might of Persia, which had now been broken, but the anti-democratic regime of Sparta, and therefore he support the attempt of Pausanias to overthrow it. But the Athenian people, whose nationalist passions had been inflamed by the war, could not be persuaded that Persia was no longer the enemy, especially as the prospect of enrichment offered by the conservative opposition was substantial.[25]

It is interesting to note here that Aeschylus, who had also been 'inflamed' by the same 'nationalist passions' in the aftermath of war, did not succumb to the same populist sentiments and, instead, chose to back the position espoused by Themistocles, which undoubtedly would have seemed the less obvious one. Both Themistocles and Aeschylus perceived that Sparta posed a greater threat to Athens' democracy than Persia had or would. Both made their case for democracy directly to the people, though via different means. Both supported the abolition of the last vestiges of aristocratic rule in Athens. And both spent their final years absent from the city of Athens.

Though ostracized, Themistocles' cause was not abandoned in Athens. Rather, it would be taken up in the 470s and 460s by a raft of other notable democrats – chief among them being the elder statesman Ephialtes and the young Pericles of Athens. The effects of Ephialtes' opposition to Cimon, the pro-Spartan leader of Athens, would eventually lead to a more democratic city-state, but not without dire consequences for both these statesmen. The general outcome and the uproar it caused within the city, as has already been intimated at various points in this book, was taken up by Aeschylus in his *Oresteia*. The main point of contention in this political dispute, besides Athens' alliance with Sparta, was whether the aristocratic *Areopagus* should be stripped of its remaining powers. Cimon, a supporter both of Sparta and the *Areopagus*, appealed to Athens' conservative faction, while Ephialtes and Pericles asked the citizens to take full responsibility for the governing of their own city. Initially, given his political connections, Cimon managed to do enough to convince the city that any moves to strip the *Areopagus* of its powers would lead to a destabilization of the entire polis. But, despite that, it was his steadfast allegiance to his Spartan allies that would eventually lead to his political demise. Indeed, had it not been for a costly miscalculation on Cimon's part to send an Athenian contingent to assist Sparta against a rebellion at Mount Ithome, the Athenians might not have turned against Cimon as they did. Humiliated by Sparta's request for the Athenians to return home, the citizens of Athens formally put an end to their alliance with Sparta before concluding a new alliance with Argos, the long-time enemies of Sparta. Cimon was promptly ostracized and the democratic faction of Athens, lead by Ephialtes, soon denuded the *Areopagus* of all but its most basic powers. These powers, in turn, were transferred directly to the people, to be exercised collectively by the democratic *Ekklesia*. The significance of this reform should not be underestimated because, as Thomson notes, it resulted in Ephialtes' assassination in the short term and, in the long term, was immediately repealed by the conservatives at the end of the Peloponnesian War.[26]

Aeschylus supported these democrats and their initiatives to strengthen democracy in Athens. For him, perhaps as for these democrats, it was the lesson of restraint that was key to the success of democracy. Aeschylus, in Robert Holmes Beck's estimation,

> did not think that the reward of virtue was joy but good health, prosperity, fecundity and other good things in an economy in which even the most wealthy or powerful were not so wealthy or powerful that they could afford to ignore the moral teaching: be sparing in desire for wealth, power and position.[27]

And unlike Sophocles or Euripides, Aeschylus, according to Sommerstein's analysis, presents the community as actors, not as victims. He asks, as Sommerstein continues, the question that Shakespeare would make his Lucrece ask much later:

> Why should the private pleasure of some one
> Become the public plague of many mo[r]e? . . .

> For one's offence why should so many fall,
> To plague a private sin in general?[28]

Aeschylus' answer: where institutional constraints are absent to prevent the hegemony of the one, the many will suffer. These institutional constraints must be overseen by the many and applied to each and every one without discrimination. For Sommerstein then:

> Democracy remains ... as the only form of government that can in principle reliably control and contain the consequences of the disputes, conflicts and crimes of individuals. And Aeschylus, who lived through the birth, growth and coming of age of Athenian democracy, is found over and over again embodying that proposition in dramatic forms. We have abundantly seen that that is not, by a long way, all there is to his plays, but it is enough to entitle him to be called the prophet, the forth-teller, of democracy.[29]

Aeschylean tragedy and democracy

If Sommerstein's assessment is not too far off the mark, then we can safely say that Aeschylus' tragedies, like Aeschylus himself, were not too far removed from the concerns consuming democracy in Athens. And though we should not, as Sommerstein warns, reduce Aeschylean tragedy solely to its democratic function, neither should we think that a prominent democratic figure that lived through the birth and development of democracy had nothing to say about the potential and the pitfalls of democratization in his own day through his own way.

Though less renowned or at least lesser known to audiences today than Sophocles and Euripides, Aeschylus can claim to have achieved something that neither of his two contemporaries did: developing tragedy into the form of drama that we know today.[30] Due in large part to his innovations, we now have tragedies that capture both the specific and the universal, and often in one fell swoop. As Stoessl eloquently surmises, '[h]is genuinely Attic spirit made him see in the individual things that which is general, in the present moment that which is eternal, in the event the law, in the appearance the idea'.[31] The particular moment, dilemma or individual at the centre of Aeschylean tragedy was never far removed from the heftier, immutable characteristics of life. The suffering hero and the lament of the chorus were Aeschylus' starting point, a convention he inherited from his dramatic predecessor, Thespis.[32] Yet, he sought deeper answers as well as a more fundamental state of awareness. The technical transformations that ensued were but attempts to grapple with the troubled soul, the need for peace, the desire for good and the capacity for evil.[33]

More specifically, Gerald Else identifies a set of nine technical innovations in the tragic art form, all of which can be traced back to Aeschylus.[34] The first involved the expansion from one to two, sometimes three actors or protagonists. Now, the glory or ruin that traditionally befell only one individual came to impact on entire families and perhaps even the city as a whole.[35] The second innovation was the more acute dramatization of the conflict or dilemma facing the protagonist internally, which would frequently be externalized through the discord between the protagonist and the chorus. A third development was the creation of a clearer structure, which utilized episodes to lead into and away from the conflict at hand. Fourth was the novel focus on the fear and apprehension surrounding the conflict and fifth was the hope for a clear and lasting resolution. The sixth, seventh, eighth and ninth traits of Aeschylean tragedy revolved around the use of trilogies; the reinterpretation of myths for dramatic and political effect; the use of visual effects onstage and an increased consciousness towards time and space in drama.

Thanks to Aeschylus' intervention, tragic theatre therefore transformed more fully into a representation that centred on clashing wills and insurmountable crises, that is, on the human soul, its desire for good and its susceptibility towards evil intermixed with the determining presence of fate and the will of gods.[36] Such was the structure of the tragedies which Aeschylus first presented at the City Dionysia in Athens in 499 BC, the same tragedies which would eventually give him his first victory in 484 BC.[37] This was a prize he would go on to win 13 times in total, becoming the first great tragedian in the immediate decades following Athens' democratic revolution.[38] Of course, the exact number of tragedies that Aeschylus produced during his lifetime is disputed today, as all but six plays were either lost or destroyed – along with a large body of classical literature – after the demise of the Roman Empire. But despite this, the numbers that are most commonly cited sit somewhere between 70 and 90 plays.[39] Some say that 89 plays is probably the most precise figure.[40] Specifically, what we are in possession of today include *Persians* (472 BC), *Seven against Thebes* (467 BC), *Suppliants* (463 BC) and the *Oresteia* trilogy of *Agamemnon*, *Libation Bearers* and *Eumenides* (458 BC).

In this period, during which Aeschylus was at his most creative, Athens was the site of more than just a democratic revolution. It was the epicentre of an artistic and intellectual broadening which, as has been described, was coincidental with the democratic way of life. Aeschylus' work should be viewed as a product of this broadening and, explicitly, of what emerges from the intersection of politics, art and philosophy. The myths that he selected for dramatization, as such, were not selected purely for their aesthetic qualities, though that was certainly a determining consideration. Instead, the myths he subsequently transformed into drama were selected because they spoke in moral terms and were themselves commentaries on such events as the birth of democracy, Athens' victory over Persia and the uncertain path towards greater democracy. It is quite possible, as Louis Spartz puts it, 'that he viewed his poetry as part of his duty as a citizen'.[41] Because of this, what Herington observes makes a great deal of sense: that there was an intensification of Aeschylus' plays late in his life when, as previously noted, debate over the abolition of the *Areopagus* was at its most vehement and the course of Athens' democracy at its least certain.[42] It may even be the case that one of the many functions of Aeschylean tragedy was to dramatize the travails of democracy and to extol those who had wagered their lives and livelihoods for its sake.

Of course, it is worth reiterating that this point, though not incorrect, should not be overstated. It is easy, writes Ireland, to reduce Aeschylus' plays to political allegories: to perceive Agamemnon as Cimon, the Danaid Suppliants as Themistocles, Eteocles as Pericles and Prometheus as Protagoras.[43] Given what we already know about Aeschylus, this would not be an inconceivable leap to make. Aeschylus would no doubt have been involved in the goings-on within his city. But '[b]y the same token', according to Ireland, 'few have expressed any sympathy with attempts to convert the plays into cryptic propaganda or political allegory'.[44] This is a position that A.F. Garvie, another notable scholar of Aeschylean drama, also holds. Aeschylus, according to Garvie, is a dramatist first and a politician second.[45] Those wishing to make concrete allusions about the political dimension of Aeschylus' plays thus require a great deal more historical detail and biographical accounts than we have available to us. Yet, even with these details and accounts, we still cannot ignore the fact that, as a tragedian competing at the City Dionysia, Aeschylus' primary goal would have been to win first prize. This is something that he would not have been able to do had he used his plays merely as political propaganda. Remember: Aeschylean drama was evocative of the times more broadly and the times dictated that anything worthy would be a composite of politics, art and philosophy. Without appealing to these other facets and faculties, as well as to the majority of the audience and judges in the theatre, dramatists simply could not have secured victory.[46]

On these matters, this book does not wish to make a case that simply cannot be substantiated by the available evidence. It does not want to insinuate that historical records definitively prove that Aeschylus was a democrat and that his tragedies were framed as democratic messages. Rather, the aim is to show that among the numerous notable features that Aeschylean tragedy is famous for, maybe one of them is the fact that they were created and performed during a time when democracy unsettled old conventions and asked citizens to answer questions that they would have never before considered. These shifts in thought and in ways of being would almost certainly have influenced Aeschylus and his work, even if they were not always the meaning of his work.

To this end, democratic or not, one of the most enduring characteristics of Aeschylean tragedy is its ability to expose the intricate flows, conditions and dilemmas that mark out existence in a community of disparate individuals. By being concerned with how people live together, or how they relate or often fail to relate to each other, his tragedies had a political edge about them. They were, despite their mythical and poetic dimensions, chiefly concerned about 'human beings in their capacity of citizens'.[47] This statement by Sommerstein makes clear that at the forefront of Aeschylus' artistic consideration was the topic of how human beings could become 'citizens', a role or status which was without precedent up to that time. We may or may not wish to label these pursuits democratic, but they were certainly directed at how a collective of human beings coexist together, as more or less equals. For his inspiration, Aeschylus drew, to a much greater degree than did Sophocles and Euripides, on the issues that had been thrown up by contemporary political events. As Sommerstein writes, in Aeschylus' day, 'politicians themselves were capable of using tragedy as an instrument of their competitive struggles', so it is quite conceivable that the tragedians, at least in part, drew on politics as an instrument in their own dramatic struggles.[48] Taken together, what we can conclude from this is that, for Aeschylus, every single thing mattered. Every single thing interconnected. A man's plight could not be understood independently from his social, religious, political and familial background. This is why a dramatic depiction of a political situation can be as instructive, and possibly even as incisive, as the musings of a statesman or a philosopher. We cannot discard 'the interaction of all the forces that make up our world, all between the home of heaven and the recesses of hell', if we are to take Aeschylus' tragedy seriously.[49] Rather, we must view his work as that which reconciled matters of the soul with matters of the state.[50] The communal bonds and the sociality of the human being that form the crux of his tragedies are therefore indicative of how central the rise of the state and the creation of a politics of popular rule were to him.[51]

And so, for all these reasons, it is probably imprudent for us to explicitly equate any particular Aeschylean tragedy with this or that political event or policy. There is simply insufficient evidence to draw such concrete conclusions. But, what we may instead want to do is to see things another way. After all, it is quite plausible to say that a number of Aeschylus' plays offered his contemporaries dramatic insights into the communal struggles and dilemmas that were being experienced by the newly empowered citizens and statesmen, not to mention those who were still denied a place in the public sphere: the slaves, women, children and foreign residents of Athens. It was the struggles of the collective that Aeschylus took up and dramatized before a cross-section of Athens' population. In his art, as such, it was his preoccupation with 'the spirit of man as a social being' that, for Stoessl, conferred Aeschylus with the qualification to speak so authoritatively about questions of the state and politics.[52]

Suppliants

This is why the tragedies of Aeschylus make for a good study into the democratic potential of tragic drama. In his dramas, what we see is precisely tragedy's multivocal form and its capacity to draw to the city's attention the cast of otherwise marginalized stories, characters and voices. To this end, in the following two chapters, this book will look specifically at how Aeschylus did this and how we can, drawing inspiration from him, possibly do the same in our own day.

To do so, we will analyse one of Aeschylus' more politically intriguing tragedies, *Suppliants*. Though a tragedy that has, as Herbert Weir Smyth argues, suffered from the neglect of subsequent generations, it nevertheless achieves something which neither the *Persians*, *Oresteia* nor any other tragedy for that matter manages to do.[53] It explicitly makes reference, albeit somewhat anachronistically, to a democracy ruled by the people while, at the same time, being a story drawn from the mythic past that may or may not have been speaking to the political events surrounding its performance in the mid-fifth century. In this sense, we can say that this tragedy remains something of an ancient democratic document to the extent that it depicts the workings of a democratic polity and articulates the type of political dilemmas the citizens of a democracy would have come together to debate and decide. In short, what separates this Aeschylean

tragedy from all others is that the stories, characters and voices which it dramatizes are set against the backdrop of a democratic city-state. This would have
spoken to audiences gathered at the City Dionysia, but it also has the capacity to
speak to contemporary audiences too.

Unfortunately, the precise meaning of this tragedy has continued to elude
many of its interpreters, given that it is pockmarked with inconsistencies, uncertainty and unresolved tensions.[54] On top of this , *Suppliants* remains the only play
that we possess from the *Danaid* trilogy. As a result, no definitive conclusions
can be drawn about the tragedy. It remains open to interpretation – both with
respect to its poetic and political dimensions. While this may trouble classical
and cultural historians, it need not necessarily detain us here. This is because our
goal is not to provide a historically accurate or philologically astute reading of
the play. The goal, instead, is to draw on the framework established towards the
end of the previous chapter in order to foreground the tragedy's ability to dramatize democracy's concerns by bringing otherwise marginalized stories, characters and voices onto the public stage and into democratic debate. It is enough
that, in the absence of definitive historical evidence, the allusions made within
the play do not preclude but rather encourage interpretations which point to the
workings and pitfalls of democratic government more broadly.

And it has certainly been in this same spirit that has allowed Aeschylean tragedies such as *Suppliants* to be adapted so freely and frequently by subsequent
generations – a case in point being the American playwright Charles L. Mee's
play *Big Love*, an adaption of *Suppliants* which will be analysed in Chapter 5.[55]
As such, if we were to take anything away from this, it might be that Aeschylus'
continuing significance should not be wedded to a narrow reading of the classics, available only to those classical and cultural historians who are well-versed
in this or that philological methodology. It is significant only to the extent that
it remains open to us all. 'Underlying the ancient metaphorical, mythical, and
religious language in which Aeschylus necessarily expressed himself', Herington
believes there 'to be insights into our world that might still make good sense to a
contemporary geneticist, environmentalist, or, indeed, psychologist'.[56] To his list,
this book will now add a contemporary democratic thinker.

4

Marginal Women, Marginalized Stories: Democracy and the Politics of Fifth-Century Supplication

The key questions posed by Aeschylus in his *Suppliants* are, according to Weir Smyth, simple ones at heart: 'is mercy due the suppliant when hospitality spells peril? Is neutrality possible when the choice lies between war and the recognition of the rights of the oppressed?'[1] The 'primitive right of refuge' and the broader principle of 'Greek humanitarianism' are thus the central concerns dramatized as inseparable from democracy itself in this tragedy about fifth-century supplication.[2] But, as a tragedy that had its dramatic premiere in the mid-fifth century, amid a turbulent political backdrop, it is not inconceivable that Aeschylus' tragedy also touched upon certain movements that were conspiring to unsettle the political orthodoxy in and around Athens at the time. Might it have been a tragedy which Aeschylus used to highlight political alternatives, which is to say, a multivocal tragedy that brought a greater variety of otherwise marginalized stories, characters and voices onto the public stage and into democratic debate?

This is the question that detains the present chapter, one that seeks to explore how tragic drama engaged democracy at the height of its popularity in fifth-century Athens. To do so, it will analyse the multivocal form of Aeschylus' *Suppliants* by reading it as a democratic text apt to dramatize particular political and existential dilemmas which emerged in the wake of the democratic revolution. Deploying the multivocal form as an analytical tool enables us to better understand how the interplay between order and disorder and reality and fiction was disclosed through an actual tragedy. That said, it perhaps needs to be acknowledged that the veracity of the multivocal form may, for philologists and cultural historians, constitute something of an inadequate analytical apparatus. For example, it is not concerned with analysing Aeschylus' tragedy according to the structure typical of suppliant dramas where, as Chad Turner points out, the focus is on there being a persecutor, victim and protector.[3] Nor is it solely concerned with erecting comprehensive definitions of what amounts to tragic plots, characters and language. As an analytical framework, it is informed by the works of classical thinkers and contemporary classical scholarship, though its ultimate aspiration is to draw out the democratic allusions that are available to us through tragedy. Because of this, methodologies conventional to studies in the classics constitute a helpful guide, but they do not curtail the parameters of this reading. This reading, instead, is about analysing the multivocal form of this Aeschylean tragedy and how it intervened in democratic thought and practice in reality.

Such a reading, as the chapter will suggest, can in the first instance, reveal one of two things. First, it shows how by giving pride of place to a band of foreign and tempestuous women, by humbling otherwise powerful statesmen and by heeding the cry of those in need, even when this comes at a detriment to oneself, Aeschylus' tragedy juggled the search for order with the spectre of disorder and depicted a universe that was the inverse of the democratic universe known to the Athenians in reality. Secondly, by reading *Suppliants* as a tragedy performed against a backdrop of political upheaval, it is evident just how Aeschylus may have used his play – as we know he did on other occasions – to provide indirect commentary on the nature and limits of democracy more broadly. While we may not be able to draw concrete links between play and politics, we can speculate whether the key events which were leading to the eventual abolition of the aristocratic *Areopagus* in Athens could have been an implicit source of inspiration for this dramatic text. After all, overcoming the pettiness of politics, the draw of aristocratic nostalgia and an increasingly hostile international arena were the stuff that consumed both Aeschylus' drama and the Athens of his day. Exploring how the two intersected, if at all, holds possible lessons about the fluid relationship between reality and fiction.

Plot

But before we can say anything about that, first we need to establish just what Aeschylus' play was about. Did it enact a real crisis or conflict – one that invoked a duel between values, wills and circumstances serious enough to shake the foundations of society? And how, if at all, did it dramatize the world's complexity and foster an understanding that one's world view is never the only or even the best world view?

Threatened with a destiny not of their own choosing, Aeschylus' tragedy presents his audience with a group of 50 sisters who have fled from their homeland of Egypt to Argos, a democratic city-state of Greece. Met by a kindly king, the suppliants request that he decide their fate. Will he accept these women as suppliants and face a hostile reprisal from their Egyptian suitors? Or should he opt to let them die by their own hands and befoul the city's gods? Structured around the suppliant maidens' plea for political asylum in a foreign land, the plot line of this Aeschylean tragedy thus sparked a variety of competing values, wills and circumstances that would, in time, bring this city-state and its people to their knees.

It all begins, as Aeschylus' tragedy opens, with a band of sisters who have fled their Egyptian home with the intention of escaping an arranged marriage scheduled to take place with their 50 Egyptian cousins. In Argos, they seek not only to find a safe haven that can shield them from their marital woes, but also a new city to call their home. In the opening scene, the chorus of suppliant maidens sing:

> Hallowed netherland whose sunbruised
> boundaries graze desert leaving it
> we flew
> not outlaws hounded publicly for murder's blood on our hands
> but fugitives
> escaping self-built prisons for our own flesh.[4]

Terrified, they plead for asylum. They have no other recourse than supplication. Not long after their arrival, they are met personally by the king of Argos, Pelasgus. Initially, the king is warm in his reception and visibly moved by the suppliants' predicament. He cannot be otherwise as the suppliants' bid, at least at the outset, is candid and impassioned, yet also deferential to the king's authority. But that does not last long. Rapidly, their tone changes as Pelasgus wavers. When he admits that he may not, despite being the Argive king, be capable of reaching a determination in his own right, supplication quickly turns into something more forceful. The suppliants despair, but not before they provide him with an ultimatum: accept them into his city walls as suppliants or live with the knowledge that their blood will be on his hands. If their demands are not met, the suppliants threaten Pelasgus that they will commit an act of mass suicide on the altars of the city's gods outside Argos' city walls. Such an act would displease the gods and pollute the city as a whole.

Why Pelasgus is reluctant to accede to the suppliants' demands, as pointed out by a number of more contemporary scholars, is because he finds himself faced with having to resolve an issue that pits a set of rather incompatible values, wills and circumstances together. Whatever he decides, his society will not remain unaffected. As Janet Lembke writes of his predicament:

> The petition presents [him] with a choice of evils. If sanctuary is refused, the gods, offended by such sacrilege, will surely punish Argos. But if the Suppliants are sheltered, war with Egypt is a certainty, for the Egyptians do seem to have a valid legal claim upon the women. In either event the Argive people will suffer.[5]

This, for both Pelasgus and the suppliants, seems to be a lose–lose situation. If they are denied asylum, the suppliants surely risk reprisal from their would-be grooms and, after that, a lifetime of repression and violence. Unable or unwilling to face such a prospect, the sisters rightly turn their thoughts, at the very least their threats, to the idea of suicide on the altars of the Argive gods. But an act seemingly directed at the gods was actually directed no less at Argos. Dirtying the gods' altars, in other words, would have, in effect, been no different from befouling the city of Argos as a whole. And so, if the king does not act, those who will suffer the most will be none other than the Argive people. By the same token, however, if Pelasgus does decide to act and receive the suppliants into the city, he will most certainly antagonize his Egyptian neighbours, who are already in pursuit of the women they see as rightly theirs. Action, as such, will constitute an act of war. Either way then, it appears that the Argives cannot escape what is coming to them. From this one crisis – the suppliants' bid for asylum in a foreign land – Pelasgus is made to adjudicate between a set of irreconcilable values, wills and circumstances. This is the crux of the plot line of this Aeschylean tragedy.

But, as it quickly transpires, Pelasgus may not need to make this decision by himself. It is true that his concern for the Argive people and his compassion for the suppliants weigh on his heart and deny him a final decision. Be that as it may, he is relieved from the duty of reaching a final determination alone because, as Aeschylus makes clear, Argos is a democratic city-state. Pressed by the urgent ultimatum presented to him by the suppliants, Pelasgus has no other choice than to defer this question directly to the people for debate and judgement. Taking his leave from the foreign refugees, he returns to the city to put their case before the Argive Assembly. Only they, not Pelasgus, can rightly determine the suppliants' fate. Though the city's king, Aeschylus has him defer to the citizens. And perhaps indicative of their democratic predisposition, the Argive people are similarly moved by the harrowing situation faced by these foreign women. But unlike their king, who was paralysed by indecision, Aeschylus unanimously makes the people of Argos back the suppliants' claim for entry. They vote as one to recognize the suppliants' plea and to accept them into their city.

It is a decision that the Argives make to their detriment, however – this being a tragic drama, a reversal of this sort is perhaps to be expected. In what evidence survives of *Egyptians* and *Danaids*, the second and third plays of the *Danaid* trilogy, we learn that soon afterwards Argos falls under the weight of an Egyptian invasion.[6] As the suppliants had so rightly feared, an Egyptian Herald was then followed by a full-scale Egyptian invasion. Pelasgus and, we can only assume, the Argives who rose in defence of their city are slain. In his place, Danaus, the suppliants' father, is crowned the new king – but not a democratic king as Turner suggests.[7] He takes power by force and without popular support. Forced to honour the original betrothal of his daughters to the 50 sons of King Aegyptus of Egypt, Danaus and his daughters conceive a plot of murder: to kill their husbands on the wedding night. The plan is agreed to by all, that is, except Hypermestra, who discovers love for her new husband and unravels the entire sequence of events.

Perhaps had love been discovered sooner, and by all the sisters, then the bloodshed might have been avoided. But it was not and Aeschylus' tragedy illuminates what happens when individuals are unwilling to look beyond their own world view and negotiate what they desire with the desires of others. The suppliants may have, according to their own logic, fled with just cause. Yet they refused to bend or concede their position. This was evident in the ultimatum they presented to Pelasgus: either he let them in or they will pollute the city with their corpses. There was no pause to contemplate what their imposition would mean for Argos or what right they have to flee from Egypt. As for the Egyptian brothers, little is known about the agreement that has guaranteed them their brides. All that is known is that they have come in search of what, they claim, is theirs by law. Either Argos returns the 50 brides to their grooms, or Egypt will wage war on the city and take back the women by force. There can be no concession. There is no willingness to recognize these women's rights – which, of course, was custom throughout the ancient world. In the middle of it all was the city-state of Argos and its citizens who, for their part, voted to take the side of the suppliants, even with the threat of warfare looming down upon them. Perhaps, this was Aeschylus' intention: to dramatize the complexity of a situation that had no obvious answers and was not devoid of risks. The need to understand the world view of others, which may very well have been a point Aeschylus was hoping to communicate with his tragedy, is both a necessary and fraught undertaking in a democratic polis. The costly decision that the democrats of Argos made was right, even though it was made to their own eventual detriment.

Characters

To make these decisions, Aeschylus populated his tragedy with a cast of characters that would have resounded with a good cross section of his Athenian audiences. Indeed, though not all were liked or familiar figures, they were, according to Mary Ebbott's classification, 'multidimensional, sublime, profoundly complex whole – all character traits without which no tragic fall could have been possible'. And given the varied cast, it also became possible for him to manufacture 'zones of interaction' for characters from different worlds to engage with one another.

But, of the four main characters in *Suppliants*, it is arguably the group of 50 suppliant women who are the most noteworthy. Because of their number, Aeschylus has made them take the place of the chorus within the tragedy. In itself a unique feature, the chorus of suppliant maidens essentially constitutes the protagonist in Aeschylus' tragedy, given that more than half of the play is composed of suppliant choral lyric.[8] The three remaining characters include Danaus, the suppliants' father, Pelasgus, the king of Argos and the Egyptian Herald, who enters late in the tragedy to forcibly seek the return of the suppliants to Egypt.

As women, the suppliants' prominence within the tragedy would have been highly significant. For both the Argives within the tragedy and the Athenian audiences who witnessed the performance of it at the City Dionysia, these were not like the typical women they would have confronted in their daily lives. They were impetuous and exotic Egyptian women. Here, the words of Danaus and Pelasgus are a testament to this:

> Remember, bend!
> You are in want, strangers, fugitives,
> and rash tongues do not suit
> the part of weakness.[9]
>
> Where
> have you come from? A congregation
> glittering, bizarre in alien robes and diadems,
> and womanly, yet gaudy as no women
> I have ever known or dreamed . . .[10]

The words of their father and later of the king depict the suppliants as women eccentric in their status and aspiration. Not only that, but they are foreign both in their physical and political constitutions. They dictate the action as public figures, something which no woman of Greece was. Women, in Greek society, were private figures who had no public voice or democratic vote. By contrast, the Egyptian sisters of Aeschylus' tragedy dominate the dialogue and, before long, turn into Pelasgus' inquisitor: what cause has he to deny them entry into the city? This is all the more astounding since Pelasgus is the sovereign of the land in which they are seeking asylum. Regardless of their lowly position, these women take charge. They assume the role that is conventionally reserved for the father figure, Danaus. As a result, all he can do is caution his boisterous daughters to 'trust | in the elder wisdom of your captain-father'.[11] But, these words have little weight. They are more a plea than a command. From beginning to end, Danaus appears insignificant; a wise sage turned servant. There is little that Aeschylus does with him, at least within this tragedy. For a man of stately prestige, this would indeed have amounted to an inversion of ancient norms.

Yet, this is only where the state of inversion begins. The character of Pelasgus is also intriguing as he accedes both to the women and then to the polis. A strong and benevolent ruler, he boasts of the land in which the suppliants have come in search of asylum. However, through his interaction with this lowly group of women, his strength and benevolence are reduced to fear and apprehension. Their words strike unease into his heart and he is quickly incapacitated by these women. A dilemma that would see the ruin of his beloved Argos and put his compatriots at risk is not one that he can easily overcome. He is torn. Perhaps then, what is most peculiar about Pelasgus – as a tragic hero faced with an insurmountable dilemma – is his incapacity to face tragedy head on. Unlike an Oedipus or an Antigone, Pelasgus cannot decide either way. That is, until the people have decided as one. This means that the democratically empowered Argive people in effect take the place of the tragic hero and become the final arbiter of the tragedy's crisis.[12] At least symbolically, it is the everyday citizens and the democracy of Argos that take centre stage in this Aeschylean tragedy.

Finally, the minor character of the Egyptian Herald is of note because he is the embodiment of the political autocracy from which the suppliants are seeking to escape. Compare his engagement with the Danaids to that of Pelasgus':

I order: stop this madmouth
crazy woman cursing.
You and you, all of you,

get up, march down to the landing craft.
You – honorless, homeless,
Not worth my love or fear.[13]

. . . I am amazed.
But the branches
that lie besides you in godshadow
seem lawhonored signs that you claim asylum.
At this one point perhaps your world meets mine.[14]

A more contrary state representative could not be found in these two characters. While to the Herald the women are neither deserving of his honour or love, Pelasgus is moved by compassion and understands that two civilizations have met together outside his city walls. This exemplifies for us the zones of interaction in this tragedy that allow for such characters as the suppliants, Danus, Pelasgus and the Herald to come face to face. Moreover, through this interaction, what we find is that characters like Danaus, Pelasgus and the Herald – the wise, stately and authoritarian men who would have dominated the ancient world – are made to bow to the will of the many: first to the people of Argos who themselves bowed to the will of the 50 suppliant women of Egypt.

Language

Unlike most other tragedies of its day though, what would have really set *Suppliants* apart is its language, more than half of which is composed entirely of choral lyric. The 'many-voicedness', both rational and non-rational, of the characters staged would have vocalized a polyphony of viewpoints quite likely to provoke the 'freedom of others' points of view to . . . reveal themselves'. The lyrics, in Peter Burian's assessment, amount to some of 'the densest, most opulent, most purely lovely things in all Greek poetry'; there to give voice to the suppliants' ecstatic irrationalities, their intense yearning and their deepest despair.[15] What can be heard at length in these choral lyrics is what could not be expressed rationally. It is poetic and seizes their innermost mood. Take these two passages for example:

io io ioioioioio
No flight
no time to hide
Inhuman cruelty leaves no escape

My heart beats darker
dashes like a small trapped creature
A father's eye snares me, fear haunts me

Let my bondage to doom
end in a slipnoose
Before a man
I wish unborn
Can touch my flesh, O come
husband me, Death.[16]

If terror, angst, defiance and arrogance could be verbalized in one single outburst, perhaps it is the choral lyrics of these ancient tragedies that came the closest. Indeed, in the above two passages it is made clear that, despite their best efforts, the suppliants may not be able to escape their own fate. Their words give form to this realization. There is no sense or logic to be salvaged at these moments. With no middle ground, no escape route, the tension stretches to hyperbolic dimensions. Will the suppliants escape the one thing they have led us to believe they cannot tolerate? Logic cannot easily explain such a predicament.

And as women from faraway lands, they would have been hard-pressed to do so before Pelasgus, the Argives as well as the audiences at the City Dionysia in Athens. Their language, unintelligible at times, voiced the unheard predicaments of women from foreign countries. It made audible certain fears and aspirations that the Athenians had suppressed within the political realm. And yet, for the women, foreign residents and even the slaves who from time to time attended the Dionysia and Lenaia festivals, these were concerns that they, as marginalized individuals, may have been quite capable of relating to. The chorus gives voice to these facets of ourselves and societies.

Set against the choral odes are the passages of Danaus, Pelasgus and the Egyptian Herald. As already touched upon, Danaus' words express a father figure whose authority resembles that of a mother's. Without any real authority, he is not so much the suppliants' spokesman as their aid and messenger. As for the language of Pelasgus and the Herald, they are indicative of their political differences: one even-handed, open to debate and democratic; the other cold, rigid and dictatorial. The opposition between empathetic paralysis and a crude one-sidedness is starkly visible in the words of Pelasgus and the Herald.

Taken together, the tragic language in this tragedy gives voice to the divergent perspectives and aspirations of the characters. The choral lyric of the suppliants, which dominates the dialogue within the whole play, expresses their arrogance and their fears. Danus, who actually says very little, is dictated to by his pestilent daughters. As a conciliator, Pelasgus speaks in uncertain terms and attempts to balance competing arguments and possibilities. He pauses, often for too long, to process the claims made before him. He urges restraint but also understands the dire situation that the suppliants are faced with. By contrast, the Egyptian Herald's language conveys that he is not there to negotiate. He has no desire to listen to the reasons offered by the suppliants nor does he recognize the democratic principles and laws of humanitarianism that has apparently compelled the Argives to receive the suppliants as refugees from a foreign land.

The multivocal form of Aeschylus' *Suppliants*: A dramatic representation of Athens' democracy

Read together, there are therefore three interrelated points of note. The first and most obvious is how prominent the suppliants are within the tragedy – a fact that is affirmed by the relative weakness of Danaus and Pelasgus. Aeschylus' tragedy is one where the women take centre stage. It is their agency, their personal aspirations and, ultimately, their repudiation of men's authority around which the tragedy's plot revolves. In this sense, it can be said that the tragedy attempts to foreground certain things that had habitually been suppressed in the public domain of the polis. The mass intrusion of the foreign, alien and anti-democratic into a democratic city-state of Greece shows just what a democratic city-state of Greece should endure in the name of its democracy. Related to this is the second point: that issues of inclusion and exclusion are near indivisible. Here, the suppliants' plea for inclusion raised the question of what it was a democratic polis should, by its nature, be able to tolerate. But such a plea was soon shown to be inseparable from existence itself. Exclusion would have resulted in the suppliants' suicide at the altar of the gods. Inclusion did result in Argive deaths. Accordingly, the third point made by Aeschylus' *Suppliants* is that inclusion and exclusion are at the heart of democracy, and this is why it is so tragic.

Through these three points, this tragedy would have problematized for its audiences the two dichotomies crucial to democratic politics at the time. The first is the interplay between order and disorder and the second between reality and fiction. Order, dramatized as what the suppliants seek and what the Argives possess, coexists intimately with disorder in Aeschylus' tragedy. Indeed, it was the very nature of the Argives' democratic existence that demanded they take the suppliants' plea into account. Their comfortable existence as such could be ruptured at any time. This was what their democracy demanded of them. And so, by recognizing the suppliants' appeal, Argos effectively brought about its own capitulation at the hands of the Egyptians. Pelasgus, chief among the Argives, was to pay the greatest price. In that instant, the idea and ideal of democracy must have reverberated around the theatre of Dionysus in Athens. We know this because *Suppliants* premiered at a time when the issue of democracy's future raged within the Athenian Assembly and courts. Performed just years after Themistocles, one of Athens' more notable democrats, was ostracized for championing a stronger and more egalitarian democratic make-up, the tragedy would have had unmistakable political overtones. While the similarities between the plot line of *Suppliants* and Themistocles' ostracism are interesting, and possibly more than mere coincidence, the differences that emerge between them also raise intriguing questions. And thus, by blurring or problematizing reality and fiction, this tragedy would quite likely have been a medium which the citizens of the day turned to in an attempt to think through some of the more intractable obstacles impeding democracy's expansion during the fifth century.

Order/Disorder

But just how exactly can we say that the multivocal form of Aeschylus' tragedy brought a variety of otherwise marginalized stories, characters and voices onto the public stage and into democratic debate? That is the question which detains us here and, in the first instance, it will be answered through an exploration of the interplay between order and disorder – something that Aeschylus' *Suppliants* manages to traverse to powerful effect.

After all, it is the issue of order that the tragedy broaches from the very outset when, through the suppliants, it begs the question: 'Land? shall you welcome | our coming?'[17] Yet, as a question which concerns the inclusion of the foreign other into the polis, it also touches upon the spectre of disorder. Weighed down by the impending clash and the prospect of destruction, Pelasgus thus proclaims to the suppliants: 'At this one point perhaps your world meets mine.'[18] What order is to result in the aftermath? This is arguably the first fundamental theme *Suppliants* broaches: the necessity of order.

Indeed, even in the tragedy's opening lines, Aeschylus makes clear that the suppliants have fled their homeland solely because of their animus towards the violent order where forced marriage and male domination are only the external by-products:

> Never
> not ever
> may the power of a male fist crush me
> With help instead from sailorguiding stars
> I chart my own course flight
> from a loathsome marriage . . .[19]

Driven by pure self-will, they desire unfettered sovereignty over their lives.[20] Their demands for asylum are unyielding, 'even insolent', as Meier writes.[21] For them, it is either success or failure, acceptance or death. They push Pelasgus to make his decision. As king, the suppliants argue that he alone possesses the right to warrant their entry. As king, the women believe that Pelasgus is just like a pharaoh of Egypt, whose single-voice and single-hand dictates to all people, willing or otherwise, their place and rights in the world. He is the one who sanctions what is and what is not in his city. To him, they cry:

> You the people! You the government!
> A pharaoh chosen, unimpeachable you
> sustain the fire blazing on the country's altarhearth
> with single-voiced decrees, your own,
> and single-handed from your sovereign bench you
> bring all debts to final reckoning . . .[22]

What the king decrees, they argue, is what will come to pass. Their insistence reaches a climax when, faced with Pelasgus' continual diffidence, the suppliants threaten their own deaths on the altars of the gods:

> If you can make us no firm promise –
> New strange offerings to give the godstone splendour . . .
> To hang myself, and now, AND FROM THESE VERY GODS![23]

Their threat, in this sense, echoes the primal human need to secure meaningful order, which for them would have been impossible under the rule of the sons of Aegyptus. But neither would it be possible in the wilderness, a place of nothingness and death. The means they have chosen in procuring order is indicative of the despotic order they have known.[24] As women without political status or physical might, their forceful words, their imposition and their hoped for acquiescence on the Argive part are their only weapons – weapons that ultimately prove to be successful.

For democratic Argos, however, the question of order – for the suppliants and themselves – is approached differently. The Argos of Aeschylus' *Suppliants* seems a place that appears worthy of envy. Pelasgus regales of its glory early on in the play:

> Over plains, over valleys
> where rivers curl redgold
> toward the sunset, I hold all power.
> Beyond eye's north horizon
> to mountains that build immense palisades
> against the wild tribes,
> to foothills where oaktrees
> rustle their oracles . . .[25]

But that is not entirely accurate. Being a democratic polis, the leader is found on more than one occasion referring to the power of the people. On this particular occasion, after agonizing over the suppliants' situation, Pelasgus ultimately delegates the issue to the people. Can Argos cope with the implications of the suppliants' presence within its walls? Can it cope with the difference of the women and the potential destruction they bring? Can it cope, in short, with what they are not and those who would bring them their end? These are the questions the Argive people assemble to decide. The decision they make, reached after a democratic vote, is recounted by the suppliants' father, Danaus, who accompanies Pelasgus to the Assembly:

> The men of Argos voted not ambivalently
> but so that my old veins ran hot and young again.
> In full assembly every man raised his right hand –
> air bristled! – to confirm this resolution:
>
> THAT WE BECOME SETTLERS IN OUR MOTHERLAND,
> FREE, SECURE IN OUR PERSONS
> AGAINST ALL SEIZURE AND HUMAN REPRISAL;
> THAT NO MAN, EITHER NATIVEBORN OR ALIEN,
> DRIVE US OUT INTO CAPTIVITY,
> BUT, IF FORCE BE EXERCISED,

HE WHO DOES NOT AID US,
THOUGH IT IS HIS RIGHT AND DUTY TO BEAR ARMS,
SHALL LOSE ALL RIGHTS,
HIS EXILE MANDATED BY HIS PEERS.[26]

With this democratic resolution, Argive order is reaffirmed anew. But as the final line shows, order is always laced with its opposite.

Disorder, in this sense, can come in many forms, though it will always appear in a manner and at an interval just beyond one's grasp. In *Suppliants*, symbolic reminders of the presence of disorder are littered throughout the tragedy. However, the two most overt instances are the suppliants' threat of suicide and the final destruction of Argos by the Egyptians.

Pitched as their ultimate threat, the suppliants inform Pelasgus that if they do not receive asylum within his city, they will have no option except to hang themselves from the statues of the city's gods. To threaten such a profane act implied two things. The first is the state of desperation these women must have been in. Toying with the thought of suicide insinuates just how despondent they were becoming at the possibility of returning to Egypt or dying in the desert. It was with this mentality that they entertained the idea of death. However, to hang themselves from the statues of the gods signified that these women had also lost faith in the gods and, by extension, the order they symbolized for human existence. What better way to show this than to defile the gods and the city of Argos with their bodily remains. Both their afterlives and the life of Argos as a community would be put in jeopardy – but, if we are to believe the suppliants' threats, this was something that these women neither cared about nor believed in any longer. Yet, for Pelasgus, who clearly did still care and believe, the suppliants' words were like 'whips that flay my heart'.[27] And how could they not, for such an act would, according to him, '[befoul] both gods and men',[28] thereby polluting the very core of Argos and presage its eventual doom at the hands of those gods.[29] Had the suppliants' committed suicide, all of Argos would have been thrust into disorder. But luckily for all involved, this prospect was averted at the last minute, when the Argive people voted to accept the suppliants into their midst.

Despite this, as the tragedy ends, we realize that Argos would not to be spared. Having chosen to recognize the suppliants as one of their own, the Argives in effect elected to destroy themselves. Their destruction, in this sense, was not up to them, being intrinsic to the way they lived. What Pelasgus had sought so desperately to avoid when he mulled over what he would do with these women is ultimately proved true:

> But if I stand, back to the wall, and battletest
> the issue with your cousins, Egypt's sons,
> shall not the cost be bitter: men drenching
> trampled earth with blood, and all in the name of women?[30]

According to the myth, the lost plays of the *Danaid* trilogy tell precisely of the deaths of Pelasgus and the Argive defenders at the hands of the Egyptians. To this end, the order which the Argives sought so hard to preserve was the very order that called them to accept the suppliants. And this was what brought disruption and death to their city. But even if the Egyptians had not come to seek the return of these women, the women themselves would have disrupted the natural flow of this Greek society. Their absolute denunciation of marriage and, with it, conventions of family, fertility and community went against deeply held Greek beliefs.[31] As such, even without war and destruction, the Argives would have subjected themselves and their society to the foreign beliefs of these Egyptian women.[32]

Order, accordingly, exists in a problematic relationship with its opposite. Certainly, the question of inclusion and the spectre of destruction go hand in hand in *Suppliants*. The dilemma faced by Pelasgus and the Argives pit foreigners against citizens, inside against outside, women against men, war against peace and the gods against the city. For this reason, Pelasgus, in his own assessment, is instantly

> . . .made weaponless.
> Fear beat in my body like a pulse:
> to act, or not to act and let chance deliver
> its blind verdict.[33]

Is he to accede to the laws of the gods, the moral law of humanitarianism or does he save the city from the prospect of war with Egypt? All pertain to order, and all bring with them the prospect of an impending disorder that terrorizes Argive existence. To be physically secure and prosperous at the expense of moral wholeness or to be morally upright at the cost of the city's destruction? These are the questions which tear at Pelasgus' heart. Responsibility is due both to the Argives and the suppliants, both to the city and the gods. There are no easy, inconsequential answers. Indeed, as Pelasgus pleads,

> There is no facile judgement for the case.
> Choose not me as judge.
> I have told you, tell you now, not without
> the polity's consent
> may I act on the question, not even though I rule, . . .
> *Aliens. When you honored them, you damned your people.*[34]

For Kitto, Pelasgus is a man on the brink of the abyss, forced like typical tragic heroes to choose between two evils.[35]

But as is clear, it is a choice which Pelasgus ultimately relinquishes to the Argive people as a whole. Here, Podlecki makes the critical point that while Kitto is correct to see Pelasgus as an individual thrust to the brink of the abyss by Aeschylus, he does not realize that Aeschylus ultimately fails to push Pelasgus over that edge.[36] Instead, Aeschylus transfers the right and responsibility of this choice onto the people. The transfer of power and focus is significant since it presents not Pelasgus as the ultimate tragic hero around which the tragedy centres, but the citizens of democratic Argos. While the king is paralysed by vacillation, the people possess the gall to decide as one and confront the consequences together. By identifying the people as the tragic heroes of this play, we are reminded of the dangers of overstepping individual limits.[37] Living with the prospect of disorder is best done together. Not that this makes life any easier. Individually, the fate of Pelasgus attests to this. And as a collective, so did the fates of the Argive people, whose decision to receive the suppliants signalled open hostility against their Egyptian suitors; this, the harbinger of their ultimate demise.

Reality/Fiction

These issues and themes, central to Aeschylus' *Suppliants*, were also central to fifth-century Athenian politics. Refuge in a foreign, democratic land; eminent figures turned into suppliants; the onset of political strife and the broadening of the democratic franchise – these were the very dilemmas faced by Athens in reality in the mid-460s, when *Suppliants* had its premiere. From what we now know about the tragedy, it would not be a stretch of one's imagination to read Aeschylus' play against – and indeed as indirect commentary of – these political dilemmas. It would not be a stretch of one's imagination to think that this was what the Athenians themselves did, what Aeschylus intended for them to do. For, this was how fictional accounts legitimately entered political lexicon in ancient Athens.

But aided by both hindsight and the historical accounts that we do have, we can conjecture a more specific way in which Aeschylus' *Suppliants* might have entered Athens' political debates. As a tragedy that touched upon the topics of exile, democratic franchise and war, it would have also touched upon or rephrased a number of the key questions that were reverberating around Athens at the time. These questions, first raised during the ostracism of Themistocles from Athens, which occurred just years before the premiere of Aeschylus' tragedy, were eventually resolved when the aristocratic *Areopagus* was finally abolished in 462/461 BC. Wedged in between these two events, notable in the history of democratic Athens, can we say that Aeschylus used his tragedy, in part, to illuminate the broader trajectory which democracy was at that time on?

Ostracized from Athens most likely around 471/470 BC, Themistocles was a notable Athenian democrat and one of only 20 recorded individuals ever to be ostracized from Athens.[38] Though already touched upon in previous chapters, the procedure of ostracism is interesting as it exemplified perfectly the democratic balance between order and disorder in Athenian life. Here was a procedure created, first, to stem the resurgence of autocracy and, second, to enable citizens to keep each other in check.[39] Preventing the absolute rule of one was the ultimate aim of this procedure. Effectively, ostracism permitted citizens to elect and vote particular members of the community into a 10-year exile from Athens for reasons of political arrogance, mismanagement or fraud. According to Donald Kagan, '[t]he law doubtless had the stated intent of preventing the recurrence of tyranny, and being enacted when it was [after the democratic revolution], it was sure to be popular'.[40] More than this, he argues that ostracism could accommodate the bigger, constitutional question which confronted the nascent democracy, which was 'how to prevent the dangers of faction and subversion while avoiding the extremes of inquisition, violence and mass expulsion resorted to by other Greek democracies with tragic consequences'.[41]

Unlike intra-elite exile, therefore, ostracism provided the people with the right, as citizens, to determine the make-up of their world and those who would rule therein. Because of this, questions about and decisions to ostracize were not taken lightly nor before sustained public debate. It was not arbitrary, exclusive and imposed from above, but an open, fair and judicious mechanism to rid the polis of its most violent and oppressive constituents.[42] But none of this, it should be made clear, prevented ostracism from being used or misused to achieve particular political ends. Indeed, given that democracy was the rule of majority sentiment, whatever sentiment happened to be in the minority could end up being branded as violent and oppressive. Because of this, even the most powerful Athenians could, if they fell out of favour, with the majority, find themselves lowered to a position that was often worse off than the worst off in Athens: the women, children, foreign residents and slaves. They could find themselves in the clasp of disorder, even as they strove to institute greater order.

While fought over specific policies and against one particular opponent, Themistocles' ostracism was evocative of a greater schism which had developed in Athens after the democratic revolution. Put simply, this schism was one which divided the aristocrats of Athens from the democrats or those who supported the *Areopagus* from those who did not.[43] In the aftermath of the Cleisthenic reforms of 508/507 BC, the continued existence of the *Areopagus* remained a topic of some contention. It came to symbolize the greater struggle between democracy and aristocracy in Athens, that is, until its eventual abolition in 462/461 BC, one year following the first staging of *Suppliants*. Themistocles achieved prominence during these years, as a renowned activist for democracy in Athens.

The precise cause of Themistocles' ostracism, of course, arose from a much more specific, yet nonetheless divisive, issue: Athenian foreign policy. The conventional wisdom that continued to grip Athens, even in the post-Persian Wars era, was that Persia nevertheless constituted the city's greatest adversary. For Themistocles, however, this fear was ill-conceived. Instead of Persia, he believed that it was actually Sparta which posed the greatest threat to Athens following the capitulation of Persia. Buoyed by its victory in the Persian Wars, Athens' ascendancy rightly troubled Sparta. They would, Themistocles thought, not rest long in the Hellenic alliance which had united the two city-states in opposition to Persia.[44] Because of this, war with Sparta would eventually be inevitable – as would Athens' eventual conquest, if it did not do all it could to suppress a resurgent Sparta. In view of this, Themistocles is recorded as having pushed for closer ties with the enemies of Sparta, most prominently Argos.[45] For him, a compact of democratic states was envisioned to counter the rise of an aristocratic one.

To be expected, the aspirations of Themistocles did not find favour, with many of Athens' most powerful elites. These powerbrokers were largely sympathetic to Athens' aristocratic heritage and believed that an authoritarian Sparta was obviously preferable to an exotic and aggressive Persia that had

only years before undertaking an invasion of Greece. One of the key propo-
nents of this position, and an ardent political opponent of Themistocles, was
Cimon, whose animus towards Persia and support for Sparta distinguished him
from Themistocles. Crucially though, unlike Themistocles, Cimon enjoyed the
majority of the people's backing. Being a man who esteemed tradition and, by
extension, a politically robust *Areopagus*, Cimon's views reflected a large cross-
section of Athenians who desired greater stability within their domestic and
foreign affairs.[46] As the stronger of the two parties, Cimon quickly outmanoeu-
vred Themistocles politically. In an alliance led by Cimon and other pro-Spartan
elites, Themistocles, therefore, found himself accused and convicted of treason –
for allegedly conspiring to betray Hellas to Persia.[47] Portrayed as unpatriotic,
Cimon and his Spartan backers managed to convince the Athenian voters to
ostracize Themistocles.[48]

Exiled from Athens, Themistocles, perhaps to be expected, sought asylum
in Argos – the city-state which he had tried to ally Athens with. Astoundingly,
Argos granted Themistocles asylum knowing full well what consequences
might ensue. By receiving Themistocles and aiding his plan to subvert Athens
and Sparta, Forrest notes that Argos effectively signalled open hostility to both
Sparta and Cimonian Athens.[49] What evidence there is indicates that Argos had
been a democracy from the outset of the fifth century, sharing many parallels
with her Athenian sister state.[50] Hence, its decision to receive Themistocles as a
suppliant must have, to some degree, met with the approval of a significant portion of the citizens within Argos, perhaps as a result of a democratic vote similar
to the one which took place in *Suppliants*.

But what happened next was both curious and unexpected. Almost as quickly
as he had entered Argos, we read that Themistocles fled his newfound haven.
This we know from a passage in Thucydides, who recounts that, upon learning of a combined Spartan-Athenian embassy charged to pursue and 'take him
wherever they found him', Themistocles fled of his own accord.[51] For Sparta,
these measures were justified. Themistocles, who 'was in the habit of visiting
other parts of the Peloponnese',[52] presumably to shore up democratic resolve and
establish an anti-Spartan league, provoked tremendous suspicion and anxiety
from Sparta.[53]

But, the exact reasons as to why he left Argos remain unknown. Did he no
longer have the support of his Argive hosts? Was there internal turmoil brewing
within Argos itself? Or, did Themistocles simply wish to avert the bloodbath
which would have ensued had he stayed? The answers to these questions

remain unclear. All that is clear is that he did flee, to Corcyra which, though 'under obligations towards him ... could not venture to shelter him at the cost of offending Athens and Lacedaemon, and they conveyed him over to the continent opposite.'[54]

Whatever the reasons then, the Argos of this story escaped the wrath that the Argos of Aeschylus' *Suppliants* could not. Even so, the similarities and differences between Aeschylus' tragedy and the political consequences of Themistocles' ostracism are fascinating and worthy of some further speculation.

For one, a consensus now exists confirming that *Suppliants* was probably first performed at the City Dionysia in Athens sometime around the mid-460s, most likely in 463 BC.[55] The temporal proximity between Themistocles' ostracism and the performance of Aeschylus' *Suppliants* could quite conceivably have spoken volumes to the Athenian audiences, as well as to the visiting dignitaries of neighbouring Argos and Sparta. The overwhelming resemblance and chronological immediacy between what took place in reality with what was staged through fiction meant that the tragedy could, at least in the interpretation of some, be viewed as a political metaphor for the events of the recent past.[56]

But this symbolism was not merely historical. The politics surrounding Themistocles' ostracism was not a thing of the past. Certainly, by the time Aeschylus' *Suppliants* was performed in Athens, it was becoming clear that these issues were still very much alive. If anything, Themistocles' ostracism had only been a prelude to the bigger shift that was set to occur: the abolition of the *Areopagus* and the move to greater democracy in Athens.

Aeschylus' tragedy sat between the key political events of Themistocles' ostracism, which coincided with the rise of Cimon/Sparta, and Ephialtes' reforms to abolish the *Areopagus*, the harbinger of Cimon's eventual downfall and ostracism from Athens. Amid the political commotion, Meier makes the point that '[q]uestion upon question was bound to arise, questions which could hardly be aired before the Assembly without arousing suspicions of vested political interests.'[57] Think here of what had happened to Themistocles for suggesting that the Athenians had misplaced their efforts in seeking to defend against another Persian attack. Exempt from these restraints, tragedians like Aeschylus used their fictional creations to air, problematize and even resolve these political questions in a manner and forum accessible to all. Aeschylean tragedy was certainly a culprit of political commentary and contemplation, in both a narrow and broad sense.[58] However, we must again remember that Aeschylus' intentions and his tragedies were not mere 'charades on contemporary events'.[59] Instead, the political purpose and treatment of Aeschylean tragedy was always more meta-phorical, abstract and redolent.[60]

Insofar as Aeschylus was broadly inspired by the political connotations of Themistocles' ostracism, *Suppliants* did not amount to mere 'political allegory'.[61] Rather, Aeschylus reinterpreted the myth to remind the Athenians of the hero-ism of the Argives when they received Themistocles, even with the knowledge of looming hostilities. But the drama also acted as a personal medium for Aeschy-lus to air his appreciation to the democrats – both within and beyond Athens.[62] Aeschylus' constant emphasis on the people's power in *Suppliants*,[63] in this regard, was not only astounding because it was anachronistic from a mythologi-cal perspective but also because of the democratic sympathies and developments rife within Athens at the time.[64] Too many similarities exist between the Argives' democracy, as recounted by Danaus in *Suppliants*, and the Athenians' democ-racy of the mid-460s to have been mere coincidence.[65] But more than this, the tragedy also alluded to some of the most pressing concerns on Athens' political horizon, even suggesting a possible way forward.

Just take Themistocles' seemingly self-imposed flight from Argos, for exam-ple. Aeschylus, as we know, chose to recreate a different ending for his tragedy. But why? As has already been mentioned, the precise reasons for Themistocles' departure are unknown. But if they were, in fact, to do with internal turmoil within Argos, that is to say, a battle between its own democrats and aristocrats, then Aeschylus' tragedy may have had one of two effects. If, on the one hand, Argos was no longer dependable as a democratic ally – for Themistocles and the Athenian democrats – then Aeschylus' *Suppliants* may have acted both as encouragement and reproach: first, to the Argives and, second, to the Athenians. It may, therefore, have been the case that Aeschylus made his fictional Argos stand firm, even against all odds, so as to encourage Argos to do the same in reality. Yet, if this was Aeschylus' message, it would have been aimed no less at Athens. In the late 460s, we know Athens was reaching the final stages of its democratic ascension with the abolition of the aristocratic *Areopagus*. Aeschy-lus understood that the reform's success or failure in Athens depended on the people, a people strong enough to bear the new burdens of democracy as the mythical Argives had done in *Suppliants*. This is why Turner argues that '[i]n the *Supplices*, all of Greece is Argos and Argos, Athens'.[66] Through his mythical dramatization, Aeschylus used Argos to encourage the citizens of Athens.

Having said all this, the question still needs to be asked: did the multivo-cal form of *Suppliants* actually inspire, remedy and complement democracy in

Athens? Did it influence the Athenians' vote to abolish the aristocratic *Areopagus* so that they too could vote as one like the Argives of Aeschylus' *Suppliants* had done? These questions are, of course, difficult to answer with any certainty. And doing so is certainly beyond the scope of this current reading. However, that the momentous push towards democracy and the significant realignment of foreign policy occurred only one year after the performance of *Suppliants* suggests that a connection of some sort did exist. Establishing a quantitatively precise chain of causation is, of course, quite another matter. But, one thing is certain. Given the proximity in time and the parallels between reality and fiction, we can safely assume that tragic dramatizations such as this formed part of and, perhaps, even helped shape the political discourse that fed directly back into the events of the day. They were timely and valued interventions into democratic life, though of a qualitatively different kind.

5

Civilization and Violence: A New Vision for Contemporary Democracy

The times certainly have changed since Aeschylus' *Suppliants* was first performed. But, different as things are between then and now, at least some of these changes – particularly 'the political, technological and other radical changes in our postmodern times' – suggest that the veracity of the Greek classics will not have waned.[1] Even though two-and-a-half millennia have lapsed since the tragedies of Aeschylus (and, by extension, Sophocles and Euripides) were first performed in ancient Athens, contemporary dramatists, historians, philosophers and political thinkers have returned time and again to these cultural artifacts. They do so, in part, out of a fascination for times past and for what we moderns have since misplaced or forgotten. But, they also return to Greece in order to rescue lost lessons and to resuscitate, for the sake of our own societies, important texts which were once indispensable to the life of societies past.

The latter has been a motivation for a number of contemporary thinkers and dramatists who have revived Aeschylus' *Suppliants* in more recent times. With little apparent respect for theatrical customs or conventional philological methods, what has concerned many of these dramatists is more the political impact and the affect that tragedies had in antiquity and how we can best recapture these today. For them as such, tragedies like Aeschylus' *Suppliants* are imbued with lessons that have the potential to transfer and translate into our own societies. It is up to us whether we choose to see them that way, to take certain liberties when we approach tragedy today, or whether we choose to designate them as categorically from another time and place.

Opting firmly for the former option, the American dramatist Charles L. Mee has translated Aeschylus' *Suppliants* into a play that reflects our own age. Equally celebrated and maligned by critics, Mee's *Big Love*, therefore, pushes the ancient dramatist's tragedy into modernity and beyond. According to this once historian turned playwright, what the Greeks provide him with is a 'model' with which to recapture the lives they lived but also to transport the past into the present. The Greeks, as he puts it,

> looked into the abyss of human life and human nature with open eyes and understood that the thing to do is to feel life as it is, in all its anguish as well as its aspiration, its missed opportunities and its savored beauties, never to falsify it, never to pretty it up; but rather to look at it bravely, unflinchingly. In the sheer steadiness and clarity and courage of that gaze will you achieve real understanding of the complexity of life; and from that comes acceptance, grace and enduring peace.[2]

Mee's charge is thus to 'take all this', like the Greeks did, 'and make a civilization of it'.[3]

Using Aeschylus' *Suppliants* as his model, this is what Mee has sought to do with *Big Love*. For Mee, the sociological insights and political bearing of Aeschylus' tragedy are not limited solely to the antique past. Though tragic dramas are no longer considered a legitimate form of political discourse, there is still something about them which can provide cutting commentary on our own political, and indeed democratic, aspirations. All that is needed is a little updating and tweaking. We must do with the Greeks' tragedies what they did with their own and that is, argues Mee, 'to take a Greek tragedy, smash it to ruins, and then, atop the ruins, write a new tragedy'.[4] For Savas Patsalidis, how Mee does this is by taking

> the body of the old tragedy [i.e. Aeschylus' *Suppliants*] and its basic issues and disembodies them, wrecks them, reduces them to rubble . . . Mee's main concern is not so much to pay any special attention to the myth itself as to give the correlations between the Aeschylean plot and current social and political issues; that is, to comment on what is happening today, 2,500 years later, regarding the plight of international refugees, the problem of political asylum, the problem of violence, gender relations, selfhood and otherness and, of course, love.[5]

He has, in this sense, revised Aeschylus' tragedy. The result is a contemporary play that, because of the disjuncture that emerges from pitting old with new, the familiar with the peculiar, actually possesses the capacity to bring otherwise marginalized stories, characters and voices onto the public stage and into democratic debate – but in a rather unexpected manner.

And so, even though it owes a great deal to Aeschylus' *Suppliants*, the themes that *Big Love* brings to stage are quite unique. As a tragedy that, at first glance, grapples with issues of political asylum and gender, *Big Love* actually turns on something altogether different. Simply put, *Big Love* is a contemporary tragedy that scrutinizes the supposed schism between civilization and violence. For a play which ostensibly evokes a 'dream-like world' where 'characters work themselves from philosophical musing into emotional frenzies',[6] Mee manages to make a serious point: that civility and the benefits which accrue from civilization are purchased at a cost that is violent at heart. Dichotomies that separate civilization from violence are erroneous and dangerous, though prevalent. And they must be uncovered. His tragedy sets about to unravel this dualistic perception, to bring to the fore what has been sustained and then concealed by our civilizational constructs, but in a highly dramatic and unconventional style.

The purpose of this chapter is to read the multivocal form of *Big Love* using the same analytical framework that was deployed to read the Aeschylean original. Given Mee's claims about his dramatic productions, can it be said that *Big Love* manages to do what he claims it does: to re-present Aeschylus' *Suppliants* for today? Does he manage to bring a variety of otherwise marginalized stories, characters and voices onto the public stage and into democratic debate as Aeschylus did with his tragedy? In short, does the multivocal form of *Big Love* dramatize the interplay between order and disorder and reality and fiction in a contemporary fashion?

This chapter, through the reading that follows, makes the argument that *Big Love* certainly has the potential to do all these things. By erecting and then destroying the schism between civilization and violence, it will suggest that *Big Love* too evokes the central democratic interplay between order and disorder and reality and fiction that we saw in Aeschylus' original. Civilization – the concept, the physical manifestation, the aspiration – connotes here that drive to instill order in one's world. It is an enterprise that seeks to enlighten the self and educate others. Violence – or barbarism, degeneration and meaninglessness – connotes the opposite drive. Such a schism, as Monaghan notes, is a defining feature of tragedy: the 'play between order and disorder, civilization and bestiality'.[7] But this schism also echoes what we have heard more broadly, in reality, about the problematic effects of our civilizing missions. Indeed, despite the proclamations that civilization represents everything that violence does not – that democratic zones of peace, for instances, are incongruous with autocratic zones of violence – Mee's tragedy demonstrates how, in reality, the two are intrinsically entwined. Civilization is founded upon and sustained by violence. That is the tragedy's indictment against a contemporary capitalist society; one which can be read to critique the perceived links between democracy, progress and peace at the heart of current efforts to extend democracy globally.

Plot

A decade ago, when interviewed by the *Drama Review* journal, Erin Mee remarked that her father's philosophy of political dramaturgy was premised on the destruction of conventions and the creation of new spaces for the previously marginalized, rejected and outcast.[8] The plays that he creates are more often than not 'broken, jagged, filled with sharp edges, filled with things that take sudden turns, career into each other, smash up, veer off in sickening turns'.[9] There is, in other words, usually some sort of crisis or conflict within his plays – out of which emerges a profusion of conflicting values, clashing wills and different circumstances. *Big Love* is no exception.

Like Aeschylus' *Suppliants*, *Big Love* tells the story of 50 sisters who have fled their homes, which this time is set in modern-day Greece. Like their Danaid ancestors, they have been promised to their 50 cousins in marriage. And like them, they have made a pact of resistance and fled to neighbouring Italy. At the doorsteps of Piero, their host, they plead their case for asylum in a scenario that quite simply seems odd. But, before Piero has time to assess the sisters' claims, their 50 would-be grooms arrive by helicopter to take back the women by force. Neither party, the brothers nor the sisters, is willing to negotiate or move from their position. Because of this, according to the sisters' logic, they have no other option left to them than to murder their grooms on their wedding night. They do so in a scene that is bloody and chaotic. Lydia is the only sister who resists because, unlike her siblings, she allows herself to discover love.

Within this tragedy, there is clearly a crisis at hand, but it is not, as we may expect, primarily concerned with questions of political asylum and gender as it was in the case of Aeschylus' *Suppliants*. Instead, the crisis lies deeper – beneath *Big Love*'s overt folly, hilarity and gratuitousness.

We first glimpse the plot's crux when Piero enters to greet the sisters. Though kind and welcoming, Piero quickly rejects the sisters' pleas and any responsibilities which they claim he owes towards them, saying:

> [A]s for the difficulties you find yourselves in
> disagreeable as they are

and as much as I would like to help
this is not my business.[10]

Thyona, the most ardent sister, immediately rebuts:

Whose business is it
if not yours?
You're a human being.[11]

With these words, Thyona invokes their predicament not predominately as a political or personal one, not one about refuge per se. Rather, the crisis emanates from something deeper. As a human being, Thyona reasons, Piero should be able to recognize her and her sisters as fellow human beings – human beings in need. If he cannot, then he is to her no different from the brothers who, as she later reveals, are less than human.

In other words, the then-implicit reason which Thyona invokes for leaving Greece is based on a dichotomy she erects that separates the human from the inhumane and, more importantly, what is civilized from what is uncivilized. For her, the sisters have fled from what they believe to be uncivilized in search of a civilization at odds with the violence and repression enacted upon them by the men they have known. These men are the metaphors of civilization's antithesis, something which these women want nothing more to do with. But, this is something that Mee's tragedy suggests is never so simple. The break, if indeed it is possible, will never be clean. Indeed, as the plot unravels, we see that civilization all too frequently has its foundations in what it classifies as its opposite. Though crudely presented at times, this seems to be the heart of Mee's tragedy: disclosing civilization's more ambivalent underbelly, the side that many inhabitants of affluent and secure societies – here represented by the 50 sisters and the inhabitants of Piero's villa – rarely see and yet directly benefit from.

The parallel monologues of Thyona and her groom-to-be Constantine are particularly instructive of the issues at stake. Of the three sister protagonists, Thyona is the most virulent about their predicament. She despises the very idea of patriarchy and male bondage and renounces any social contract that would pledge her so freely to man's authority. Men are, in her eyes, biological accidents, incomplete females, half-dead lumps of flesh that will never be made whole, regardless of how many women they consummate.[12] 'Boy babies', so she believes, 'should be flushed down the toilet at birth'.[13] They are subhuman, the antithesis of what is civilized, because that is how they act. Together with her sisters, Thyona has come in search of a new civilization that is devoid of these things.

Constantine, manly and brutish as he appears, comes into the tragedy to remind these women that the civilization they seek is actually no different from the one they have escaped. There is no concrete perimeter that cordons off what is civilized from what is uncivilized. More often than not, without the one, the other cannot exist. For Constantine, as for Thyona, men are metaphors for the violent, brutish and exploited undersides of civilization. They constitute civilization's keeper which, paradoxically, requires them to know, and do, the most uncivilized things. In the process, they become inhuman. But rather than being upfront and transparent, civilization shrouds the fact that there is no natural justice or morality, no principle of equality among individuals and no unambiguous dichotomy between good and evil. As the theatre critic Rush Rehm writes of *Big Love*, '[m]ale violence reveals the truth buried under the myth of civilization that permeates the upper-class world of the tragedy. Humans are really brutes, and the proof is the fact that we need (and reward) brutishness in our ongoing fight to civilize other brutes'.[14] While this arrangement benefits certain humans, others are burdened with the mechanics of its reality. That knowledge and obligation can be excruciating: to kill with a smile, to hate and then love, to lose all control while feigning normality and then to realize that these things are no different, all immensely human, all part of what it means to be civilized. And then, when the job is done, the keepers of civilization are expected to dull their savage impulses, to forget the horrors they have seen and enacted and, above all, to conceal civilization's violent underbelly for the sake of those around them. In Constantine's words:

> [S]uddenly
> when this impulse isn't called for any longer
> a man is expected to put it away
> carry on with life
> as though he didn't have such impulses
> or to know that, if he does
> he is a despicable person.[15]

This quality is what makes him civilized. It is also what makes him uncivilized. But what he knows of 'this noxious world' he seeks to divulge to women – the symbol of civilization's benefactors – who, he believes, cannot claim ignorance or indemnity. He needs to inform her:

> about what it is that civilization really contains
> the impulse to hurt side by side with the gentleness

the use of force as well as tenderness
the presence of coercion and necessity.[16]

These things are not external to her nor are they the inverse of what she claims to be. They belong to all humanity – both men and women, the civilized and uncivilized. No one, therefore, should deny it:

[P]retending it belongs to another
rather knowing it as her own
feeling it as her own
feeling it as a part of life as intense as love
as lovely in its way as kindness
because to know this pain
is to know the whole of life
before we die
and not just some pretty piece of it
to know who we are
both of us together.[17]

By speaking about this aspect of civilization, Constantine complicates the foundations of Mee's fictional society and intimates at what rests beyond the simple dichotomies espoused by Thyona. The civilization we create, as he claims, depends upon violence and death. It is unjust. Its glossy surfaces and rational discourses, its laws and systems of knowledge, feed themselves on the destruction and exploitation of others. They are its foundations. Consequently, if it is the role of men to martyr their bodies for the sake of civilization, as it is in Constantine's logic, then it is the place of women to submit themselves and to have their bodies exploited by men. Their consent is their continued acquiescence to the benefits provided for them through civilization. This is the insidious social contract that binds their world together.

The crudities of Constantine's gendering and generalizations aside, of which there are many, his point is a tragic one. It is tragic because, through his clash with Thyona, we see how sworn adversaries who claim to have nothing in common with each other are not so different, both merely pawns of something greater than themselves, the chief of which is the civilization they sustain and are sustained by: violent, vengeful and, perhaps, ultimately meaningless. Instead of the gods and fate, it is the structure of civilization that denies modern humans their agency. This 'noxious' world demands that some individuals forfeit their sense of decency, control and hope. But having done so, it then ridicules and alienates them when they act violently, lose control or sink into the depths of despair. Women, the patrons of something they never agreed to, somewhere along the line became the default stimulants and recompense for sustaining this frightening cycle. Even if they think they can refuse to take part, to shun their life of privilege, the realities of doing so are often more complicated. Ultimately, in Constantine's eyes, women are simultaneously civilization's beneficiary and its recompense. Men, who rightly or wrongly have sacrificed so much, are deserving of their dues. This is why he demands his bride, a bride who would rather kill him – and herself – than be with him. This is the insidiously violent nature of their civilization.

Characters

Given what Mee is trying to do through his plot, the let-down is the cast of characters he has chosen to populate his tragedy with, who at first glance do not seem 'multidimensional, sublime, profoundly complex, whole', something which Mary Ebbott believes tragic characters should be. The characters of *Big Love* are not striking for their foreignness. Though the sisters claim otherwise, they are not really individuals marginalized in any genuine sense. They carry none of the stigma – women, barbarian – attached to the suppliants in Aeschylus' original. Despite this, Mee's characters are exemplary in one important sense: they each are the embodiment of a unique opinion or viewpoint that, through their interaction, constitutes an entire world view. The result is indeed the creation of particular 'zones of interaction' where these characters can sound off against each other.

Of the 11 characters within this tragedy, the most prominent are the three representative sisters (Lydia, Olympia and Thyona) and brothers (Constantine, Oed and Nikos) around whom the tragedy's crisis is located. Besides them, there is Piero, the head of the house which the sisters have come to, Bella, his mother, and Giuliano, his nephew. There are also Piero's two house guests, Eleanor and Leo. Significantly though, unlike Aeschylus' original, *Big Love* has no chorus, but it does include anywhere from 6 to 47 additional brides and grooms – to make up the 50 – during the wedding and murder scenes near the tragedy's end.[18] Also absent is Danaus, the father of the brides in *Suppliants*.

Despite this, what stands out about Mee's characters is that they are each made to be representative of a particular ideological perspective. Each embodies a distinct position. Through them, Mee scrutinizes the key values, the different wills and the varying circumstances that have triggered the crisis at hand. Specifically, each issue that is confronted by these characters is scrutinized through synecdochical trios, leading to a contrast of hues which eschews simple black or white perceptions.[19]

Here, we can look at the three sisters' heated dialogue, late in the tragedy, when they put Lydia on trial for her failure to kill her husband like they have done as an example.[20] This dialogical encounter between the three sisters captures well the differences in perspectives.

In the first instance, Lydia offers her reasons for not killing her husband:

> I have to somehow go on my gut instincts
> because sometimes
> you can convince yourself in your mind
> about the rightness of a thing
> and you try to find fault with your reasoning
> but you can't
> because no matter how you turn it over in your mind
> it comes out right.[21]

In these words, Lydia reveals the disjuncture between emotion and logic. The logic spun by the sisters, following from their rationale for leaving Greece and their search for asylum, has consumed their every action since the tragedy began. They have sacrificed too much for their murderous decision to not make sense. Thinking in the terms they have delineated for themselves, there is no fault in their reasoning irrespective of how Lydia turns it over in her mind. And yet, her 'gut instincts' tell her differently. For all the sense that killing Nikos makes, it feels completely wrong. And because of that, she could not go through with it.

Thyona feels differently, which is to say, she deduces logically that

> [f]irst comes justice,
> and if there is no justice
> then those who are being taken advantage of
> have every right to take their oppressors
>
> . . .
>
> to hurl their corpses into wells
>
> . . .
>
> Because there are times
> when this is justified

there are times, though you may not like it,
when this is all that human beings may rightly do and to shrink from it
is to be less than human.[22]

She is blithely unaware, but the reasons she offers here are the very same ones which Constantine attempted to make her aware of: that civilization is founded precisely upon this kind of violence. His death at her hands is testament to this fact. Indeed, the new civilization which she and her sisters erect has been purchased with the spilt blood of Constantine and his brothers. Tragically, having failed to realize how similar she and Constantine are, Thyona has slaughtered the only person that could, in time, have truly come to understand her.

Seeing the problematic foundations of their decision exposed, Olympia finally understands how she never fully understood the decision which she helped reach. In fact, as she says,

I was just following orders in a way
I should kill myself probably
now that I see the kind of persona I am.[23]

She now sees the dangers of blindly following instructions. With bloodstained hands, she realizes she is no longer able to cope. But that Olympia was able to reach this conclusion at all was because she finally saw in her sisters something of herself or, more precisely, of what she is not.

As individuals, Mee's characters may, therefore, not be 'multidimensional, sublime, profoundly complex, whole'. Yet, as a collective, the varying perspectives, rationales and emotional responses they offer, or embody, demonstrate that to truly grasp the multivocality of existence, one must explore the 'Self *through* the Other'. It is through others that we, in turn, become more multidimensional, sublime, complex and whole.

Language

This is a point that is echoed through the language used in *Big Love*. There are many voices, some rational while others less so, that come together to convey a diversity of perspectives. Mee, as Daniel Mendelsohn notes, 'thought hard about not only what this tragedy meant, but *how* it meant – about the figurative forms and allusive structures that might allow tragedy, after twenty-five centuries after the demise of Athens, to keep signifying'.[24]

Worth noting in the first instance is the fact that all the characters speak. Some speak through reasoned debate and argument; some through anecdotes, while others use physical movement, from the faintest gesture to full body gesticulations and others still speak the loudest through their failure to speak up for themselves. This is arguably *Big Love*'s most daring feat: the bold and experimental ways it enables expression.

Particularly crucial here is the tragedy's radical synthesis of text, physical movement and music. Each of these mediums, as was the case with tragic dramas in ancient Greece, is equally important to the tragedy's language, its overall message and affect.

The most compelling demonstration of the tragedy's merging mediums takes place in two parallel scenes – two of its most notable – where the sisters and brothers literally throw themselves with violent loathing to the stage floor. 'I don't need a man! | I don't need a man!' Thyona grunts, as she throws herself to the floor over and over again.[25] Only seconds before Piero, who had previously vowed to defend the sisters, requested the brothers join him to 'have a smoke, | get things sorted out'.[26] Outraged, Thyona bellows her fury to no one in particular. Yet, this is not enough. Her ire cannot be fully contained or expressed, and so, in Mee's production notes for the tragedy,

> she is throwing herself to the ground over and over,
> letting her loose limbs hit the ground with the rattle of a skeleton's bones,
> her head lolling over and hitting the ground with a thwack,
> rolling over, bones banging the ground,
> back to her feet,
> and throwing herself to the ground again in the same way over and over.[27]

Over this, music begins to play. Bach's *Sleepers Awake* from Cantata No. 140 is Mee's suggestion.[28] A largely sombre piece with eschatological connotations, it engenders a stark contrast, which if anything, only amplifies the wrath of Thyona and, soon, of all three sisters who follow her lead. Their invective – protracted, dynamic and cutting – is meant to be barely comprehensible at times, despite the ferocity with which it is delivered. Their frenzied physical movements sit uneasily against Bach's composition. Along with serene beauty, there is physical brutality and madness. The contrast speaks of uneasiness: the sisters' inability to reconcile their hearts' content with the world around them. Despite the case they have made against the brutalities of the brothers, Piero seems adamant that conciliation is possible. Layer upon layer, the language builds and undercuts itself until, together, the sisters all yell against the grain of the music and collapse into one pile, exhausted and overwhelmed. They have spoken with their words and, when this was not enough, with their screams and their bodies.

Marc-Antoine Charpentier's Prelude to *Te Deum*, at full volume, frames the brothers' outbreak. Like the sisters, these men hurl themselves, but with even greater physical force, to the ground. Oed tears off his shirt. Fiercer than the women, these men scream at each other, over each other, repeating each others' words, until a chaotic rhythm and synchronization emerges. Nothing is supposed to be heard with clarity – though a reading of the text delineates what it is they are saying:

> Then everybody told me
> you're just a jerk
> this macho stuff
> big man
> bullshit
> and then I thought my instincts are off
> my instincts are all off.
> . . .
> I said to my dad
> I don't want to do this
> this isn't me
> I felt so ashamed.[29]

The brothers begin to question the wisdom of what they have been told, of what is supposedly required of them. Is it really necessary that men bear the burdens of civilization? Do women really need their protection? Does civilization really hinge on violence? If the answer is yes, then why are they so hated by the very individuals they have supposedly given so much to protect? And why are they overshadowed by such a sense of shame? Unable to find adequate answers, or to fully express themselves, the brothers find release in this chaotic and senseless manner.

The brothers' and sisters' inability to express themselves is a central theme which Mee returns to. Using Lydia, he states:

> [B]ut really there are some things
> when you want to know the truth of them
> you have to use not just your mind or even your mind and your feelings
> but your neurons or your cells or whatever

to make some decisions
because they are too complicated
they need to be considered in some larger way
and in the largest way of all
I know I have to go with my whole being.[30]

What Mee says through Lydia here, he echoes elsewhere. Life, as the Greeks appreciated, is complex. Reductionist explanations and rigid forms of expression are insufficient. For this reason, 'Greek theatrical events were a combination of music, movement, and text'.[31] Life is not easily expressed or captured through rational discourse alone. In fact, sometimes it is precisely the excess of rationalism that precipitates an outbreak of non-rational impulses. Rationalism does not eliminate violence but rather triggers it. Both the sisters and brothers are testament to that. This outbreak, as Mee's language suggests, is not neat; sometimes it is prone to excess, unruliness and kitsch. Still, when one represses oneself for prolonged periods, this may be the only release that can depress the situation. Multivocal language gives in to this release.

The multivocal form of Mee's *Big Love*: A dramatic representation of civilization and violence

In this way *Big Love*, like Aeschylus' original, provides a meditation on the precarious balance between the need for order in our lives and how quickly that order can be undermined. But more than that, it is also a tragedy which, despite seeming apolitical and dreamlike, conveys a message that is very much inured in political reality. The way *Big Love* does this is by asking us to question the almost natural schism that separates civilization from violence. 'At the crossroads of theater and history', as Kara Reilly argues,

> the postmodern Mee is like high modernist Walter Benjamin because he possesses the understanding that "without exception the cultural treasures he surveys have an origin, which he cannot contemplate without horror. There is no document of civilization that is not the same time a document of barbarism".[32]

Mee's tragedy exposes this historical violence that at once marks and is shrouded by our civilizational constructs. There is barbarism where we least expect it. More than that, it is this violence that enables the cogs of civilization to turn. Secure and complacent at the centre of civilization's promise, we remain ignorant.

Order/Disorder

Indeed, it is *Big Love*'s dramatization of obscured realities that gives it the ability to bring a variety of otherwise marginalized stories, characters and voices onto the public stage and into democratic debate. From a tragedy that begins with a dispute about sex and gender, race and political asylum, *Big Love* quickly hints at deeper claims. These claims, in short, are about the nature of human existence and the civilization we have created that has gradually enabled us to become more and more civilized. Out of chaotic nothingness, or human existence in its barest form, order was erected. This order has made possible creative and cultural pursuits as well as more complex systems of political governance and theories of knowledge. Gradually though, this ordered life broke away from its founding disorder and, in its wake, civilization and the civilized became categorically dissociated from their antitheses.

Constantine comes into the tragedy to remind us that this is not always so. Today, the nexus between civilization and violence remains, even though it is hidden from view. All civilizations are founded upon a generating violence – against indigenous populations, the environment, even against one's own people. Wars continue to be fought and blood spilt in the name of civilization, humanity and democracy. Even the creation of knowledge and the pursuit of self-awareness, a cornerstone of all civilized peoples, are not immune. Think here of the playwright Timberlake Wertenbaker's comments when she said:

> It was one of the frightening conclusions of the twentieth century, after the horrors of the Second World War, Chile, and the hot sores of the Balkan wars and Afghanistan, that we do not seem to progress morally as human beings: we know more, but we seem to understand less and less about ourselves.[33]

There is something that civilization, and our obsession with it, has neglected to emphasize. The order we erect, and have benefited from, comes at a cost that is not always visible or easy to bear. More than this, what we understand as order remains insidiously rooted in something more sinister. This is Constantine's point exactly. Through him, Mee begins to reveal what lies beneath the civilizational order the sisters live in. When we forget these things, we fail to appreciate just how precarious our situation is, how the civilization we erect is an insidious assemblage that depends upon individuals, institutions and practices we may find repulsive, vicious or violent.

It was, according to Hall, a crucial characteristic of tragedy to question the distinction between civilization and barbarism in ancient Athens. As she reiterates, '[t]he democratization of the political system at Athens was made possible only by expanding the slave sector, and almost all Athenian slaves were barbarians'.[34] Democracy, in other words, was sustained by inequality, bondage and violence. The schism between civilization and violence was a key component to democratic order, and tragedy was key in problematizing that often unquestioned relationship. And even if democracy may no longer speak in the language of slaves and barbarians, it certainly continues to sustain a raft of rather insidious practices. One such practice is its continued dependence on democratic violence, despite its proclamations of democratic peace.

Unfortunately, the links between civilization and violence have been all but forgotten, at the very least eschewed, in contemporary times. Especially in the West, as Zygmunt Bauman argues, public opinion largely discredits the notion that Western civilization was founded upon 'pre-social barbarity'.[35] Instead, the modern civilizing process has enshrined the belief that civilization, by definition, represents the antithesis of violence and barbarism.[36] Keane affirms this, saying that '[t]he journey towards civilization was seen to be a slow but steady elimination of violence from human affairs'.[37] Civilization was responsible for drawing sovereign borders – so as to separate the civilized from the uncivilized.

However, for Bauman, a society of civility is rarely ever possible without violence kept in reserve.[38] Civility, he writes, is produced when everyday violence is repressed with the threat of state-sanctioned violence. When this occurs, ordinary people 'potentially become the playthings of sinister managers of coercion, whose own barbarism is a form of question for civilization'. In this regard, the creation of the sovereign state is a prime example of how state-building is intrinsically founded upon generative violence.[39] As Michael Shapiro writes in *Violent Cartographies*, the founding of America, the birthplace of modern democracy, is inextricably fused with the systematic and brutal extinction of indigenous populations. Here, he lays claim to the fact that the idyllic haunts of his childhood summers in New England were 'a place of violence and erasure'.[40] But the horrors of America's foundation, the price of its peace, prosperity and natural beauty, have long since been buried and erased from the nation's collective memory.[41] 'Soil' and 'minerals', not dispossession and murder, are 'the stuff from which modern "prosperity" was produced'.[42] Holocausts, this one and the one which followed suit during the World War II, are not aberrations of civilization. They are intrinsic to it.[43] Even more than that, holocausts are more often than not the result of excessive rationalism, not unfettered irrationalism.[44] Rational violence constitutes a way forward, a means of producing a stable 'political and social order'.[45]

Today, the eruption of violence continues to go hand in hand with the spread of progress.[46] Though it scarcely seems possible, the world of concentration camps, economic exploitation and violent conflicts is not incongruous with economic prosperity, high culture, improved living standards and political stability.[47] Even in the new Europe, as Chan reminds us, the 'sense of its painfully achieved civilization' will forever be associated with 'the European periphery slaughtering itself in what had been Yugoslavia'.[48] That is why, for Chan, 'almost every contemporary savagery is accomplished with the technology of civilization'.[49]

For those like Constantine and his brothers – who are thrust into the confluence of civilization and violence – all this may seem obvious. But it is not. That is what their presence reminds the sisters of. Due in equal parts to the forgetfulness that violence can induce and civilization's tendency to repress alternate histories, we need reminding of this.[50] *Big Love* uncovers the differing notions of civilization and violence and demonstrates that, ultimately, those who claim to have no involvement in violence inevitably do. This, Mee demonstrates particularly well in two consecutive scenes: first, the murder of the brothers and, second, the trial of Lydia.

Having reached the conclusion that there are no alternatives left, Thyona proposes to her sisters to 'meet force with force', to 'kill them | one by one'.[51] They will marry the brothers as planned, but then they will murder each one on the wedding night. Presumably, the murder scene in Aeschylus would have been equally horrific, if not as absurd as Mee's rendition. In Mee's production notes, he has the brides and grooms enter the stage in a 'stately fashion', each in their wedding dresses and tuxedoes. In the backdrop to the wedding procession, Wagner's 'Wedding March' from Lohengrin plays. But as soon as the procession begins, chaos descends. It all begins when the brides and grooms smear their wedding cake into each others' mouths and onto their faces, over their tuxedoes and dresses. As Constantine and Thyona wrestle each other to the ground, the music shifts to Handel's 'Arrival of the Queen of Sheba' and then again to the Dionysian Widor's 'Toccata' from Organ Symphony No. 5. The mood now is ecstatic as the stage is overtaken by women and men dancing, playing and fighting. Brides burn themselves with cigarettes, women and men begin to play with fire, while others hurl plates and knives across the stage. There are sisters and brothers eating cake only to regurgitate what they have consumed. Brides tie their grooms onto boards and lash at them. All control is surrendered in this scene.

Then, with no warning, Thyona takes to Constantine with a kitchen knife. She stabs and kills him. Her sisters follow suit. Blood stains the women's dresses and covers their hands. There is a sense that the murder is only the climax, not the antithesis, of this orgiastic release. It may appear crazed, the antithesis of everything that the audience has witnessed up to now. But it is not. Only when the action begins to subside does the silhouette of Lydia and Nikos making love become visible.

The madness of this scene is starkly contrasted with the following scene. Led by Thyona, the sisters turn their rage towards Lydia; the blood of the murdered still fresh on their hands. They demand to know why Lydia reneged on her promise, why she betrayed them. Thyona quickly reminds Lydia that she would be put on trial in any 'civilized society', which through Piero's intercession is what they agree to do.[52] Here again, the division between civilized and uncivilized is erected. However, the trial ends promptly with a reconciliation that is enforced by Bella:

You did a dreadful thing, you women, when you killed these men.
What could be worse than to take another's life?

. . .

[But] For the sake of healing
for life to go on
there will be no justice.[53]

Bella commands the women to forget this episode and the violence they have committed for the sake of healing. She advocates the return to normality.

For all the silliness and incongruity of these scenes, Mee manages to do something quite subtle. With these two scenes, Mee offers a metaphor for what Constantine pointed to earlier in the tragedy. Civilization requires that we forget or eschew what creates and underpins it. Its existence rests on the continual denial of otherwise unpleasant realities. By asking the sisters to forget and forgive, instead of making them confront their violence, Bella does not understand that she is endorsing what these women have done, what the men would have done to them had they not been murdered first. Yet, that is to be forgotten. And the madness of the preceding scene soon gives way to reconciliation and the resumption of everyday life. It is worth stressing, as Mendelsohn does, that beneath the 'familial, social, and civic order' which Bella enforces, there lies generative, if repressed, violence.[54] Though we do not see it, one suspects that the sisters' future with Bella may not be so different from their past.

By juxtaposing the disorder of the wedding and murder scene with the ordered restraint of the trial scene, Mee makes audiences acutely aware of contrast, complexity and paradox in situations where the opposite seems true. By setting the sisters and brothers against each other, *Big Love* enacts the agonistic nature of existence. First comes violence, then comes civilization.

In doing so, the multivocal form of *Big Love* brings to bear a frequently forgotten truth about Western civilization: that it at once breeds, depends upon and then veils violence.[55] In the stories, characters and voices that *Big Love* brings to stage, this is the otherwise marginalized message that it reiterates.

Reality/Fiction

Conveyed in its highly unconventional form, this is a point that would not have been lost on the ancient Greeks. By reading *Big Love*, as we would a Bauman, Keane, Shapiro or any other authority on civilization's violence, we can come to understand how all political orders rest on violence. But by reading *Big Love*, we would come to understand it from a dramatic perspective that neither Bauman, Keane nor Shapiro's work can provide. Although outwardly frivolous and abstract at times, if *Big Love* was read democratically – as this chapter has begun to do through a reading of the tragedy's multivocal form – it becomes possible to see this story as an alternate source of democratic insight that can impart very real lessons for how we engage with each other in reality.

But at most, Mee's tragedy allows us to ponder questions of democratic peace and democratic violence only indirectly. As a tragedy, the concept of democracy is never explicitly raised. Yet, its message – to get at what is otherwise shrouded by our civilizational norms and constructs, to expose its vicious, destructive and nihilistic tendencies – is a uniquely democratic one. The need to disclose hidden truths about our own way of life, even when what is unearthed may be unsavoury and capable of implicating us in acts we might never personally condone, speaks of the democratic need to balance order with disorder. As *Big Love* does this, it begins to touch upon very real issues that are taking place in the real world.

As a somewhat unconventional dramatist, Mee's references to real places and events – most prominently the Kosovo conflict of 1998–1999, the 1994 Rwandan genocide and the Nigerian-Biafran War of 1967–1970 – demonstrate that his is no ordinary sense of reality. Being a former historian by trade, Reilly notes that his works are ultimately based on 'stuff that [is] stolen from the world'.[56] What he brings to stage is the 'cultural debris that surrounded him in his work as a historian'. But as a collage artist, whose patchwork plays evoke both what is 'historical and mythological', he incites what Patsalidis calls 'a multiplicity of vision' whereby what is familiar appears strangely new and bizarre, if not out of place.[57] For this reason, his tragedies do not seem real nor do they authentically represent the historical events he draws inspiration from.

Instead, his fictions draw freely upon what prevails in reality, but he does so in order to create new visions of reality. The regrettable fact of doing this is that it has the potential to make those of us who are not so used to seeing reality as fluid and changeable, question whether or not he is actually making light of the issues and events that he invokes. As such, though his dramatizations might come across as if he is being dismissive of the severity of such matters as warfare, genocide, refugee crises, ethnic division and gendered violence, what he does is frequently the opposite. By appearing to joke about serious matters, he is actually making the point that we as a society do not take these issues and events seriously enough. In *Big Love*, for instance, he admonishes that when refugees come in search of asylum, the collective thoughts of our societies are too often consumed, almost by default, by apprehension, defensiveness and dissociation. This makes us little different from Piero, who fears that if he were to grant the sisters refuge in this instance, 'the next thing I know I would have a refugee camp here in my home. | I'd have a house full of Kosovars and Ibo and Tootsies'.[58]

Mee gets that message across by drawing certain scenarios from reality, scenarios we are all familiar with, such as refugee crises, threats of gendered violence and portraits of the good life. Yet, with these real issues and events, which in reality often seem unrelated, his dramatic representations undertake to invert and then distort the reality in which they take place. After all, scenarios where refugees have fled their homes because of the violence threatened to them are all too real in our world. What is less real is a story that has 50 sisters fleeing to a foreigner's villa in Italy, claiming that had they stayed in Greece, they would have been forced to marry their 50 cousins.

Big Love, as such, is real and serious to the extent that it is a metaphor for otherwise very real and serious concerns. This is how Mee uses this tragedy to address and resolve fundamental problems which take place in reality all the time, but which, for reasons of political correctness or bureaucratic ineptitude, cannot be questioned or debated publicly. His play takes place in an alternate universe, which is modelled on our own, to dramatize questions that are very real. Freed from the constraints of our own world, he then goes on to lay bare the contradictions and duplicities which seem somehow natural within own our world but that, when relocated to the fictional realm, appear illogical and hypocritical.

Specifically, beneath the overt folly, hilarity and gratuitousness that *Big Love* brings to the stage, what we are given a sense of is that the civilization we have created – refined, just and progressive as it seems on the surface – depends for its sustenance on repressed violence. This is a claim that could not be any less real or any less serious. Every civilization, *Big Love* shows, is sustained not just by what is esteemed but also by what it proclaims as its opposite: for example, violence, greed, barbarism, inequality, hatred and exploitation. Understanding this, for Constantine, is to understand why those who benefit from civilization's fruits might ultimately be called into account by those who sacrifice their lives to sustain civilization as a whole. It requires that we try to understand, confront and embrace what, until now, we have found too difficult to do. We must understand, to use an analogy that Nietzsche was particularly fond of, the connection between the rose, which is beautiful, and its roots, which can often be repulsive. Still, '[i]t might even be possible', as Nietzsche wrote, 'that what constitutes the value of those good and honoured things resides precisely in their being artfully related, knotted and crocheted to these wicked, apparently antithetical things'.[59] And though he was referring more to how emotions like hate, revenge and anger may ultimately produce feelings of love, gratitude and good nature, the metaphor applies equally well to Constantine's point.

Subject to this kind of scrutiny, we may similarly realize that the supposedly democratic zones of peace in which we live are actually premised on their being democratic zones of violence. Despite the associations of democracy with peace, progress and consensus, we continue to see wars fought under democracy's banner, wars fought – and lost – in the promotion of democratic values and democratic rights revoked, sometimes to brutal effect, so that democracy might ultimately be preserved. In recent years, neoconservative democratization has been particularly guilty of all these charges.[60] In bringing democracy, liberty and justice to places like Afghanistan and Iraq, great violence and destruction have resulted. Rarely a day passes now in the world's two newest democracies when threats of violence, mass murder and civil unrest do not disrupt these societies. Given this, creating a new civilization – or expanding the perimeters of our own democratic civilization – amid decay requires a daily military presence and is met with an equally deadly response. From the prisoner abuses at Abu Ghraib to the advent of daily suicide bombings, the new global democracy is now being erected on bloodied ground. To the extent that it is broadcast and debated in the news media, violence is always portrayed as an aberration – a regrettable but temporary by-product – of democratization. Rarely do commentators acknowledge the debts that democracy owes to violence.

As the logic of *Big Love* helps to make clear, this is an inescapable aspect of politics. Democracy, if we think seriously about it, is no exception. Today, as scholars like Michael Dillon and Julian Reid remind us, global liberal democracy retains a martial face.[61] Modern constructs of democratic politics that we celebrate and promote, such as republicanism, liberalism and market capitalism, are all committed to a project of procuring peace through violence. Democratic peace is sustained by democratic forms of violence and, as a consequence, continues to justify the use of force as a legitimate democratic possibility.[62] 'The zone of peace', writes Reid, 'is infused with the logics of war'.[63] Violence, therefore, is a means to a democratic end which, as Daniel Ross contends, adds 'to the increasingly violent essence of those worlds that proclaim themselves, violently, democratic'.[64] This is *Big Love*'s end message: violence is at the core of all you see and all you do not.

And so, when Mee suspends reality, what he is doing is to make us rethink the connections between order and disorder, something he enacts by problematizing the schism between civilization and violence. Though all of this occurs within the topsy-turvy world that Mee has constructed, one in which our reality has been suspended but only just, none of the broader themes and issues which are thrown up as a result, are alien or artificial to us in the twenty-first century. That is why his tragedy can make us uncomfortable: because beneath its excess, we are given a glimpse of something that would usually be shrouded by our civilizational assemblage. Mee's tragedy forces us to ask the question: how does my way of life exacerbate and make necessary the themes and crises which the sisters and brothers speak of in the tragedy? Can I really claim to be ignorant and independent of them?

For Mendelsohn, these sorts of questions are fundamentally similar to those which tragedy would have posed to its audience during its heyday in ancient Athens. Mee's tragedy, as Mendelsohn notes, possesses all the intellectual and theatrical veracity of an ancient Greek tragedy – wrestling with pertinent political and moral questions in the way which Aeschylus would have done in his day.[65] By entwining the personal with the political, the real with what barely resembles reality, *Big Love* is a tragedy that leaves us 'arguing . . . about women and men and violence and sex and power'.[66] For Mendelsohn, then, what Mee has produced is a tragedy for today that preserves all the fundamental social and political tensions that the tragedies in Athens did – 'in a way that allows the work, after so many centuries, not merely to work but to be heard'.[67] 'Don't think for a moment', writes Marshall, 'that it doesn't apply to you'.[68]

6

Towards a Multivocal Democracy

The question that we are faced with now is how to translate these insights, specific and archaic as they have been at times, into something of an ethos capable of producing a more vibrant, open-ended and multivocal democracy? In spite of all that has been said in the preceding pages, we would nonetheless be mistaken if we thought that the link between democracy and tragedy was anything other than fraught. After all, it is not so much tragedy as notions like representation, equality, freedom and rationality that have most frequently been associated with democracy today. So, what can we really learn from viewing democracy through a tragic lens?

For one, we might, like the Greeks who lived through democracy's adolescent years, find ourselves more likely to see the injustices, hypocrisies and exclusions that democracy is supposed to uncover and overcome but which it is not always capable of doing in reality. Democracy in our eyes would become a commodity, valuable for its ability to make apparent the interplay between order and disorder and reality and fiction. So invigorated, we would become dissatisfied with delimiting our democratic endeavours solely to national congresses, parliaments or conventional venues of popular participation. Though vital, we will begin to understand that to extend democracy, we necessarily must search out disorder and fiction, neither of which are typically found within official institutions and practices of democratic politics. Accordingly, what we would become increasingly aware of were we to view democracy through a tragic lens is that formal institutions of democracy are not always enough, that instead of unearthing what we do not know and giving voice to those who are all too often ignored, it can actually suppress difference and work to revoke democratic rights in the promotion of entrenched democratic values. Our objective, even before we think about taking the next step of establishing any new body, convention or concert of democracy, is to recalibrate how we are to balance order with disorder and reality with fiction in politics.

This is where the Greek's experiment can still be of use. When statesmen, citizens and the institutions of popular rule they had molded to provide unequalled access to the ruling of their ancient city stalled, as often became the case in a city-state mired down by international warfare and domestic turmoil, it was the dramas performed in the theatre of Dionysus that offered political insights of unusual clarity. Faced with geopolitical instability, personal greed and political overconfidence, the tragedies of Aeschylus, Sophocles and Euripides taught audiences the lesson that life is ephemeral, filled with unknowns, which can trigger in them the need for certainty and immortality – pursuits quite capable of producing arrogance, conflict and downfall. These were lessons in the lures of hubris and the dangers of nemesis, all of which sit at the heart of any democracy. Unlike today, theatre was public and political, seen by the people as political education. Performances in the theatre created a polis that, as Hannah Arendt once said, 'properly speaking, is not the city-state in its physical location; it is the organization of the people as it arises out of acting and speaking together'.[1]

Elevated by democracy, tragedy checked the political excesses unleashed after the democratic revolution. From what we now know, the birth of democracy occurred at a time when repression, inequality and injustice dominated political affairs. The aristocratic order which had existed and that, at the expense of the many, had served the few so well, roused widespread discontent and anger. Eventually, it became too much to bear. Discontent and anger boiled over, rupturing the traditions of the once unquestionable hierarchy as it did. It is not difficult to see why tragedy rapidly came to prominence within this tumultuous environment. The space that was once sure, now became a vacuum, begging to be filled with new dreams and expectations as well as more inclusive norms and structures.

Tragedy became a vital theoretical backbone of democracy. It debunked the absolute certainty and life force that had sustained the aristocratic world, without debunking the certainty and life force needed to sustain the Greek world as a whole. It gave back to democracy, when democracy faltered, what it had first given Athens: the fleeting realization that no single voice or way of life was absolute and wholly true; that even the greatest among them was not all great. By doing so, tragedy proved itself to be an intrinsically democratic art form.

Tragedy's ability to do this was due in large part to its multivocal form. By bringing a variety of otherwise marginalized stories, characters and voices onto the public stage and into democratic debate, the multivocal form represented tragedy's most direct intervention into democratic politics. It was an explicit reminder to the masses who attended these performances that democratic rights and freedoms had severe limits. It acknowledged that, when faced with unknowns and life's transience, it can be all too easy to seek reassurance by reaffirming what one knows and erecting structures that immortalize one's own way of life. In short, what tragedy's multivocal form did was to impart the lesson that democracy was not perfect, especially when it sought to conceal its own limits by pursuing its own self-perfection. When it did this, tragedy could speak paradoxically more candidly about democracy than could be done in reality.

How tragedy did this, as this book has shown, was through its capacity to draw out the core democratic interplay between order and disorder and reality and fiction. By dramatizing the underbelly of existence, the multivocal form reminded audiences that disorder exists at the heart of all orders, as unpleasant a realization as that is. Through staging a diversity of plots, characters and languages, order was, in effect, made perpetually susceptible to the threat of disorder. But that, at its core, was precisely what democracy had been created to encourage in the realm of politics: to self-institute and then self-limit. Having toppled the order of aristocracy in Athens, democracy was conceived to defy every closed system of thought. Tragedy extended this when democrats, impeded by the triviality of politicking and the threats to existence they faced both within and beyond their city walls, applied the political brakes in reality. It showed to the polis that, at sites and times of disorder, new perspectives, foreign peoples and anathema beliefs can encroach into the ordered existence of Athenian life, and that this could be both necessary and potentially enriching.

In such a world, where nothing was known with any degree of certainty, how one should understand and deal with political reality was a task that opened itself up to logical deduction, rational dialectic as well as unbound creativity. For this reason, the Greeks did not restrict themselves to the use of only factual accounts to understand reality. On the contrary, fictive sources were often considered as legitimate and expedient as their non-fictional counterparts in the conduct of politics. It was normal – even prudent – to draw from political, philosophical and aesthetic sources in an attempt to resolve democratic dilemmas. Self-institution, being an act of creation, demanded that the Athenians boldly imagine a new future distinct from their aristocratic past. It required them to think, imaginatively, about what was possible in reality as well as about what reality was itself. The multivocal form, in this respect, was one particularly crucial if unconventional source that helped to enrich democratic politics. Tragic art dramatized the paradoxes of politics and existence – through its resort to fictional plots, characters and language. By drawing on fiction to reinterpret and better understand reality, the Athenians were able to learn from and discuss experiences that had been silenced or vilified in reality.

Through the multivocal form of tragedy, audiences therefore became privy to the realization that life under democracy would be a tragic one and that whatever greatness they, as a civilization, had laid claim to would never be dissociated from the horrors of slavery, warfare, colonization and exploitation that, together, comprised the democratic way of life.

A multivocal democracy today

Given the importance of tragedy to the development of the West's first great democracy, this book has laboured under the assumption that it constitutes a rich, if untapped, source of democratic insight today. Perhaps, like the ancient Greeks, tragedy might be capable of aiding contemporary efforts to extend the institutions and procedures of democracy – especially from a rigidly defined national realm into a more post-national configuration befitting of today's global flows of people, ideas and capital. Might tragedy's multivocal form possess something capable of inspiring contemporary democrats to revive the interplay between order and disorder and reality and fiction as a premise for our own democratic initiatives?

It is true that we probably will not, as a result of this study, be directly equipped to begin to articulate concrete institutions and procedures amiable to a more democratic world. Nor would we, by returning to ancient Greek politics and theatre, be able to see immediate if any overlaps between our own democratic ways and a democratic way of life that has since elapsed into the annals of history. But before we can begin to redress these questions and undertake such tasks, problematic due to their novelty and scale, we might find it necessary to first remind ourselves of what essentially it is about democracy that we would wish to see made available on a global scale and what a world crying out to be heard really wants out of a democracy. It has been to this end that the forgotten link between democracy and tragedy has been revived: so as to place us in a better position to think through some of the more trenchant and vexing global challenges confronting contemporary democracy – in critical, unorthodox and imaginative ways.

With this in mind, this book established a novel analytical framework, based around an unconventional reading of tragedy's multivocal form, to guide its analysis of the democratic insights of two tragedies: the first being Aeschylus' *Suppliants* and the second Charles L. Mee's contemporary adaptation *Big Love*. It argued in each instance that learning to read these dramatic plays as possible democratic texts is to re-read 'historical', 'artistic' and 'fictional' artifacts as key political texts – which is precisely what the ancient Greeks would have done with their own tragedies. The benefits of such an undertaking would not merely enrich our cultural horizons, though it inevitably would, but it would allow us the opportunity to reinvigorate democracy and debates germane to the prospect of a post-national democracy in two key ways.

Democracy is predicated on both the presence of order and disorder

In the first instance, as this book has stressed, one of the foremost effects of tragedy's multivocal form is the capacity it has to leave its audiences with a more nuanced appreciation of how their sense of order – namely, the life, knowledge and civilization they have erected – could never be detached from the forces of disorder. To think of these two conditions as opposites, somehow unrelated, is to misconstrue the nature of existence. The democratic urge arose in Athens, in part, as a recognition of the tensions that existed between order and disorder in Greek life. Tragedy dramatized this, personally, for each individual audience member. Yet, the realization that the life we lead might somehow not be as incorruptible as we had thought is of no less significance today than when the Greek tragedians of the antique past first dramatized it. Shielded by the ever-expanding knowledge base that we have acquired through increasingly scientific means, we have curiously become less self-aware of just what our civilization has wagered for the sake of its own survival. Arriving at a more nuanced appreciation of the crucial links between order and disorder in our own political struggles should therefore continue to be a pressing political objective – one that, in turn, would work to enhance how we conceive of democracy and our capacity to engage in politics more openly.

Especially because the concept and procedures of democracy today are often considered synonymous only with the search for order, the tragic intervention may oddly be particularly timely. Order here connotes the regime of meaning which has come to be composed of notions like representation, equality, freedom and peace, which together have given form and function to the way of life known as democratic. Order, according to most mainstream democratic discourses, is the by-product of progress and rationalism in the political realm.[2] Being entwined with the project of modernity, the current agenda to democratize the global realm effectively holds that to be democratic is to value teleological development and rational discourse.[3] As Bruce Russett, one of the intellectual forefathers of democratic peace theory, states: 'if history is imagined to be the history of wars and conquest, then a democratic world might in that sense represent "the end of history"'.[4] For his part, Francis Fukuyama confers. His argument is that with the end of the Cold War, a resounding global consensus arose with regard to the prevalence and legitimacy of liberal democracy as the best system of governance.[5] Given this, he equates liberal democracy with the 'end point of mankind's ideological evolution and the final form of human government' – as such, the end of history.[6] Unlike previous ideologies and systems of governance whose intrinsic 'defects and irrationalities' caused them to self-corrupt and capitulate, liberal democracy represents the pinnacle of an 'evolutionary process [that] was neither random nor unintelligible' but 'would end when mankind had achieved a form of society that satisfied its deepest and most fundamental longings'.[7] With his prescriptions, democracy becomes interlinked with a teleological order made possible through a rational ideology and a system of governance.

As a result, it has not so much been the search for disorder rather the creation of order that has become the lynchpin of contemporary democratic configurations at every level, from the local to the global.[8] Without order, we have been told repeatedly, 'there can be no society. And without society there can be no civilized life'.[9] Democracy is no different.[10] It seeks, at the level of the community, the nation and the society of nations, to bring about norms and institutions specifically designed to encourage a certain social and political formation. The point, through democratic procedures, is to establish some sort of order that is broadly conceived by the constituents of that society to be the precondition of the good life.

This is a model that we now know would have only been considered partly democratic according to the Greeks. For them, it was the threatening presence of disorder that initially gave rise to the need for order. Disorder provided the greatest inspiration for democratic inclusion and change. In this endeavour, tragedy's multivocal form played a key democratic role by bringing a variety of otherwise marginalized stories, characters and voices onto the public stage and into democratic debate. A true democracy, tragedy reiterated, should not just be about the eradication of conflict, the solidification of rational knowledge and the creation of distinct territorial, structural and epistemic boundaries. Perhaps more important than that, it needs to become a kind of 'rhetorical vocabulary that neither masks nor apologizes for the disorderly, agonistic, unkempt, and fundamentally unstable character of democratic politics'.[11] Open to what is unknown and beyond questioning, democratic politics should aspire towards the creation of a precarious balance between that which is and that which is not in the world. Disorder, in this regard, would necessarily take its rightful place on the public stage and be incorporated into democratic debate. This was how democratic politics was conceived as an idea and a practice that has become as much about self-realization as about self-negation.[12]

Reading tragedy's multivocal form democratically, perhaps we too can begin to uncover democracy as a vital interplay between order and disorder. When contemporary democracy seems struck above all else by the promise of unfettered progress, the logic of tragedy may help to slowly peel back what has been concealed by our modern life, knowledge and civilization, and ask such questions as what lies beyond, at whose expense have we prospered and what might they have to say to us?

Problematizing the notion of order through disorder is a democratic act. Being open to the presence and demands of disorder, even as we strive to erect an overarching global order, is crucial to any truly democratic ethos. Tragedy's multivocal form has shown us that democracy should not be solely about the creation of order. Order, though vital, can frequently conceal more than it reveals. Order privileges the status quo and threatens to continually delegitimize individuals, issues and events currently struggling for recognition on the margins of society. Automatically suppressing what threatens order can mean that we might never get the chance to move beyond our present injustices and problems. It can mean that we continue to make light of stories, characters and voices marginalized in contemporary political struggles. Sites of disorder, as such, are as crucial as sites of order in politics. Seeking out the fluid connections between order and disorder is central to understanding what democracy is all about – or so the Greeks would argue.

Indeed, for all our talk of order, it is often forgotten or accepted as unproblematic that all orders exist only because they have been superimposed, sometimes violently and at other times incongruously, onto some form of pre-existing disorder – and that this is deemed to be both natural and desirable. Rarely do we question the allure of order or see disorder as an alternative form of order which, though undeniably different, might also offer some alternative form of comfort, security, stability and knowledge. All orders cover up and smooth over something that once appeared too dangerous, incomprehensible or repugnant to tolerate unadulterated.

It is this theme that, in various ways, has animated much of the preceding reading of Aeschylus' *Suppliants* and Charles L. Mee's *Big Love*. In both tragedies, we sense that the elimination of political crises and conflicts do not in themselves produce understanding and peace. Understanding and peace exist only because they were slotted abruptly into the place where crisis and conflict stood. But, where crises and conflicts are artificially averted or ignored, the disorder that has been eliminated or suppressed is likely to be shrouded and kept falsely at bay. To redress this, appropriate mechanisms for widespread political contestation and dispute must be put in place within any political order. This, as Derek Barker writes in *Tragedy and Citizenship*, is what the 'art form of tragic drama provides'.[13] Through it, he continues, students of tragedy can begin to recognize the 'paradoxical sense that the reconciliation of conflict is an indeterminate and even impossible task . . . . [which] requires both a yearning to mediate and cope with conflict and an understanding that conflict in omnipresent and ineliminable'.[14] Coming to terms with this is how we can come to terms with the democratic utility offered to us through these sites of disorder.

Similarly, by forcing us to see stories where before we may have only seen one story and a set of conflicting narratives in lieu of the official narrative, tragedy's multivocal form reminds us that in any order there is always a corresponding disorder. In this process, writes Howard Stein, what we actually learn is how 'to reflect and illuminate human life, to know ourselves a little better, to be reminded of ourselves – both our civilized and uncivilized elements – over and over and over again' – a lesson entrenched within *Big Love*.[15] When the civilized come into contact with the uncivilized, without obliterating the other, is when we can truly see and hear multiple stories, characters and voices. When our world view comes into dialogue with the world views of others, however trying, imperfect and momentary that exchange may be, we initiate the process of complicating the world or, rather, of realizing just how complex a place our world can be. There is no one world view, regardless of its perceived preponderance, that can effectively bring into relief the countless realities that exist all together and all at the same time.

The overall message that we can therefore take away from this is that where there is order there will be disorder too. Even Hedley Bull, the international relations scholar famed for delineating the existence of an international order from a realm better known for its anarchy, admitted that 'the element of disorder looms as large or larger in world politics than the element of order'.[16] We need to better recognize this at the global level and at the domestic level. Additionally, we need to learn to countenance the troubling predisposition in politics that attempts to dissociate order from disorder: to see them as separate categories if not as polar opposites. Order exists where disorder does not – and vice versa. For them to coexist is both a contradiction in terms and illogical. It is for this reason that the world is often uncritically categorized into distinct and separate zones: one of democratic peace, for instance, and the other of violent turmoil.[17]

Yet, reality is never quite as simple. Order is rarely divorced from disorder. Oftentimes, it exists because of it. At other times, what may be considered as order for some might rightly represent chaotic disorder for others. As Bleiker notes, '[j]ust as order can be the basis of terror and repression, disorder can provide the opportunity for freedom and justice'.[18] At a more primordial level, all orders are but an arbitrary set of facts, truths, institutions and norms that have been selected and then imposed against a broader, if less cohesive, array of facts, truths, institutions and norms. Without realizing this, we can neglect to take seriously those stories, characters and voices whose existence contravenes what we have identified as real and pressing. Uncovering the arbitrariness of our own order, from time to time, and identifying with those who have been delegitimated through the course of our ordering is, in essence, a democratic act which intrinsically re-evaluates power relations, scrutinizes the realities of our political ideals and practices and reinvents a broader, more inclusive society than what had previously existed. Through this process, we can come to see the potential tyranny of order and the opportunities that are available to us in disorder. Seeing order and disorder as two sides of the same coin, not as separate or distinct, is to see reality as it really is. Especially when orders become too repressive and totalizing in their claims to legitimacy, 'disorder can be both the only reality we have and a valuable source of democratic politics'.[19]

Analysing tragedy's multivocal form helps turn our attention to the existence of both order and disorder. This becomes democratic to the extent that it asks us to eradicate the dissociations we may have possessed between order and disorder, peace and turmoil, knowledge and understanding, civilization and violence, so as to reveal their connections. Geographical, political and epistemic divides misconstrue the complex political realities and unnecessarily sideline a vast number of stories, characters and voices. In this regard, zones of peace – or order – do not represent the condition that prevails in the absence of turmoil – or disorder. A real democracy is drawn from both conditions; it is the composite of both conditions.

By reading tragedies like *Suppliants*, *Big Love* and others, what we are left with is precisely a more astute awareness of the interplay between order and disorder – the upshot of which can help to institute a more vibrant and dynamic global democratic system. By seeing order and disorder as valuable sites of democratic understanding and practice, we would place ourselves in a more secure if less stable environment. While we all have a need for order – as 'orders', writes Richard Devetak, 'are always established against threats' – so too do we have a need to understand what threatens order.[20] Especially when threats change, as they inevitably do, the order that was created to hold them at bay can become ineffective and, worse still, even more arbitrary and exclusionary than when it was established. If orders do not undergo periodic self-examination – or self-limitation – they can themselves become a threat to ongoing security, peace and justice. Tragedy's multivocal form, by drawing on insights gleaned from a variety of otherwise marginalized stories, characters and voices, is a reminder of this. The multivocal form, in this sense, seeks to draw explicitly from disorder to help renegotiate the parameters of what order best accommodates life in the present. What may be antithetical to order now, may, in time, come to inspire a more just and other-inclusive order. Collectively questioning the composition of our orderly world is thus crucial. At times, this requires that we actively engage in discussion of what threatens to intrude, invert and rupture our orderly world.

But tragedy's multivocal form does not just remind us of the democratic need to search out and locate disorder. More importantly, it reminds us that order – our order, any order – is itself a form of disorder, just as disorder can be a nascent site of order. Examining disorder is to examine how others choose to live their lives and to understand the reasons why they might find the lives we lead problematic. Seeing how marginalized stories, characters and voices intervene and intertwine with those at the rational centre is to see the connections that exist at all levels. It is to come to grips with both the oneness and the plurality of our world. This is the challenge that, for Walker, has faced us for some time now: to 'see Many Worlds not as the negation of One World but as the condition for its possibility'.[21] When we see disorder not as the negation of order in our world but as the condition for its possibility is when we can ensure that any institutions and procedures of democratic politics that we establish at both the national and post-national level are more attuned to a greater number of stories, characters and voices than ever before.

Democracy understands the dichotomy between reality and fiction fluidly

Though all this sounds relatively reasonable and even desirable in theory, none of it can actually come about without a fundamental rethinking of what we deem as legitimate and illegitimate in the political arena. Too often, our retreat to the shores of order, hastened by our fear of disorder, has been the result of an unnecessarily narrow and rigid demarcation of what is politically acceptable from what is not. Thus, increasing our sensitivities to the intricate interplay between order and disorder will not be possible without an equal commitment to the destruction of another entrenched modern dichotomy: the false opposition that partitions reality from fiction.

What we glean from tragedy's multivocal form also speaks to this overdrawn distinction. By its very nature, tragedy dramatized stories, characters and voices that the tragedians had imagined and reinterpreted. They were dramatic representations that, in today's parlance, operated in the realm of fiction, as a form of popular entertainment. And yet, the Greeks regarded what they encountered in the theatre to be just as politically incisive as what had been taught by their statesmen and philosophers. Although only fictional representations, tragic dramas were, nonetheless, regarded in Athens as a legitimate form of political discourse in reality.

All this suggests that the fundamental dichotomy which we have erected in modern times between the realm of reality and the realm of fiction was a notion foreign to the ancient Greeks.[22] To them, fictional forms of representation, such as tragedy, could legitimately draw on and be drawn upon by rational understandings of reality. Fiction was just another resource that thinkers and practitioners of politics looked to for inspiration and guidance. It broadened reality, especially if what constitutes reality is rigidly ordered and beyond dispute.

Put differently, institutions such as democracy and tragedy drew their inspiration from factual and fictional sources alike. Together, the intellectual and aesthetic horizons of both institutions, and of their patrons, were broadened and put in better stead to give expression to a greater range of issues and individuals in a greater variety of ways. In Thomas Docherty's words, the key task of a democracy of this kind is 'to make culture happen, to bring about the event that reveals the extraordinary by making us step out of that which is ordinary for us'.[23] Crucial, in this regard, is fiction or the 'truth of the private realm', which gives political representation to the irrational and unrepresentable.[24]

The understanding that sometimes rational discourse is not enough to convey the world's complexity – that instead of giving expression to it, complexity can actually be suppressed and belittled – is a fundamental truth latent within the multivocal form of tragedy. Resorting to sources that to us are better known for their literary, artistic and sensory qualities, the Greeks sought to retrieve what had been suppressed by rational understandings of reality alone. Tragedy's multivocal form grasps that when the former is suppressed by the latter for too long, it will find expression in any way it can. In *Suppliants*, it is externalized through the widespread psychological despair and political violence that descended on Argos not long after the sisters landed on its shores. And in *Big Love*, it emerged through the physical release, the Dionysian outbreak that both the sisters and brothers gave in to.

As a result, when rational discourses are incapable of conveying the complexity of reality, there is a need to explore other forms of expression – to free language from the official discourse – so that others, too, can have a legitimate voice in political deliberations. As Anna Agathangelou and Ling remind us, '[s]howing the spaces where gaps exist between voices does not signal an end to understanding but a beginning to negotiations across these gaps in a location that is suspended, if only for the moment, between locations of power'.[25] A multivocal democracy must enable individuals to search out new languages and sources of knowledge as they seek to further understand and give expression to a life where crisis and conflict are the inevitable corollaries of their own disparate values, wills and circumstances.

This goes against the grain of most contemporary political discourses, which have come to view these fictional sources of knowledge with suspicion. The reason for this, as Bleiker laments, is because these discourses continue to be wedded to a Newtonian frame of mind and, as a consequence, maintain a rather myopic conception of what equates to real knowledge.[26] The effect of this has been that more artistic representations of politics have tended to be 'routinely ghettoised' within political debates.[27] Legitimate political knowledge of reality is produced through rational and social scientific methods. There continues to be a preconception that if observation of political reality utilizes rational and social scientific methods, then the information gathered will equate to facts about political reality. We can see this logic at work, for instance, in one of the foundational twentieth-century political texts on international relations: Hans Morgenthau's *Politics Among Nations: The Struggle for Power and Peace.*[28] Though a vast and sprawling book, covering topics from power, imperialism, ideology and morality to diplomacy, *Politics Among Nations* had fairly strict objectives and methodologies. The 'theory of international politics' it set out to establish was 'this-worldly',[29] to be

> judged not by some preconceived abstract principle or concept unrelated to reality, but by its purpose: to bring order and meaning to a mass of phenomena which without it would remain disconnected and unintelligible. It must meet a dual test, an empirical and a logical one: Do the facts as they actually are lend themselves to the interpretation the theory has put upon them, and do the conclusions at which the theory arrives follow with logical necessity from its premises? In short, is the theory consistent with the facts and within itself?[30]

The objective and methodology are quite clear. Reality and facts about it are of the utmost importance. Through rational and social scientific methods, order can be garnered from a mass of phenomena that would otherwise be disconnected and unintelligible. Other sources of knowledge – namely, those that emanate from fictional representations – have no legitimacy in the politics among nations. Importantly, the desire to possess these facts about political reality is no different from the desire to give political reality a definitive order. Disorder, or so the logic goes, can be kept in check if the correct methodology is applied.

There is little freedom for scholars, politicians and policymakers to appreciate the democratic benefits of utilizing factual as well as fictional accounts to engage political matters. Fiction symbolizes the lack of real knowledge. It does not, as Damon Young writes, divulge those truths which are 'hidden by superfluous facts, interpretations, myths'.[31] And it certainly does not have the potential to reveal the *arche*: 'the primal theme or tension at work in a person, a relationship or a situation'. That remains the preserve of factual analyses, that is, those carried out through rational and social scientific methods.

Important though these facts about reality are in the creation of a rational political order, they are not enough. Political analysts who are serious about democracy must also subject order to question. And one way that this can be done is by interrogating, from time to time, 'how reality is seen, framed, read, and generated in the conceptualisation and actualisation' of political reality.[32]

In her innovative textbook, *International Relations Theory: A Critical Introduction*, Cynthia Weber gives us some concrete examples of how one might do this in the conceptualization and conduct of international affairs.[33] Using popular films such as *Lord of the Flies*, *Wag the Dog* and *The Truman Show* to re-read dominant theories of world politics, Weber reveals how reality can be mediated through various mediums and modes of representation – some deemed legitimate, while others not. For her, pairing dominant international relations myths (e.g. Waltz's theory of anarchy) with popular films (such as *Lord of the Flies*) enables us to see them as stories or as 'a particular vision of the world', not as unquestionable, objective facts about reality.[34] It is only by doing so that we can understand how mediated or fictional our so-called facts about politics are; how what may erstwhile amount to fiction can, in turn, possibly be a source that can show us new realities. And, more importantly, how the facts of 'IR theory may not be located in the realm of "truth" and "reality" any more than popular films are'.[35] Consequently, where dominant facts fail to adequately explain or accommodate marginalized stories, characters and voices, Weber shows us that it is possible to turn to fictional sources and representations of politics. There, we may be able to find the answers which evade us in reality.

Another scholarly illustration of what such an endeavour might look like is Chan's recent book, *The End of Certainty*.[36] Chan's book is, as he openly acknowledges, written as if it were 'a meandering novel'.[37] Because of this, his writing – how he writes, what he writes of – betrays the discipline he proclaims to speak of. That is to say, we are familiar with many of the stories he tells about global politics. We have after all heard them many times before: stories about the 'end of history' by Francis Fukuyama; the 'clash of civilizations' by Samuel Huntington and even Robert Kagan's story 'of paradise and power'. Yet, we have never heard them quite like this. Drawing from a truly global cast of characters, Chan delves deep into the texts, myths and cultures that international relations scholars in the West have long proclaimed to understand – though often, as it turns out, have little if any understanding of. To make his point, he populates his book with other stories told by and about Jean Sibelus' *Finlandia*, Kwame Gyekye's *An Essay on African Philosophical Thought*, Jacques Lacan's *Antigone*, Ayi Kwei Armah's *The Beautyful Ones Are Not Yet Born*, Vargas Llosa's *The War of the End of the World* and Ngugi wa Thiong'o's *Petals of Blood*. It is a book that draws on fictional sources to illuminate the factual realities of the political world in a fashion that the dominant theoretical frameworks are often at a loss to do.

The chaotic unity or 'doubling' (Chan's term) that comes from fusing reality and fiction this way brings these otherwise disparate and excoriated figures, stories and philosophies to the fore.

All this can be seen as democratic because, through fiction, we expand facts about reality. As Hayward Alker writes, 'the world of fiction leads us to the essential heart of the real world of action by playing the unreal'.[38] That, in itself, is a democratic endeavour. Seeing the dichotomy between reality and fiction as inherently fluid is to see and hear stories, characters and voices marginalized through factual accounts alone.[39] It is to locate the 'cracks and fissures and dissent of difference', which is where we can find the 'micro-personal story' that belies the 'macro-structures' of our grand political narratives.[40] In short,

> [a]ccepting a fiction/reality binary among texts as unproblematic therefore allows "reality" to continue as the privileged signifier, making it harder to challenge those who claim special access to this "reality" and ignoring the meaning we derive from other sources of information.[41]

By expanding and exploring a greater range of accounts, we can interrogate political order and disorder wherever they occur: in canonical texts, institutional practices, university classrooms, as well as in fictional representations of reality.

In this enterprise, tragedy can once again become an explicit source precisely because its multivocal form brings into relief the fluid connections between reality and fiction. Reading tragedies as a democratic source reminds us that there are truths in fact as well as in fiction, and both have the potential to offer new and relevant political insights. Tragedy cultivates a democratic sensitivity that relays both official narratives and forgotten stories of personal repression, struggle and survival. Drawing actively on factual and fictional sources as part of democratic deliberations has clear and practical benefits. It can open up opportunities to learn from and discuss experiences that would otherwise be impossible: foreign perspectives, silenced opinions and uncomfortable truths. Not all of these efforts will necessarily provide political insights of equal worth. Nevertheless, we must learn to encourage fictional accounts which 'not only provides voice but [can also demonstrate] the variety and scope of voices, thereby curbing the hegemony of one'.[42] Our inability to 'see another as fully human' has, according to Martha Nussbaum, much to do with the technocratic forms of rationalized knowledge we have become accustomed to.[43] To liberate us from this bind, she encourages the cultivation of a literary imagination which, with the help of literary sources, makes it more possible for us to enter 'imaginatively into the lives of distant others and to have emotions related to that participation'.[44] New perspectives, greater empathy and more introspection can emerge in the wake of such aesthetic explorations. Only then can we begin to think more expansively, even imaginatively, about the sites, peoples and structures most in need of democratic intervention.

When certain stories, characters and voices remain imprisoned by the dominant discourses of fact, true democratic politics must dare to look further. Through fiction – where private, repressed and sordid truths lie – we can see and hear more than we did; things we may not have seen or heard in political discourse before. A revival of such a holistic approach to knowledge is perhaps more timely now than ever.

And so, radical and short-lived as it was, maybe the Greeks' experience still has something to teach us about our own democratic tendencies? Maybe we can even draw from their tragedies in order to create our own, so that we may better understand our own?

When the Greeks expanded democracy to the courts, festivals, marketplaces and, of course, to the theatre, they soon heard voices beyond the official political purview. Individuals who would have otherwise remained invisible began to take centre stage, along with the daily struggles that marked their existence. Were we to do the same, we might just find that our answers to Sheldon Wolin's question – 'What has Athens to do with Washington?' – are actually more than we think. And that would be a good place to start.

Notes

Introduction

1 Ruth Thomson. 'Witnessing, weeping and outrage – Modern contexts and ancient woes in Euripides' The Trojan Women at the State Theatre Company of South Australia, November 2004'. *Didaskalia* 6.3 (2006). http://www.didaskalia.net/issues/vol6no3/thompson.html.

2 See, for instance, Richard Ned Lebow. *The Tragic Vision of Politics: Ethics, Interests and Orders.* Cambridge: Cambridge University Press, 2003; Mervyn Frost. 'Tragedy, ethics and international relations'. *International Relations* 17.4 (2003); Nicholas Rengger. 'Tragedy or scepticism? Defending the anti-Pelagian mind in world politics'. *International Relations* 19.3 (2005); Richard Ned Lebow. 'Tragedy, politics and political science'. *International Relations* 19.3 (2005); Chris Brown. 'Tragedy, "tragic choices" and contemporary international political theory'. *International Relations* 21.1 (2007); J. Peter Euben. 'The tragedy of tragedy'. *International Relations* 21.1 (2007); Richard Beardsworth. 'Tragedy, world politics and ethical community'. *International Relations* 22.1 (2008); Mervyn Frost. 'Tragedy, reconciliation and reconstruction'. *European Journal of Social Theory* 11.3 (2008); Richard Ned Lebow and Toni Erskine (eds), *Tragedy and International Relations.* New York and Basingstoke: Palgrave Macmillan, 2012. Also see, for instance, the symposium on 'The 2500th anniversary of democracy: Lessons of Athenian democracy'. *PS: Political Science and Politics* 26.3 (1993). Of the five essays in this symposium, Athenian tragedy's connection with democracy was only mentioned once, and only in passing in J. Peter Euben. 'Democracy ancient and modern'. *PS: Political Science and Politics* 26.3 (1993), 481.

3 See, for instance, Cynthia Farrar. *The Origins of Democratic Thinking: The Invention of Politics in Classical Athens.* Cambridge: Cambridge University Press, 1988; M. I. Finley. *The Ancient Greeks.* Harmondsworth: Penguin, 1963; Simon Goldhill. *Reading Greek Tragedy.* Cambridge: Cambridge University Press, 1996; Christian Meier. trans. Andrew Webber. *The Political Art of Greek Tragedy.* Cambridge: Polity Press, 1993; David M. Pritchard (ed.), *War, Culture and Democracy in Classical Athens.* Cambridge: Cambridge University Press, 2009; Richard Sewell. *In the Theatre of Dionysos: Democracy and Tragedy in Ancient Athens.* Jefferson:

McFarland, 2007; M. S. Silk. *Tragedy and the Tragic: Greek Theatre and Beyond.* Oxford: Clarendon Press, 1996; John J. Winkler and Froma I. Zeitlin (eds), *Nothing to Do with Dionysos? Athenian Drama in Its Social Context.* Princeton: Princeton University Press, 1990.

4   Sheldon Wolin. 'Democracy: Electoral and Athenian'. *PS: Political Science and Politics* 26.3 (1993), 475.

5   David Held. 'Democracy and globalization', in Daniele Archibugi, David Held and Martin Kohler (eds), *Re-imagining Political Community: Studies in Cosmopolitan Democracy.* Cambridge: Polity Press, 1998, pp. 21–2.

6   Jean Grugel (ed.), *Democracy without Borders: Transnationalization and Conditionality in New Democracies.* London and New York: Routledge, 1999.

7   See, for instance, Michael W. Doyle. 'Kant, liberal legacies, and foreign affairs'. Parts 1 and 2. *Philosophy and Public Affairs* 12.3–4 (1983); Bruce Russett. *Grasping the Democratic Peace: Principles for a Post-Cold War World.* Princeton: Princeton University Press, 1993; Bruce Russett. 'A structure for peace: A democratic, interdependent, and institutionalized order', in Takashi Inoguchi, Edward Newman and John Keane (eds), *The Changing Nature of Democracy.* Tokyo: United Nations University Press, 1998; Immanuel Kant. *Perpetual Peace.* New York: Columbia University Press, 1932; Thomas J. Knock. *To End All Wars: Woodrow Wilson and the Quest for a New World Order.* New York: Oxford University Press, 1992; Daniele Archibugi, David Held and Martin Kohler. 'Introduction', in Archibugi, Held and Kohler (eds), *Re-imagining Political Community*; Edward G. Mansfield and Jack Snyder. 'Democratization and war'. *Foreign Affairs* 74.3 (1995); James M. Lindsay. 'The case for a concert of democracies'. *Ethics and International Affairs* 23.1 (2009); G. Schmitt and T. Donnelly. 'The Bush doctrine'. *Project Memorandum* 30 January 2002. http://www.newamericancentury.org/defense-20020130. htm; Michael Hirsh. 'Bush and the World'. *Foreign Affairs* 81.5 (2002); Daniele Archibugi and David Held (eds), *Cosmopolitan Democracy: An Agenda for a New World Order.* Cambridge: Polity Press, 1995; John S. Dryzek. *Deliberative Global Politics: Discourse and Democracy in a Divided World.* Cambridge: Polity, 2006; John S. Dryzek. 'Transnational democracy'. *The Journal of Political Philosophy* 7.1 (1999).

8   Euben. 'Democracy ancient and modern', 479.

9   See, for instance, Oliver Taplin. 'Spreading the word through performance', in Simon Goldhill and Robin Osborne (eds), *Performance Culture and Athenian Democracy.* Cambridge: Cambridge University Press, 1999; Kurt A. Raaflaub. 'Contemporary perceptions of democracy in fifth-century Athens', in Loren J. Samons II. ed. and intro. *Athenian Democracy and Imperialism.* Boston: Houghton Mifflin, 1998.

10 Robert J. Bonner. *Aspects of Athenian Democracy*. New York: Russell & Russell, 1967, pp. 117–18; Michael X. Zelenak. *Gender and Politics in Greek Tragedy*. New York: Peter Lang, 1998, p. 6; Goldhill. *Reading Greek Tragedy*, p. 77.

11 See, for instance, Christian Meier. trans. David McLintock. *The Greek Discovery of Politics*. Cambridge: Harvard University Press, 1990, pp. 88–9; Zelenak. *Gender and Politics in Greek Tragedy*, p. 11.

12 Eric Csapo and William J. Slater. *The Context of Ancient Drama*. Ann Arbor: The University of Michigan Press, 1994, p. 286.

13 Lebow. *The Tragic Vision of Politics*, p. 361.

14 Nicole Loraux cited in Zelenak. *Gender and Politics in Greek Tragedy*, p. 11. The democratic revolution is often associated with Cleisthenes, but it also involved and included the demos as a whole. See Josiah Ober. *The Athenian Revolution: Essays on Ancient Greek Democracy and Political Culture*. Princeton: Princeton University Press, 1996, 4, 35.

15 Cornelius Castoriadis. 'The Greek *Polis* and the creation of democracy', in Cornelius Castoriadis. trans. and ed. David Ames Curtis, *The Castoriadis Reader*. Oxford: Basil Blackwell, 1997, p. 274.

16 Costas M. Constantinou. 'The beautiful nation: Reflections on the aesthetics of Hellenism'. *Alternatives: Global, Local, Political* 31.1 (2006), 56.

17 Rush Rehm. *Radical Theatre: Greek Tragedy and the Modern World*. London: Duckworth, 2003, p. 87.

18 Edith Hall. 'The sociology of Athenian tragedy', in P. E. Easterling (ed.), *The Cambridge Companion to Greek Tragedy*. Cambridge: Cambridge University Press, 1997, p. 94; Rehm. *Radical Theatre*, p. 87.

19 Charles Segal. *Interpreting Greek Tragedy: Myth, Poetry, Text*. Ithaca and London: Cornell University Press, 1986, 45, 75, 78.

20 Hall. 'The sociology of Athenian tragedy'.

21 Id., 92.

22 Mary Ebbott. 'Marginal figures', in Justina Gregory (ed.), *A Companion to Greek Tragedy*. Malden: Blackwell, 2005, p. 366.

23 Damon A. Young. *Distraction: A Philosopher's Guide to Being Free*. Melbourne: Melbourne University Press, 2008, p. 94; J. J. Pollitt. *Art and Experience in Classical Greece*. Cambridge: Cambridge University Press, 1972; Andrew Stewart. *Classical Greece and the Birth of Western Art*. Cambridge: Cambridge University Press, 2008; Damon A. Young. 'Sparta for our times'. *Meanjin* 66.2 (2007), 175.

24 Nicholas J. Rengger. *International Relations, Political Theory and the Problem of Order: Beyond International Relations Theory?* London and New York: Routledge, 2000, p. 9.

25 N. Katherine Hayles. 'Introduction: Complex dynamics in literature and science', in N. Katherine Hayles (ed.), *Chaos and Order: Complex Dynamics in Literature and Science*. Chicago: The University of Chicago Press, 1991, p. 1.

26 Rengger. *International Relations, Political Theory and the Problem of Order*, p. 9.

27 Hayles. 'Introduction', p. 2.

28 Kurt A. Raaflaub. 'Introduction', in Kurt A. Raaflaub, Josiah Ober and Robert W. Wallace (with Paul Cartledge and Cynthia Farrar). *Origins of Democracy in Ancient Greece*. Berkeley: University of California Press, 2007, p. 3; Cornelius Castoriadis. 'The "end of philosophy"?', in David Ames Curtis (ed.), *Philosophy, Politics, Autonomy*. New York: Oxford University Press, 1991, pp. 20–2; Castoriadis. 'The Greek *Polis* and the creation of democracy', p. 275.

29 J. Peter Euben. 'The polis, globalization, and the politics of place', in Aryeh Botwinick and William E. Connolly (eds), *Democracy and Vision: Sheldon Wolin and the Vicissitudes of the Political*. Princeton and Oxford: Princeton University Press, 2001, p. 259.

30 Cornelius Castoriadis. trans. Kathleen Blamey. *The Imaginary Institution of Society*. Cambridge: Polity Press, 1987, p. 156.

31 Kate Grenville. 'The writer in a time of change: Learning from experience'. *Griffith Review* 26 (2009), 58.

32 Carmel Bird. 'East of the sun and west of the moon: Fiction and the imagination'. *Griffith Review* 26 (2009), 119.

33 John S. Dryzek. *Deliberative Democracy and Beyond: Liberals, Critics, Contestations*. Oxford: Oxford University Press, 2000.

34 Authors who have broadly written about these global political developments include, for instance, Jim George. *Discourses of Global Politics: A Critical (Re) Introduction to International Relations*. Boulder: Lynne Rienner, 1994; Samuel P. Huntington. *The Clash of Civilizations and the Remaking of World Order*. New York: Simon and Schuster, 1996; Rajani K. Kanth. *Breaking with the Enlightenment: The Twilight of History and the Rediscovery of Utopia*. Atlantic Highlands: Humanities Press, 1997; Thomas F. Homer-Dixon. *Environment, Scarcity, and Violence*. Princeton: Princeton University Press, 1999; Zygmunt Bauman. *Liquid Modernity*. Cambridge: Polity Press, 2000; Roland Bleiker. *Popular Dissent, Human Agency and Global Politics*. Cambridge: Cambridge University Press, 2000; Manfred Steger. *Globalism: The New Market Ideology*. Lanham: Rowman and Littlefield, 2002; Amy Schrager Lang and Cecelia Tichi (eds), *What Democracy Looks Like: A New Critical Realism for a Post-Seattle World*. New Brunswick: Rutgers University Press, 2006.

35 Christopher Rocco. *Tragedy and Enlightenment: Athenian Political Thought and the Dilemmas of Modernity*. Berkeley: University of California Press, 1997, pp. 7–8.

36 Page duBois. 'Toppling the hero: Polyphony in the tragic city'. *New Literary History*
    35.1 (2004), 77.

37 Ibid.

38 Rocco. Tragedy and Enlightenment, p. 5.

39 In recent times, a range of political thinkers have begun to see in the contem-
    porary global transformations a new and radical style of democracy – or the
    need for one – which has little if anything to do with our predominant notions
    of democracy. See, for instance, Nathan Widder. 'The relevance of Nietzsche to
    democratic theory: Micropolitics and the affirmation of difference'. *Contemporary
    Political Theory* 3.2 (2004); Friedrich Nietzsche. ed. Raymond Geuss and Ronald
    Speirs. *The Birth of Tragedy and Other Writings*. Cambridge: Cambridge University
    Press, 1999; Matthias Fritsch. 'Derrida's democracy to come'. *Constellations: An
    International Journal of Critical and Democratic Theory* 9.4 (2002); Paul Patton.
    'Derrida, politics and democracy to come'. *Philosophy Compass* 2.6 (2007); Paul
    Patton. 'Deleuze and democracy'. *Contemporary Political Theory* 4.4 (2005); Alan
    D. Schrift. 'Nietzsche, Foucault, Deleuze, and the subject of radical democracy'.
    Aneglaki: Journal of Theoretical Humanities 5.2 (2000); Chantal Mouffe. *The
    Democratic Paradox*. London: Verso, 2000.

40 Castoriadis. 'The Greek *Polis* and the creation of democracy', p. 268.

41 See, for instance, Alasdair MacIntyre. *After Virtue: A Study in Moral Theory*.
    London: Duckworth Press, 1985; Paul Ricoeur. *Time and Narrative*, Volume 3.
    Chicago: Chicago University Press, 1988.

42 See, for instance, Louiza Odysseos. 'Laughing matters: Peace, democracy and the
    challenge of the comic narrative'. *Millennium: Journal of International Studies* 30.3
    (2001); Keith C. Sidwell. *Aristophanes the Democrat: The Politics of Satirical Com-
    edy during the Peloponnesian War*. Cambridge: Cambridge University Press, 2009;
    Susan Lape. *Reproducing Athens: Menander's Comedy, Democratic Culture and
    the Hellenistic City*. Princeton: Princeton University Press, 2004; Niall W. Slater.
    Spectator Politics: Metatheatre and Performance in Aristophanes. Philadelphia:
    University of Pennsylvania Press, 2002; Michael Vickers. *Pericles on Stage: Political
    Comedy in Aristophanes' Early Plays*. Austin: University of Texas Press, 1997.

43 Edith Hall. *Inventing the Barbarian: Greek Self-Definition through Tragedy*. Oxford:
    Clarendon Press, 1989.

44 Id., p. 162.

45 Edward W. Said. *Orientalism*. London: Penguin Books, 2003, p. 56.

46 Id., p. 57.

47 John Keane. *The Life and Death of Democracy*. London: Pocket Books, 2009,
    63, 64.

48 Id., p. 74.

49 Franz Stoessl. 'Aeschylus as a political thinker'. *The American Journal of Philology* 73.2 (1952), 114.

50 Farrar. *The Origins of Democratic Thinking*, p. 30.

51 Charles Mee. 'What I like'. *The (Re)Making Project*. http://www.charlesmee.org/html/charlesMee.html.

Chapter 1

1 Castoriadis. 'The "end of philosophy"?', pp. 21–2; Cornelius Castoriadis. 'The Athenian democracy: False and true questions', in Pierre Leveque and Pierre Vidal-Naquet. trans. and ed. David Ames Curtis, *Cleisthenes the Athenian: An Essay on the Representation of Space and Time in Greek Political Thought from the End of the Sixth Century to the Death of Plato*. New Jersey: Humanities Press, 1996, p. 121.

2 Raaflaub. 'Introduction', p. 3.

3 Castoriadis. 'The "end of philosophy"?', pp. 20–2; Castoriadis. 'The Greek *Polis* and the creation of democracy', p. 275.

4 Neal Curtis. 'Tragedy and politics'. *Philosophy and Social Criticism* 33.7 (2007), 871.

5 Castoriadis. 'The Greek *Polis* and the creation of democracy', p. 284.

6 Segal. *Interpreting Greek Tragedy*, p. 45.

7 Id., 75, 78.

8 Christian Descamps. 'Introduction', in Pierre Leveque and Pierre Vidal-Naquet, *Cleisthenes the Athenian*, p. 100.

9 See Barbara Goff. 'Introduction: History, tragedy, theory', in Barbara Goff. ed. and intro., *History, Tragedy, Theory: Dialogues on Athenian Drama*. Austin: University of Texas Press, 1995, p. 6.

10 Id., p. 8.

11 John J. Winkler and Froma I. Zeitlin. 'Introduction', in Winkler and Zeitlin (eds), *Nothing to Do with Dionysos?*, p. 4.

12 Ibid.

13 Ibid.

14 Ober. *The Athenian Revolution*, p. 10.

15 Michelle Gellrich. 'Interpreting Greek tragedy: History, theory and the new philology', in Goff (ed.), *History, Tragedy, Theory*, p. 40.

16 Jean-Pierre Vernant. 'Tension and ambiguities in Greek tragedy', in Jean-Pierre Vernant and Pierre Vidal-Naquet. trans. Janet Lloyd, *Tragedy and Myth in Ancient Greece*. Sussex: Harvester Press, 1981, pp. 6–7.

17   Jasper Griffin. 'The social function of attic tragedy'. *The Classical Quarterly* 48.1 (1998), 60.

18   But this, in part, can be problematized through an examination of Nietzsche's thoughts on agonism in relation to democracy and tragedy. As an advocate of tragedy's beauty and power, Nietzsche is also a staunch critic of democracy. Within his texts, a palpable elitism prevails, as does an aversion to modern notions of egalitarianism, liberalism and democracy. However, we need not conclude from this that tragedy is indeed undemocratic and vice versa. Rather, it is necessary to maintain a definite notion of democracy, a notion that perhaps precedes or negates modern, liberal democracy. Such is the importance of Athenian democracy. Beyond the mere institutions, the call for equality and the demands of openness, Athenian democracy grasped sordid truths within the individuals and their communities. From these truths came the need for agonism. This, Nietzsche would have been far from critical of. In fact, his very penchant for elitism and pessimism effectively accommodates the workings of agonism. And it is as these concepts are extended to the greater population, as they become the ethos of the polis, that tragedy will begin to flourish. There exists a fundamental unity between democracy and tragedy; a unitary disclosure via different means. For Nietzsche, this is precisely why '[t]ragedy has always contained a pure democratic character, [because] it springs from the people'. See Lawrence J. Hatab. *A Nietzschean Defense of Democracy: An Experiment in Postmodern Politics.* Chicago and La Salle: Open Court, 1995; Lawrence J. Hatab. 'Prospects for a democratic *Agon*: Why we can still be Nietzscheans'. *Journal of Nietzsche Studies* 24.1 (2002); Joshua Foa Dienstag. 'Tragedy, pessimism, Nietzsche'. *New Literary History* 35.1 (2004), 88–9; Widder. 'The relevance of Nietzsche to democratic theory'.

19   See Helene Foley's analysis of the divergence of Christine Sourvinou-Inwood's democratic reading of *Antigone* with Larry Bennet and Blake Tyrell's reading of the same play. See Helene Foley. 'Tragedy and democratic ideology: The case of Sophocles' *Antigone*', in Goff (ed.), *History, Tragedy, Theory.*

20   Sewell. *In the Theatre of Dionysos*, p. 186.

21   Constantinou. 'The beautiful nation', 54.

22   Donald Kagan. *Pericles of Athens and the Birth of Democracy.* New York: The Free Press, 1991, p. 2; Meier. *The Political Art of Greek Tragedy*, p. 17.

23   Farrar. *The Origins of Democratic Thinking*, p. 1.

24   See, for instance, Ober. *The Athenian Revolution*; Greg Anderson. *The Athenian Experiment: Building an Imagined Political Community in Ancient Attica 508–490 BC.* Ann Arbor: The University of Michigan Press, 2003; Leveque and Vidal-Naquet. *Cleisthenes the Athenian*; Cynthia Farrar. 'Power to the people', in Kurt A. Raaflaub, Josiah Ober and Robert W. Wallace. *Origins of Democracy in Ancient Greece.*

25   See, for instance, Aristotle, *Politics*, 2.12, in Cosmo Rodewald. ed. and intro.,
     Democracy: Ideas and Realities. London: Dent, 1974; Mortimer Chambers.
     'Aristotle's "forms of democracy"'. *Transactions and Proceedings of the American
     Philological Association* 92 (1961), 22–4; Farrar. 'Power to the people';
     R. K. Sinclair. *Democracy and Participation in Athens*. Cambridge: Cambridge
     University Press, 1988.
26   See Walter Eder in Farrar. 'Power to the people', p. 172.
27   Kagan. *Pericles of Athens and the Birth of Democracy*, p. 4.
28   Daniel Ross. *Violent Democracy*. Cambridge: Cambridge University Press, 2004, p. 5.
29   For more on Solon see Robin Barrow. *Athenian Democracy: The Triumph and the
     Folly*. Houndmills: Macmillan, 1973; Farrar. *The Origins of Democratic Thinking*; Sin-
     clair. *Democracy and Participation in Athens*; Robin Sowerby. *The Greeks: An Introduc-
     tion to their Culture*. London and New York: Routledge, 1995. For more on Cleisthenes
     see Anderson. *The Athenian Experiment*; Finley. *The Ancient Greeks*; Leveque and
     Vidal-Naquet. *Cleisthenes the Athenian*; Ober. *The Athenian Revolution*.
30   Ebbott. 'Marginal figures', p. 366.
31   Barrow. *Athenian Democracy*, pp. 29–30.
32   Id., pp. 21–2; Sowerby. *The Greeks*, pp. 31–2.
33   Finley. *The Ancient Greeks*, p. 75; Peter V. Jones. *The World of Athens: An
     Introduction to Classical Athenian Culture*. Cambridge: Cambridge University
     Press, 1984, pp. 202–3.
34   Jones. *The World of Athens*, p. 204.
35   Id., p. 206.
36   Ibid.
37   Id., pp. 208–9.
38   Barrow. *Athenian Democracy*, p. 30; Farrar. *The Origins of Democratic Thinking*,
     p. 22; Kurt A. Raaflaub. 'The breakthrough of *Demokratia* in mid-fifth century
     Athens', in Kurt A. Raaflaub, Josiah Ober and Robert W. Wallace. *Origins of
     Democracy in Ancient Greece*, p. 105.
39   Eric W. Robinson. 'Ancient Greek democracy: A brief introduction', in Eric
     W. Robinson (ed.), *Ancient Greek Democracy: Readings and Sources*. Malden:
     Blackwell, 2004, p. 3.
40   Anderson. *The Athenian Experiment*, 36–7, 81; Sowerby. *The Greeks*, p. 34.
41   Ibid.
42   David Ames Curtis. 'Translator's foreword', in Pierre Leveque and Pierre Vidal Naquet.
     Cleisthenes the Athenian, p. xi; Sinclair. *Democracy and Participation in Athens*, p. 3.
43   Sara Forsdyke. *Exile, Ostracism, and Democracy: The Politics of Expulsion in
     Ancient Greece*. Princeton: Princeton University Press, 2005; Robinson. 'Ancient
     Greek democracy', p. 3.

44 Sewell. *In the Theatre of Dionysos*, p. 185.

45 For instance, Aristotle asserts that Athenian democracy progressed through 11 changes (*metabolai*) in form. Chambers. 'Aristotle's "forms of democracy"', 22.

46 The word for democracy in ancient Athens is *demokratia*, which denotes the giving of *kratos* (power) to the *demos* (people). It is worthwhile noting that the etymology of *kratos* is related to 'grasp', signifying a rather physical power. Hence, as Paul Cartledge notes, the people would literally have their hands on what mattered. See Jones. *The World of Athens*, p. 197; Paul Cartledge. 'Democracy, origins of: Contribution to a debate', in Kurt A. Raaflaub, Josiah Ober and Robert W. Wallace. *Origins of Democracy in Ancient Greece*, pp. 156–7.

47 See Castoriadis. 'The Athenian democracy', p. 121.

48 Meier. *The Political Art of Greek Tragedy*, pp. 14–18.

49 Ross. *Violent Democracy*, p. 7.

50 See, for instance, Castoriadis. 'The Greek *Polis* and the creation of democracy', pp. 273–4; Gilles Labelle. 'Two refoundation projects of democracy in contemporary French philosophy: Cornelius Castoriadis and Jacques Ranciere'. *Philosophy and Social Criticism* 27.4 (2001), 78.

51 Castoriadis. 'The Greek *Polis* and the creation of democracy', p. 274.

52 Castoriadis. 'The "end of philosophy"?', pp. 20–1.

53 David Ames Curtis. 'Preface', in Castoriadis (ed.), *Philosophy, Politics, Autonomy*, pp. vii–viii.

54 Castoriadis. 'The "end of philosophy"?', p. 20.

55 Ibid.

56 Sewell. *In the Theatre of Dionysos*, p. 185.

57 Labelle. 'Two refoundation projects of democracy in contemporary French philosophy', 80.

58 Castoriadis. 'The "end of philosophy"?', p. 20.

59 Cornelius Castoriadis. 'Power, politics, autonomy', in Castoriadis (ed.), *Philosophy, Politics, Autonomy*, p. 160.

60 Castoriadis. 'The Greek *Polis* and the creation of democracy', p. 274.

61 See Kagan. *Pericles of Athens and the Birth of Democracy*, p. 9. Also for more on the coming together of opposites witnessed under democracy see Farrar. *The Origins of Democratic Thinking*, p. 1; Meier. *The Political Art of Greek Tragedy*, p. 37; Raaflaub. 'Introduction', p. 3.

62 Pierre Vidal-Naquet. 'Democracy: A Greek invention', in Pierre Leveque and Pierre Vidal-Naquet, *Cleisthenes the Athenian*, p. 108.

63 An extensive literature, both classic and modern, has emerged detailing the immense injustices, horrors and frivolity meted out by and under the West's first great democracy. See, for instance, Vidal-Naquet. 'Democracy', p. 108; Castoriadis.

'The Athenian democracy', p. 123–4; Jones. *The World of Athens*; Bernard Groffman. 'Lessons of Athenian democracy: Editor's introduction'. *PS: Political Science
and Politics* 26.3 (1993), 471; Sowerby. *The Greeks*, pp. 47–54. At the same time,
however, Castoriadis warns us that contemporary theorists should not impose
modern standards on ancient peoples, given that the notion of political universality – the complete destruction of traditional limitations, the questioning of
sensitive topics, universal suffrage – is a recent development. Castoriadis. 'Power,
politics, autonomy', pp. 160–1; Castoriadis. 'The Athenian democracy', p. 127.

64 Castoriadis. 'The "end of philosophy"?', p. 20.
65 Curtis. 'Translator's foreword', p. xi.
66 Id., p. xx.
67 Strictly speaking, it must be noted that 'Greek tragedy' is a misnomer. It was not
Greece or the Greeks per se that gave birth to tragedy. Indeed, it was not Greece
or the Greeks who needed its insights and accentuated its notoriety. Rather, it was
Athens and the Athenians. It was, for Castoriadis, the upshot of a people and a
predicament that rejected absolute singularity. This was why the genre and institution became so esteemed in Athens in the immediate aftermath of the democratic
revolution. See Castoriadis. 'The Greek *Polis* and the creation of democracy',
p. 284; Sewell. *In the Theatre of Dionysos*, p. 3; Zelenak. *Gender and Politics in
Greek Tragedy*, p. 3.
68 Hall. *Inventing the Barbarian*, p. 1.
69 Jones. *The World of Athens*, p. 301; Sowerby. *The Greeks*, p. 78.
70 Costas M. Constantinou. *On the Way to Diplomacy*. Minneapolis: University of
Minnesota Press, 1996, p. 99.
71 Segal. *Interpreting Greek Tragedy*, 32, 34; Josiah Ober and Barry Strauss. 'Drama,
political rhetoric, and the discourse of Athenian democracy', in Winkler and
Zeitlin (eds), *Nothing to do With Dionysos?*, pp. 239–40; Alfred Cary Schlesinger. *Boundaries of Dionysus: Athenian Foundations for the Theory of Tragedy*.
Cambridge: Harvard University Press, 1963.
72 G. Lowes Dickinson. *The Greek View of Life*. London: Methuen, 1960, p. 234;
Schlesinger. *Boundaries of Dionysus*, 27, 37.
73 Lebow. *The Tragic Vision of Politics*, p. 20.
74 H. M. Kellen. 'The essence of tragedy'. *International Journal of Ethics*
22 (1912), 199.
75 Eva Figes. *Tragedy and Social Revolution*. London: John Calder, 1976, p. 11; Roy
Flickinger. *The Greek Theater and its Drama*. Chicago: Chicago University Press,
1922; Jones. *The World of Athens*, pp. 301–2; William Ridgeway. *The Origin of
Tragedy*. Cambridge: Cambridge University Press, 1910, p. 71; Sowerby. *The
Greeks*, p. 77.

76 Douglas Smith. 'Introduction', in Friedrich Nietzsche. trans. and intro. Douglas Smith. *The Birth of Tragedy*. Oxford: Oxford University Press, 2000; Gerald F. Else. *The Origin and Early Form of Greek Tragedy*. New York: W.W. Norton, 1972, p. 30.

77 Else. *The Origin and Early Form of Greek Tragedy*, pp. 9–10.

78 Richard G. Moulton. *The Ancient Classical Drama: A Study in Literary Evolution*. Oxford: Clarendon Press, 1898, p. 6.

79 Id., pp. 8–9.

80 Id., p. 10.

81 Ibid.

82 Smith. 'Introduction', p. xvii.

83 P. E. Easterling. 'The end of an era? Tragedy in the early fourth century', in Alan H Sommerstein, Stephan Halliwell, Jeffrey Henderson and Bernhard Zimmermann (eds), *Tragedy, Comedy and the Polis: Papers from the Greek Drama Conference*. Bari: Levante Editori, 1993.

84 Ridgeway. *The Origin of Tragedy*.

85 J. Peter Euben. *The Tragedy of Political Theory: The Road Not Taken*. Princeton: Princeton University Press, 1990, p. 50.

86 Constantinou. *On the Way to Diplomacy*, 100, 99.

87 Bonner. *Aspects of Athenian Democracy*, pp. 117–18; Zelenak. *Gender and Politics in Greek Tragedy*, p. 6.

88 Goldhill. *Reading Greek Tragedy*, p. 77.

89 See, for instance, Meier. *The Greek Discovery of Politics*, pp. 88–9; Zelenak. *Gender and Politics in Greek Tragedy*, p. 11.

90 Meier. *The Political Art of Greek Tragedy*, p. 1.

91 Id., 1–4, 47–8; Farrar. *The Origins of Democratic Thinking*, p. 11.

92 Stephen Chan. *The End of Certainty: Towards a New Internationalism*. London and New York: Zed Books, 2009, p. 201.

93 Goldhill. *Reading Greek Tragedy*, pp. 75–8.

94 Simon Goldhill. 'The audience in Athenian tragedy', in P. E. Easterling (ed.), *The Cambridge Companion to Greek Tragedy*, pp. 55–6.

95 Id., p. 60.

96 Csapo and Slater. *The Context of Ancient Drama*, p. 286.

97 Goldhill. *Reading Greek Tragedy*, p. 77.

98 Stoessl. 'Aeschylus as a political thinker', 113–14.

99 Goldhill. 'The audience in Athenian tragedy', p. 56.

100 Hall. 'The sociology of Athenian tragedy', p. 100.

101 Bonner. *Aspects of Athenian Democracy*, p. 118; Euben. *The Tragedy of Political Theory*, pp. 55–6; Finley. *The Ancient Greeks*, p. 106; Hall. 'The sociology of Athenian tragedy', p. 125.

102 Paul Cartledge. '"Deep plays": Theatre as process in Athenian civic life', in
   P. E. Easterling (ed.), *The Cambridge Companion to Greek Tragedy*, p. 8; Zelenak.
   Gender and Politics in Greek Tragedy, p. 7.

103 Paul Monaghan. 'Managerialism meets Dionysos: Theatre and civic order'. *Double
   Dialogues* 3 (2005/06). http://www.doubledialogues.com/archive/issue_three/
   monaghan_two.htm.

104 Hall. *Inventing the Barbarian*; Zelenak. *Gender and Politics in Greek Tragedy*.

105 Christoph Menke. 'The presence of tragedy'. *Critical Horizons* 5.1 (2004), 216;
   Vernant. 'Tension and ambiguities in Greek tragedy', p. 18.

106 Meier. *The Greek Discovery of Politics*, pp. 82–4.

107 Id., 121, 123.

108 Simon Goldhill. 'The great Dionysia and civic ideology', in Winkler and Zeitlin
   (eds), *Nothing to Do with Dionysos?*, p. 126.

109 Monaghan. 'Managerialism meets Dionysos'.

110 Goldhill. 'The great Dionysia and civic ideology', 124, 127.

111 Castoriadis. 'The Greek *Polis* and the creation of democracy', p. 284.

112 Nathalie Karagiannis. 'The tragic and the political: A parallel reading of Kostas
   Papaioannou and Cornelius Castoriadis'. *Critical Horizons* 7.1 (2006), 309.

113 Ibid.

114 Castoriadis. 'The Greek *Polis* and the creation of democracy', p. 284.

115 Nietzsche. *The Birth of Tragedy*, s3.

116 Castoriadis. 'The Greek *Polis* and the creation of democracy', p. 284; J. Peter
   Euben. 'Introduction', in J. Peter Euben (ed.), *Greek Tragedy and Political Theory*.
   Berkeley: University of California Press, 1986, p. 29; Michael Janover. 'Mythic
   form and political reflection in Athenian tragedy'. *Parallax* 9.4 (2003), 41.

117 Monaghan. 'Managerialism meets Dionysos'.

118 Segal. *Interpreting Greek Tragedy*, 23, 41.

119 See, for instance, Deborah Boedeker and Kurt Raaflaub. 'Tragedy and city', in
   Rebecca Bushnell (ed.), *A Companion to Tragedy*. Malden: Blackwell, 2005,
   pp. 119–22 for full analysis.

120 A. Brown. ed. and trans. *Sophocles: Antigone*. Warminster: Aris and Phillips Ltd.,
   1987, 1–2; R. E. Braun. trans. *Sophocles: Antigone*. London: Oxford University
   Press, 1973.

121 Castoriadis. 'The Greek *Polis* and the creation of democracy', p. 286; Matthew
   Sharpe. 'Autonomy, reflexivity, tragedy: Notions of democracy in Camus and
   Castoriadis'. *Critical Horizons* 3.1 (2002), 113–14.

122 Nietzsche. *The Birth of Tragedy*, s4; Smith. 'Introduction', p. xvii; M. S. Silk and
   J. P. Stern. *Nietzsche on Tragedy*. Cambridge: Cambridge University Press, 1981, p. 65.

123 Hall. 'The sociology of Athenian tragedy', p. 126.

124 Damon Young. 'The democratic chorus: Culture, dialogue and polyphonic *Paideia*'. *Democracy and Nature* 9.2 (2003), 231–2.

125 Friedrich Nietzsche. trans. R. J. Hollingdale. *Richard Wagner in Beyreuth*. Cambridge: Cambridge University Press, 1983, p. 223.

126 Constantinou. 'The beautiful nation', 56.

127 Boedecker and Raaflaub. 'Tragedy and city', p. 123.

128 Euben. *The Tragedy of Political Theory*, p. 147.

129 Giacomo Gambino. 'Nietzsche and the Greeks: Identity, politics, and tragedy'. *Polity* 28.4 (1996), 433–4, 427.

Chapter 2

1 Hall. 'The sociology of Athenian tragedy'.

2 Sewell. *In the Theatre of Dionysos*, p. 171.

3 Gambino. 'Nietzsche and the Greeks', 416–17.

4 Hall. 'The sociology of Athenian tragedy'.

5 Ibid.

6 Segal. *Interpreting Greek Tragedy*, 45, 75, 78.

7 See David Held. *Models of Democracy* (3rd edn). Cambridge: Polity Press, 2006, p. 28.

8 Aristotle, ed. and trans. Stephen Halliwell. *Poetics*. Cambridge: Harvard University Press, 1995, Book 7.

9 Id., Book 7, 9.

10 Id., Book 14.

11 Hall. 'The sociology of Athenian tragedy', p. 93.

12 Jean-Pierre Vernant. 'Myth and tragedy', in Amelie Oksenberg Rorty (ed.), *Essays on Aristotle's Poetics*. Princeton: Princeton University Press, 1992, p. 33.

13 duBois. 'Toppling the hero', 75.

14 Ibid.

15 Paul Woodruff. *The Necessity of Theater: The Art of Watching and Being Watched*. Oxford: Oxford University Press, 2008, p. 72.

16 Aristotle. *Poetics*, Book 15.

17 duBois. 'Toppling the hero', 67.

18 Michael Chayut. 'Tragedy and science'. *History of European Ideas* 25.4 (1999), 167–8.

19 Ebbott. 'Marginal figures', p. 366.

20 Id., p. 367.

21 Claude Calame. trans. Janice Orion. pref. Jean-Claude Coquet. *The Craft of Poetic Speech in Ancient Greece*. Ithaca: Cornell University Press, 1995, pp. 97–115.

22 Alvin W. Gouldner. *Enter Plato: Classical Greece and the Origins of Social Theory*. London: Routledge and Kegan Paul, 1965, 108, 110.

23 Id., p. 114.

24 Dostoyevsky quoted in Young. 'The democratic chorus', 228.

25 Ibid.

26 Hall. 'The sociology of Athenian tragedy', p. 123.

27 Vernant. 'Myth and tragedy', p. 35.

28 See Jean-Pierre Vernant. 'The historical moment of tragedy in Greece: Some of the social and psychological conditions', in Vernant and Vidal-Naquet (eds), *Tragedy and Myth in Ancient Greece*; Vernant. 'Tension and ambiguities in Greek tragedy'; Claude Calame. 'Performative aspects of the choral voice in Greek tragedy: Civic identity in performance', in Goldhill and Osborne (eds), *Performance Culture and Athenian Democracy*.

29 Calame. 'Performative aspects of the choral voice in Greek tragedy', p. 130.

30 Vernant. 'Tension and ambiguities in Greek tragedy', p. 18.

31 Daniel W. Graham. *Explaining the Cosmos: The Ionian Tradition of Scientific Philosophy*. Princeton and Oxford: Princeton University Press, 2006.

32 'Hesiod's theory' in Id., p. 10.

33 Gi-Ming Shien. 'Being and nothingness in Greek and ancient philosophy'. *Philosophy East and West* 1.2 (1951), 16, 18; T. A. Sinclair. *A History of Greek Political Thought*. London: Routledge & Kegan Paul, 1967.

34 H. C. Baldry. *The Unity of Mankind in Greek Thought*. Cambridge: Cambridge University Press, 1965, p. 27.

35 Monaghan. 'Managerialism meets Dionysos'.

36 Farrar. *The Origins of Democratic Thinking*, p. 30; Goldhill. *Reading Greek Tragedy*, pp. 77–8; Meier. *The Political Art of Greek Tragedy*, pp. 2–3.

37 Albert Camus. 'Lecture given in Athens on the future of tragedy', in Albert Camus. ed. and trans. Philip Thody, *Selected Essays and Notebooks*. Harmondsworth: Penguin, 1970, p. 199.

38 Edith Hamilton. *Mythology: Timeless Tales of Gods and Heroes*. New York: A Mentor Book, 1969, p. 13.

39 Id., p. 17.

40 Lowes Dickinson. *The Greek View of Life*, p. 250.

41 Svetla Slaveva-Griffin. 'Philosophy and myth: A review of recent scholarship'. *The European Legacy* 12.2 (2007), 247.

42 Raymond Geuss. 'Introduction', in Nietzsche (ed.), *The Birth of Tragedy and Other Writings*, p. xiv.

43 Schlesinger. *Boundaries of Dionysus*, pp. 42–3; Bruno Snell. *The Discovery of the Mind in Greek Philosophy and Literature*. New York: Dover Publications, 1982, p. 98.

44 Walter Kaufmann. *Tragedy and Philosophy*. Garden City: Doubleday and Company, 1968, p. 78.

45 Alastair Blanshard. *Hercules: A Heroic Life*. London: Granta, 2005, p. 45.

46 Boedeker and Raaflaub. 'Tragedy and city', pp. 122–3.

47 Christiane Sourvinou-Inwood. 'Assumptions and the creation of meaning: Reading Sophocles' *Antigone*'. *Journal of Hellenic Studies* 109 (1989), 136.

48 Zelenak. *Gender and Politics in Greek Tragedy*, p. 3.

49 Vernant. 'Myth and tragedy', p. 36.

50 Aristotle. *Poetics*, Book 6.

51 Bonner. *Aspects of Athenian Democracy*, p. 89; Ober and Strauss. 'Drama, political rhetoric, and the discourse of Athenian democracy', pp. 237–40.

52 Cartledge. 'Deep plays', p. 3.

53 Lowes Dickinson. *The Greek View of Life*, p. 206.

54 Id., pp. 253–4.

55 See Martha C. Nussbaum. *The Fragility of Goodness: Luck and Ethics in Greek Tragedy and Philosophy*. Cambridge: Cambridge University Press, 1986, p. 90; Stephen Chan. 'Typologies toward an unchained medley: Against the gentrification of discourse in international relations', in Vivienne Jabri and Eleanor O'Gorman (eds), *Women, Culture and International Relations*. Boulder: Lynne Rienner, 1999, pp. 165–7.

56 Richard Tarnas. *The Passion of the Western Mind: Understanding the Ideas That Have Shaped Our World*. New York: Ballantine Books, 1991, p. 17.

57 Alfred North Whitehead. *Science and the Modern World*. New York: The Macmillan Company, 1926, p. 11.

58 Gambino. 'Nietzsche and the Greeks', 417.

59 Dennis J. Schmidt. *On Germans and Other Greeks: Tragedy and Ethical Life*. Bloomington and Indianapolis: Indiana University Press, 2001, p. 273.

60 Grace M. Ledbetter. *Poetics Before Plato: Interpretation and Authority in Early Greek Theories of Poetry*. Princeton: Princeton University Press, 2003, p. 3.

61 Stephen Chan. 'A new triptych for international relations in the 21st century: Beyond waltz and beyond Lacan's Antigone, with a note on the Falun Gong of China'. *Global Society* 17.2 (2003), 191.

62 George Steiner. *The Death of Tragedy*. New Haven and London: Yale University Press, 1996, p. 8.

63 Camus, 'Lecture given in Athens on the future of tragedy', p. 196; Albert Camus. 'Helen's exile', in Albert Camus. trans. Justin O'Brien, *The Myth of Sisyphus and Other Essays*. New York: Alfred A. Knopf, 1967, pp. 187–8.

64   Wendy C. Hamblet. 'The tragedy of Platonic ethics and the fall of Socrates'. *Ethics* 2.2 (2003), 142, 143.

65   Id., 142.

66   Tarnas. *The Passion of the Western Mind*, p. 19; Jean-Pierre Vernant. *Myth and Thought among the Greeks*. Cambridge: MIT Press, 2006, 371, 401–3.

67   Eugenio Benitez. 'Philosophy, myth and Plato's two-worlds view'. *The European Legacy* 12.2 (2007), 225.

68   Steiner. *The Death of Tragedy*, p. x.

69   William Allan. 'Tragedy and the early Greek philosophical tradition', in J. Gregory (ed.), *A Companion to Greek Tragedy*, pp. 71–2; N. G. L. Hammond. *A History of Greece to 322 BC* (3rd edn). Oxford: Clarendon Press, 1986, pp. 421–2; G. E. R. Lloyd. *Early Greek Science: Thales to Aristotle*. New York: W.W. Norton, 1970, p. 66.

70   Farrar. *The Origins of Democratic Thinking*, pp. 3–5.

71   Plato. trans. and intro. Francis Macdonald Cornford. *The Republic of Plato*. London: Oxford University Press, 1945, Ch. xxiv, p. 221.

72   Tarnas. *The Passion of the Western Mind*, p. 38.

73   Richard Kannicht. *The Ancient Quarrel Between Philosophy and Poetry: Aspects of the Greek Conception of Literature*. Christchurch: University of Canterbury Press, 1988, p. 2.

74   Kaufmann. *Tragedy and Philosophy*, p. 78; Snell. *The Discovery of the Mind in Greek Philosophy and Literature*, p. 90.

75   Lowes Dickinson. *The Greek View of Life*, 228, 230.

76   Lloyd. *Early Greek Science*, p. 66; Kannicht. *The Ancient Quarrel Between Philosophy and Poetry*, p. 3.

77   Snell. *The Discovery of the Mind in Greek Philosophy and Literature*, p. 111.

78   Walter R. Agard. *What Democracy Meant to the Greeks*. Chapel Hill: The University of North Carolina Press, 1942, p. 195.

79   Bernard Crick. 'A meditation on democracy', in Inoguchi, Newman and Keane (eds), *The Changing Nature of Democracy*, p. 255.

80   Plato. *The Republic of Plato*, Ch xxxi.

81   Paul Fairfield. 'A modest phenomenology of democratic speech'. *The European Legacy* 10.4 (2005), 359.

82   Id., 361.

83   Costas M. Constantinou. *States of Political Discourse: Words, Regimes, Seditions*. London and New York: Routledge, 2004, pp. 8–10.

84   See, for instance, T. H. Irwin. 'Euripides and Socrates'. *Classical Philology* 78.3 (1983); Helmet Kuhn. 'The true tragedy: On the relationship between Greek tragedy and Plato, I'. *Harvard Studies in Classical Philology* 52 (1941), 4–5; James I.

Porter. *The Invention of Dionysus: An Essay on the Birth of Tragedy*. Stanford: Stanford University Press, 2000, p. 88; Silk and Stern. *Nietzsche on Tragedy*, pp. 73–76; Snell. *The Discovery of the Mind in Greek Philosophy and Literature*, p. 109–12.

85 Nietzsche. *The Birth of Tragedy*, s17.

86 Id., s12; see Constantinou. 'The beautiful nation', for a more complex articulation of this perspective.

87 Curtis. 'Tragedy and politics', 860.

88 Constantinou. *States of Political Discourse*, p. 8.

89 Easterling. 'The end of an era?', pp. 561–62.

90 Constantinou. *States of Political Discourse*, p. 9. However, Georgia Xanthakis-Karamanos makes the argument that the demise of tragedy was, in fact, the result of the growing anxieties and gloominess in fourth-century Athenian life. Unlike the fifth century, when order could flourish with disorder and fact and fiction, the painful realities of the fourth century meant that audiences 'could hardly face true tragedies' onstage. See Easterling. 'The end of an era?', p. 562.

91 Also see Nussbaum. *The Fragility of Goodness*, pp. 122–34; D. D. Raphael. *The Paradox of Tragedy*. Bloomington: Indiana University Press, 1960, pp. 76–9.

92 Stephen Halliwell. 'Plato's repudiation of the tragic', in Silk (ed.), *Tragedy and the Tragic*, p. 338.

93 Tarnas. *The Passion of the Western Mind*, p. 292.

94 Isaiah Berlin. ed. Henry Hardy. *The Roots of Romanticism*. Princeton: Princeton University Press, 1999, p. 3.

95 George Steiner. '"Tragedy", reconsidered', in Rita Felski (ed.), *Rethinking Tragedy*. Baltimore: Johns Hopkins University Press, 2008, p. 43.

96 Michael Tomasky. 'It's all in the poetry – How Obama's vision and message of unity won over Iowa'. *The Guardian* 5 January 2008. http://www.guardian.co.uk/world/2008/jan/05/barackobama.uselections2008.

97 John Locke. *An Essay Concerning Human Understanding*. New York: Prometheus Books, 1995, p. 411.

98 Immanuel Kant. trans. J. H. Bernard. *Critique of Judgment*. New York: Hafner Press, 1951, s53, pp. 171–2.

99 Chan. *The End of Certainty*, p. 12.

100 Morton Schoolman. *Reason and Horror: Critical Theory, Democracy, and Aesthetic Individuality*. New York: Routledge, 2001, p. 42.

101 Euben. *The Tragedy of Political Theory*, p. 260; Martha C. Beck. *Tragedy and the Philosophical Life: A Response to Martha Nussbaum*. Lewiston: E. Mellen Press, 2006, p. 19.

102 Beck. *Tragedy and the Philosophical Life*, pp. 36–7.

103 Slaveva-Griffin. 'Philosophy and myth', 247.

104 This account is of Nietzsche's Socrates. Porter. *The Invention of Dionysus*, p. 90;
     Lee Spinks. *Friedrich Nietzsche*. London: Routledge, 2003, pp. 31–2; Walter A.
     Kaufmann. 'Nietzsche's admiration for Socrates'. *Journal of the History of Ideas* 9.4
     (1948), 475–6.
105 Hamblet. 'The tragedy of Platonic ethics and the fall of Socrates'.
106 Hans-Georg Gadamer. trans. and intro. P. Christopher Smith. *Dialogue and
     Dialectic: Eight Hermeneutical Studies on Plato*. New Haven: Yale University Press,
     1980, p. 48.
107 Hamblet. 'The tragedy of Platonic ethics and the fall of Socrates', 150.
108 Schmidt. *On Germans and Other Greeks*, pp. 7–8.
109 Alex Danchev. 'Princes and players: From a play banned in Athens to Samuel
     Beckett in Sarajevo – Why theatre still matters'. *The Times Literary Supplement* 31
     December 2008. http://entertainment.timesonline.co.uk/tol/arts_and_entertain-
     ment/the_tls/article5423443.ece.
110 Leo Aylen. *Greek Tragedy and the Modern World*. London: Methuen, 1964,
     pp. 213–14.
111 Gail Finney. 'Modern theater and the tragic in Europe', in Bushnell (ed.), *A Com-
     panion to Tragedy*, p. 474.
112 Rita Felski. 'Introduction', in Rita Felski (ed.), *Rethinking Tragedy*. Baltimore: Johns
     Hopkins University Press, 2008, p. 9.
113 David Scott. 'Tragedy's time: Postemancipation futures past and present', in Felski
     (ed.), *Rethinking Tragedy*; Michael Maffesoli. trans. Rita Felski, Allan Megill and
     Marilyn Gaddis Rose. 'The return of the tragic in postmodern societies', in Felski
     (ed.), *Rethinking Tragedy*.
114 Edith Hall. 'Why Greek tragedy in the late twentieth century?', in Edith Hall,
     Fiona Macintosh and Amanda Wrigley (eds), *Dionysus since 69: Greek Tragedy
     at the Dawn of the Third Millennium*. Oxford: Oxford University Press, 2004,
     p. 22.
115 Constantinou. *States of Political Discourse*, p. 9.
116 Chayut. 'Tragedy and science', 167–8.
117 Ebbott. 'Marginal figures', p. 366.
118 Id., p. 367.
119 Dostoyevsky quoted in Young 'The democratic chorus', 228.
120 Alan McKee. 'A beginner's guide to textual analysis', *Metro* (Issue 127/128,
     2001), 140.
121 Roland Barthes. 'Textual analysis of Poe's "Valdemar"', in Robert Young. ed. and
     intro., *Untying the Text: A Post-Structuralist Reader*. Boston: Routledge and Kegan
     Paul, 1981, p. 135.
122 Roland Barthes. 'Theory of the text', in Young (ed.), *Untying the Text*, 37, 39.

123 Id., p. 43.
124 Ibid.
125 Michael J. Shapiro. 'Textualizing global politics', in James Der Derian and Michael Shapiro (eds), *International/Intertextual Relations: Postmodern Readings of World Politics*. Lexington: Lexington Books, 1989.
126 Id., p. 13.
127 duBois. 'Toppling the hero', 64–5.
128 Id., 65.
129 Daniel Mendelsohn. 'The Greek way', in Daniel Mendelsohn (ed.), *How Beautiful It Is and How Easily It Can be Broken: Essays*. New York: Harper, 2008, pp. 410–11.
130 John Fiske. *Television Culture*. London: Routledge, 1987, p. 108.

Chapter 3

1 George Thomson. *Aeschylus and Athens: A Study in the Social Origins of Drama*. London: Lawrence and Wishart, 1966, p. 1.
2 Ibid.
3 Farrar. *The Origins of Democratic Thinking*, p. 30.
4 Stoessl. 'Aeschylus as a political thinker', 114.
5 Thomson. *Aeschylus and Athens*, p. 2.
6 Id., p. 4.
7 Thomas G. Rosenmeyer. *The Art of Aeschylus*. Berkeley: University of California Press, 1982, p. 2.
8 Robert Holmes Beck. *Aeschylus: Playwright Educator*. The Hague: Martinus Nijhoff, 1975, p. 6.
9 See Athony J. Podlecki. *The Political Background of Aeschylean Tragedy*. Ann Arbor: The University of Michigan Press, 1966.
10 John Herington. *Aeschylus*. New Haven and London: Yale University Press, 1986, p. 17.
11 Ibid.
12 Podlecki. *The Political Background of Aeschylean Tragedy*, p. 5.
13 A. F. Garvie. *The Plays of Aeschylus*. London: Bristol Classical Press, 2010, p. 7.
14 Podlecki. *The Political Background of Aeschylean Tragedy*, p. 4.
15 Marsh H. McCall, Jr. 'Introduction', in Marsh H. McCall, Jr. (ed.), *Aeschylus: A Collection of Critical Essays*. Englewood Cliffs: Prentice-Hall, 1972, p. 2.
16 Alan H. Sommerstein. *Aeaschylean Tragedy* (2nd edn). London: Duckworth, 2010.
17 Stoessl. 'Aeschylus as a political thinker', 113.
18 Herington. *Aeschylus*, p. 19.

19 Id., pp. 20–1.

20 Id., p. 27.

21 Sommerstein. *Aeaschylean Tragedy*, p. 4.

22 McCall. 'Introduction', p. 2.

23 Stoessl. 'Aeschylus as a political thinker', 121.

24 Sommerstein. *Aeaschylean Tragedy*, p. 9.

25 Thomson. *Aeschylus and Athens*, pp. 213–14.

26 Id., p. 215.

27 Beck. *Aeschylus: Playwright Educator*, pp. 37–8.

28 Sommerstein. *Aeaschylean Tragedy*, p. 299.

29 Id., p. 300.

30 McCall. 'Introduction', p. 1.

31 Stoessl. 'Aeschylus as a political thinker', 139.

32 Else. *The Origin and Early Form of Greek Tragedy*, p. 81.

33 Ibid.; Hebert Weir Smyth. *Aeschylean Tragedy*. New York: Biblo and Tannen, 1969, 9, 10.

34 Else. *The Origin and Early Form of Greek Tragedy*, p. 85.

35 Weir Smyth. *Aeschylean Tragedy*, p. 8.

36 Id., pp. 8–9.

37 Garvie. *The Plays of Aeschylus*, p. 7.

38 Sommerstein. *Aeaschylean Tragedy*, pp. 4–5.

39 Louis Spatz. *Aeschylus*. Boston: Twayne, 1982, p. 2.

40 Herington. *Aeschylus*, p. 16.

41 Spatz. *Aeschylus*, p. 1.

42 Herington. *Aeschylus*, pp. 30–1.

43 S. Ireland. *Aeschylus*. Oxford: Clarendon Press, 1986, p. 6.

44 Id., p. 5.

45 A. F. Garvie. *Aeschylus' Supplices: Play and Trilogy*. Cambridge: Cambridge University Press, 1969.

46 Ireland. *Aeschylus*, p. 6.

47 Sommerstein. *Aeaschylean Tragedy*, p. 281.

48 Ibid.

49 Herington. *Aeschylus*, pp. 12–13.

50 Raphael. *The Paradox of Tragedy*, p. 77.

51 Stoessl. 'Aeschylus as a political thinker', 138.

52 Ibid.

53 Weir Smyth. *Aeschylean Tragedy*, p. 36.

54 Aeschylus. trans. Peter Burian. *The Suppliants*. Princeton: Princeton University Press, 1991, p. xxii.

55 Beck. *Aeschylus*, p. 3.
56 Herington. *Aeschylus*, p. 11.

Chapter 4

1 Weir Smyth. *Aeschylean Tragedy*, pp. 10–11.
2 Id., p. 43.
3 Chad Turner. 'Perverted supplication and other inversions in Aeschylus' Danaid trilogy'. *The Classical Journal* 97.1 (2001).
4 Aeschylus. trans. Janet Lembke. *Suppliants*. New York and London: Oxford University Press, 1975, pp. 7–11ff.
5 Janet Lembke. 'Introduction', in Aeschylus. *Suppliants*, p. 7.
6 See Weir Smyth. *Aeschylean Tragedy*, pp. 43–5; R. P. Winnington-Ingram. 'The Danaid trilogy of Aeschylus'. *The Journal of Hellenic Studies* 81 (1961).
7 Turner. 'Perverted supplication and other inversions in Aeschylus' Danaid trilogy', 36–7.
8 Garvie. *Aeschylus' Supplices*, p. 88.
9 Danaus in Aeschylus. *Suppliants*, pp. 247–50ff.
10 Pelasgus in Aeschylus. *Suppliants*, pp. 291–5ff.
11 Danaus in Aeschylus. *Suppliants*, pp. 203–4ff.
12 Podlecki. *The Political Background of Aeschylean Tragedy*, pp. 50–1.
13 Egyptian Herald in Aeschylus. *Suppliants*, pp. 1130–5ff.
14 Pelasgus in Aeschylus. *Suppliants*, pp. 299–303ff.
15 Peter Burian. 'Introduction', in Aeschylus. trans. Peter Burian. *The Suppliants*. Princeton: Princeton University Press, 1991, p. xi.
16 Halfchorus in Aeschylus. *Suppliants*, pp. 1040–53ff.
17 Suppliants in Aeschylus. *Suppliants*, pp. 26–7ff.
18 Pelasgus in Aeschylus. *Suppliants*, p. 303ff.
19 Suppliants in Aeschylus. *Suppliants*, pp. 491–6ff.
20 Farrar. *The Origins of Democratic Thinking*, pp. 31–2.
21 Meier. *The Political Art of Greek Tragedy*, p. 85.
22 Suppliants in Aeschylus. *Suppliants*, pp. 461–6ff.
23 Suppliants in Aeschylus. *Suppliants*, 603, 605, 607ff.
24 This is further demonstrated by the Egyptian Herald, who forcefully seeks the Suppliants return without any empathy for why they fled in the first place. He seeks what is lost from his city, and is mindless to all else.
25 Pelasgus in Aeschylus. *Suppliants*, pp. 319–26ff.
26 Danaus in Aeschylus. *Suppliants*, pp. 825–38ff.

27   Pelasgus in Aeschylus. *Suppliants*, p. 608ff.

28   Pelasgus in Aeschylus. *Suppliants*, p. 617ff.

29   Stoessl. 'Aeschylus as a political thinker', 122–3.

30   Pelasgus in Aeschylus. *Suppliants*, pp. 619–22ff.

31   Turner. 'Perverted supplication and other inversions in Aeschylus' Danaid
     trilogy', 32.

32   Meier. *The Political Art of Greek Tragedy*, p. 96.

33   Pelasgus in Aeschylus. *Suppliants*, pp. 472–5ff.

34   Pelasgus in Aeschylus. *Suppliants*, 500–4, 508ff.

35   Podlecki. *The Political Background of Aeschylean Tragedy*, p. 50.

36   Ibid.

37   Meier. *The Political Art of Greek Tragedy*, 92–3, 96.

38   Meier. *The Political Art of Greek Tragedy*, p. 78; J. L. O'Neil. 'The exile of Themis-
     tokles and democracy in the Peloponnese'. *The Classical Quarterly* 31.2 (1981),
     335; W. G. Forrest. 'Themistokles and Argos'. *The Classical Quarterly* 10.2
     (1960), 221, 226; Donald Kagan. 'The origin and purpose of ostracism'. *Hes-
     peria* 30.4 (1961), 401; Jennifer Tolbert Roberts. *Athens on Trial: The Antide-
     mocratic Tradition in Western Thought*. Princeton: Princeton University Press,
     1994, p. 143.

39   Rudi Thomsen. *The Origin of Ostracism: A Synthesis*. Copenhagen: Gyldendal,
     1972, p. 11.

40   Kagan. 'The origin and purpose of ostracism', 398.

41   Id., 400.

42   Forsdyke. *Exile, Ostracism, and Democracy*, 9, 144.

43   Id., pp. 232–5.

44   Id., p. 236; Meier. *The Political Art of Greek Tragedy*, p. 79.

45   Meier. *The Political Art of Greek Tragedy*, p. 79.

46   Id., p. 80.

47   Podlecki. *The Political Background of Aeschylean Tragedy*, p. 52; Thucydides. trans.
     Richard Crawley and intro. Lorna Harwick, *The History of the Peloponnesian War*.
     Ware: Wordsworth Editions, 1997, pp. 1.135–6.

48   Forrest. 'Themistokles and Argos', 236.

49   Id., 226–7.

50   Id., 222–36; O'Neil. 'The exile of Themistokles and democracy in the Peloponnese',
     342.

51   Thucydides. *The History of the Peloponnesian War*, p. 1.135.

52   Ibid.

53   O'Neil. 'The exile of Themistokles and democracy in the Peloponnese', 335.

54   Thucydides. *The History of the Peloponnesian War*, p. 1.136.

55 Farrar. *The Origins of Democratic Thinking*, pp. 30–1; Forrest. 'Themistokles and Argos', 239; Garvie. *Aeschylus' Supplices*, p. 144; Lembke. 'Introduction', p. 4; Meier. *The Political Art of Greek Tragedy*, p. 83; Podlecki. *The Political Background of Aeschylean Tragedy*, 42–3, 60–1.

56 Meier. *The Political Art of Greek Tragedy*, p. 84; Podlecki. *The Political Background of Aeschylean Tragedy*, pp. 49–50.

57 Meier. *The Political Art of Greek Tragedy*, p. 3.

58 Forrest. 'Themistokles and Argos', 236; Garvie. *Aeschylus' Supplices*, p. 141.

59 G. Zuntz cited in Garvie. *Aeschylus' Supplices*, p. 141.

60 Farrar. *The Origins of Democratic Thinking*, p. 37.

61 Podlecki. *The Political Background of Aeschylean Tragedy*, p. 56.

62 Forrest. 'Themistokles and Argos', 240.

63 Aeschylus. *Suppliants*, 365, 397, 517, 601, 605, 739, 942, 963ff.

64 Forrest. 'Themistokles and Argos', 239; Garvie. *Aeschylus' Supplices*, p. 153.

65 Turner. 'Perverted supplication and other inversions in Aeschylus' Danaid trilogy', 42.

66 Ibid.

Chapter 5

1 Savas Patsalidis. 'Charles Mee's intertextual and intercultural inscriptions: *The Suppliants* vs *Big Love*', in Barbara Ozieblo and Maria Dolores Narbona-Carrion (eds), *Codifying the National Self: Spectators, Actors and the American Dramatic Text*. Brussels: PIE-Peter Lang, 2006, p. 105.

2 Charles Mee cited in Michael Bigelow Dixon. 'Big Love'. *Actor Theatre's Subscriber Newsletter* 2000. Actors Theatre of Louisville. http://actorstheatre.org/HUMANA%20FESTIVAL%20CDROM/tragedy_love.htm.

3 Charles Mee. 'Notes toward a Manifesto 2002', in *Big Love*. Theatre at University of British Columbia Companion Guide.

4 Charles L. Mee. 'I like to take a Greek tragedy'. *Theatre Journal* 59.3 (2007), 361.

5 Patsalidis. 'Charles Mee's intertextual and intercultural inscriptions', p. 111.

6 Signature Theatre. 'Getting to Know Mee'. *Signature Edition* July 2008. http://signaturetheatre.org/0708/iphigenia_2.htm.

7 Monaghan. 'Managerialism meets Dionysos'.

8 Erin B. Mee. 'Shattered and fucked up and full of wreckage: The words and works of Charles L. Mee'. *The Drama Review* 46.3 (2002), 86–7.

9 Mee, 'What I like'.

10 Charles L. Mee. *Big Love. The (Re)making Project*, p. 14. http://www.charlesmee.org/html/big_love.html.

11 Ibid.

12 Id., p. 18.

13 Ibid.

14 Rush Rehm. '*Supplices*, the satyr play: Charles Mee's *Big Love*'. *The American Journal of Philology* 123.1 (2002), 116.

15 Mee. *Big Love*, p. 43.

16 Ibid.

17 Ibid., pp. 43–4.

18 Mee does, however, see the chorus as important, noting it 'is like the crowd of people on the street in the evening television news. The television reporter puts the microphone first in front of each person and then another. The first person says what she thinks, the second person says what he thinks. Taken together, this is the voice of the community'. Mee. 'I like to take a Greek tragedy', 362.

19 Catherine Scott Burriss. 'Performance review: Big Love'. *Theatre Journal* 54.1 (2002), 151.

20 Mee. *Big Love*, pp. 55–9.

21 Id., p. 58.

22 Ibid.

23 Id., p. 59.

24 Mendelsohn. 'The Greek way', p. 345.

25 Mee. *Big Love*, p. 24.

26 Id., p. 23.

27 Id., p. 24.

28 Ibid.

29 Id., 40, 41–2.

30 Id., pp. 58–9.

31 Mee. 'I like to take a Greek tragedy', 362.

32 Kara Reilly. 'A collage reality (re)made: The postmodern dramaturgy of Charles L. Mee'. *American Drama* 14.2 (2000), 60.

33 Timberlake Wertenbaker. 'The voices we hear', in Hall, Macintosh and Wrigley (eds), *Dionysus since 69*, p. 366.

34 Hall. *Inventing the Barbarian*, p. 101.

35 Zygmunt Bauman. *Modernity and the Holocaust*. Ithaca: Cornell University Press, 1989, p. 12.

36 John Keane. *Violence and Democracy*. Cambridge: Cambridge University Press, 2004, 52, 66; Christina Rojas. Foreword. Michael J. Shapiro. *Civilization and Violence: Regimes of Representation in Nineteenth-Century Colombia*. Minneapolis: University of Minnesota Press, 2002, xiii, 165.

37 Keane. *Violence and Democracy*, p. 52.

38 Bauman. *Modernity and the Holocaust*, p. 66.
39 Richard Devetak. 'Globalization's shadow: An introduction to the globalization of violence', in Richard Devetak and Christopher W. Hughes (eds), *The Globalization of Political Violence: Globalization's Shadow*. Abingdon: Routledge, 2008, p. 11.
40 Michael J. Shapiro. *Violent Cartographies: Mapping Cultures of War*. Minneapolis: University of Minnesota Press, 1997, pp. 2–3.
41 Richard Slotkin. *Regeneration Through Violence: The Mythology of the American Frontier, 1600–1860*. Middletown: Wesleyan University Press, 1973; Michael J. Shapiro. *Methods and Nations: Cultural Governance and the Indigenous Subject*. New York: Routledge, 2004.
42 Shapiro. *Violent Cartographies*, p. 28.
43 Bauman. *Modernity and the Holocaust*, pp. 13–15.
44 Id., p. 28.
45 Keane. *Violence and Democracy*, p. 66.
46 Bernard Wasserstein. *Barbarism and Civilization: A History of Europe in our Time*. Oxford: Oxford University Press, 2007; Kenton Worcester, Sally Avery Bermanzohn and Mark Ungar. 'Introduction: Violence and politics', in Kenton Worcester, Sally Avery Bermanzohn and Mark Ungar (eds), *Violence and Politics: Globalization's Paradox*. New York and London: Routledge, 2002.
47 Richard Rubenstein. *The Cunning of History*. New York: Harper, 1978, p. 91.
48 Chan. The End of Certainty, p. 65.
49 Id., p. 64.
50 Keane. Violence and Democracy, p. 7; Rojas. Civilization and Violence, p. 46.
51 Mee. *Big Love*, p. 49.
52 Id., p. 56.
53 Mee. *Big Love*, pp. 59–60.
54 Mendelsohn. 'The Greek way', p. 343.
55 Keane. *Violence and Democracy*, p. 2; Worcester, Avery Bermanzohn and Ungar. 'Introduction', p. 4.
56 Reilly. 'A collage reality (re)made', 57; Signature Theatre. 'Getting to Know Mee'.
57 Patsalidis. 'Charles Mee's intertextual and intercultural inscriptions', p. 107.
58 Mee. *Big Love*, p. 15.
59 Friedrich Nietzsche. trans. R. J. Hollingdale, *Beyond Good and Evil*. London: Penguin, 1973, p. 34.
60 Schmitt and Donnelly. 'The Bush doctrine'.
61 Michael Dillion and Julian Reid. 'Global liberal governance: Biopolitics, security and war'. *Millennium: Journal of International Studies* 30.1 (2001), 44.
62 Julian Reid. 'War, liberalism, and modernity: The biopolitical provocations of "Empire"'. *Cambridge Review of International Affairs* 17.1 (2004).

63 Id., 66.

64 Ross. *Violent Democracy*, p. 1173.

65 Mendelsohn. 'The Greek way', p. 344.

66 Id., p. 345.

67 Id., p. 346.

68 C. W. Marshall. 'Aeschylus and the Foundation of Mee's *Big Love*'. Theatre at University of British Columbia Companion Guide 24 January – 3 February 2007. Telus Studio Theatre, Vancouver.

Chapter 6

1 Hannah Arendt. *The Human Condition*. Chicago: The University of Chicago Press, 1958, p. 198.

2 See Odysseos. 'Laughing matters', 711–12.

3 James Mayall. 'Democracy and international society'. *International Affairs* 76.1 (2000), 65.

4 Russett. *Grasping the Democratic Peace*, p. 138.

5 Francis Fukuyama. *The End of History and the Last Man*. New York: Avon, 1993, p. xi.

6 Ibid.

7 Id., xi, xii.

8 See, for instance, Hedley Bull. *The Anarchical Society: A Study of Order in World Politics* (2nd edn). Houndmills: Macmillan Press, 1995; Hidemi Suganami. *The Domestic Analogy and World Order Proposals*. Cambridge: Cambridge University Press, 1989; J. D. B. Miller and R. J. Vincent (eds), *Order and Violence: Hedley Bull and International Relations*. Oxford: Clarendon Press, 1990; Tim Dunne. *Inventing International Society: A History of the English School*. London: Macmillan, 1998.

9 Roland Bleiker. 'Order and disorder in world politics', in Alex Bellamy (ed.), *International Society and its Critics*. Oxford: Oxford University Press, 2005, p. 179.

10 Roland Bleiker. 'Visualizing post-national democracy', in David Campbell and Morton Schoolman (eds), *The New Pluralism: William Connolly and the Contemporary Global Condition*. Durham: Duke University Press, 2008, p. 137; Raymond Aron cited in Rengger. *International Relations, Political Theory and the Problem of Order*, pp. 17–18; Randall L. Schweller. 'The problem of international order revisited'. *International Security* 26.1 (2001).

11 Fairfield. 'A modest phenomenology of democratic speech'. 373.

12 Thomas Docherty. *Aesthetic Democracy*. Stanford: Stanford University Press, 2006, p. xviii.

13 Derek W. M. Barker. *Tragedy and Citizenship: Conflict, Reconciliation, and Democracy from Haemon to Hegel*. Albany: State University of New York Press, 2009, p. 4.

14 Id., pp. 4–5.

15 Howard Stein. 'Theater as a humanizing force'. *Arion: A Journal of Humanities and the Classics* 16.3 (2009), 177.

16 Bull. *The Anarchical Society*, p. xv.

17 See Max Singer and Aaron Wildavsky. *The Real World Order: Zones of Peace/Zones of Turmoil*. Chatham: Chatham House, 1993; Robert D. Kaplan. 'The coming anarchy'. *The Atlantic Monthly* February (1994).

18 Bleiker. 'Order and disorder in world politics', p. 188.

19 Bleiker. 'Visualizing post-national democracy', p. 137.

20 Richard Devetak. 'Violence, order, and terror', in Bellamy (ed.), *International Society and its Critics*, p. 236.

21 R. B. J. Walker. *One World, Many Worlds: Struggles for a Just World Peace*. Boulder: Lynne Rienner, 1988, p. 166.

22 Barker. *Tragedy and Citizenship*, p. 3.

23 Docherty. *Aesthetic Democracy*, p. xvii.

24 Id., p. 113.

25 Anna M. Agathangelou and L. H. M. Ling. 'Fiction as method/method as fiction: Stories and storytelling in the social sciences'. *International Affairs Working Paper 2005-5*. Graduate Programme in International Affairs. The New School. http://www.gpia.info/files/u1/wp/2005-05.pdf.

26 Roland Bleiker. 'Learning from art: A reply to Holden's "World Literature and World Politics"'. *Global Society* 17.4 (2003), 418.

27 Alex Danchev and Debbie Lisle. 'Introduction: Art, politics, purpose'. *Review of International Studies* 35.4 (2009), 776.

28 Hans J. Morgenthau. revised. Kenneth W. Thompson. *Politics Among Nations: The Struggle for Power and Peace*. New York: McGraw-Hill, 1985.

29 Joel H. Rosenthal. *Righteous Realists: Political Realism, Responsible Power, and American Culture in the Nuclear Age*. Baton Rouge: Louisiana State University Press, 1991, p. 1.

30 Morgenthau. *Politics Among Nations*, p. 3.

31 Damon Young. 'On fiction and philosophy'. *Meanjin* 67.4 (2008), 122.

32 James Der Derian cited in Roland Bleiker. 'The aesthetic turn in international relations political theory'. *Millennium: Journal of International Studies* 30.3 (2001), 531.

33 Cynthia Weber. *International Relations Theory: A Critical Introduction* (2nd edn). London: Routledge, 2001.

34 Id., p. 185.

35 Id., p. 186.

36 Elsewhere, on a related note, Chan has also made the case that international relations needs to be more mindful of narratology, that is, 'the methodology by which we might "recognise" a story'. See Stephen Chan. 'A problem for IR: How shall we narrate the saga of the bestial man'. *Global Society* 17.4 (2003).

37 Chan. *The End of Certainty*, p. ix.

38 Hayward R. Alker. *Rediscoveries and Reformulations: Humanistic Methodologies for International Studies*. Cambridge: Cambridge University Press, 1996, p. 298.

39 See, for instance, Azar Nafisi. *Reading Lolita in Tehran: A Memoir in Books*. Sydney: Hodder, 2003, p. 25–6.

40 Agathangelou and Ling. 'Fiction as method/method as fiction', 11.

41 Elspeth Van Veeren. 'Interrogating *24*: Making sense of US counter-terrorism in the global war on terrorism'. *New Political Science* 31.3 (2009), 365.

42 Agathangelous and Ling. 'Fiction as method/method as fiction', 12.

43 Martha C. Nussbaum. *Poetic Justice: The Literary Imagination and Public Life*. Boston: Beacon Press, 1995, p. xiii.

44 Id., p. xvi.

Bibliography

Aeschylus. trans. Janet Lembke (1975), *The Suppliants*. New York and London: Oxford University Press.

Aeschylus. trans. Peter Burian (1991), *The Suppliants*. Princeton: Princeton University Press.

Agard, Walter R. (1942), *What Democracy Meant to the Greeks*. Chapel Hill: The University of North Carolina Press.

Agathangelou, Anna M. and L. H. M. Ling, 'Fiction as method/method as fiction: Stories and storytelling in the social sciences'. *International Affairs Working Paper 2005-5*. Graduate Programme in International Affairs. The New School. http://www.gpia.info/files/u1/wp/2005-05.pdf.

Alker, Hayward R. (1996), *Rediscoveries and Reformulations: Humanistic Methodologies for International Studies*. Cambridge: Cambridge University Press.

Allan, William (2005), 'Tragedy and the early Greek philosophical tradition', in Justina Gregory (ed.), *A Companion to Greek Tragedy*. Malden: Blackwell Publishing.

Anderson, Greg (2003), *The Athenian Experiment: Building an Imagined Political Community in Ancient Attica 508–490 BC*. Ann Arbor: The University of Michigan Press.

Archibugi, Daniele and David Held (eds) (1995), *Cosmopolitan Democracy: An Agenda for a New World Order*. Cambridge: Polity Press.

Archibugi, Daniele, David Held and Martin Kohler (1996), 'Introduction', in Daniele Archibugi, David Held and Martin Kohler (eds), *Re-imagining Political Community: Studies in Cosmopolitan Democracy*. Cambridge: Polity Press.

Arendt, Hannah (1958), *The Human Condition*. Chicago: The University of Chicago Press.

Aristotle. ed. and trans. Stephen Halliwell (1995), *Poetics*. Cambridge: Harvard University Press.

Aylen, Leo (1964), *Greek Tragedy and the Modern World*. London: Methuen.

Baldry, H. C. (1965), *The Unity of Mankind in Greek Thought*. Cambridge: Cambridge University Press.

Barker, Derek W. M. (2009), *Tragedy and Citizenship: Conflict, Reconciliation, and Democracy from Haemon to Hegel*. Albany: State University of New York Press.

Barrow, Robin (1973), *Athenian Democracy: The Triumph and the Folly*. Houndmills: Macmillan.

Barthes, Roland (1981), 'Theory of the text', in Robert Young ed. and intro., *Untying the Text: A Post-Structuralist Reader*. Boston: Routledge and Kegan Paul.

— (1981), 'Textual analysis of Poe's "Valdemar"', in Robert Young ed. and intro., *Untying the Text: A Post-Structuralist Reader*. Boston: Routledge and Kegan Paul.

Bauman, Zygmunt (1989), *Modernity and the Holocaust*. Ithaca: Cornell University Press.

— (2000), *Liquid Modernity*. Cambridge: Polity Press.

Beardsworth, Richard (2008), 'Tragedy, world politics and ethical community'. *International Relations* 22.1.

Beck, Martha C. (2006), *Tragedy and the Philosophical Life: A Response to Martha Nussbaum*. Lewiston: E. Mellen Press.

Benitez, Eugenio (2007), 'Philosophy, myth and Plato's two-worlds view'. *The European Legacy* 12.2.

Berlin, Isaiah. (ed.) Henry Hardy (1999), *The Roots of Romanticism*. Princeton: Princeton University Press.

Bigelow Dixon, Michael (2000), 'Big Love'. *Actor Theatre's Subscriber Newsletter 2000*. Actors Theatre of Louisville. http://actorstheatre.org/HUMANA%20FESTIVAL%20CDROM/tragedy_love.htm.

Bird, Carmel (2009), 'East of the sun and west of the moon: Fiction and the imagination. *Griffith Review* 26.

Blanshard, Alastair (2005), *Hercules: A Heroic Life*. London: Granta.

Bleiker, Roland (2000), *Popular Dissent, Human Agency and Global Politics*. Cambridge: Cambridge University Press.

— (2001), 'The aesthetic turn in international relations political theory'. *Millennium: Journal of International Studies* 30.3.

— (2003), 'Learning from art: A reply to Holden's "World Literature and World Politics"'. *Global Society* 17.4.

— (2005), 'Order and disorder in world politics', in Alex Bellamy (ed.), *International Society and its Critics*. Oxford: Oxford University Press.

— (2008), 'Visualizing post-national democracy', in David Campbell and Morton Schoolman (eds), *The New Pluralism: William Connolly and the Contemporary Global Condition*. Durham: Duke University Press.

Boedeker, Deborah and Kurt Raaflaub (2005), 'Tragedy and city', in Rebecca Bushnell (ed.), *A Companion to Tragedy*. Malden: Blackwell.

Bonner, Robert J. (1967), *Aspects of Athenian Democracy*. New York: Russell & Russell.

Braun, R. E. trans. (1973), *Sophocles: Antigone*. London: Oxford University Press.

Brown, A. ed. and trans. (1987), *Sophocles: Antigone*. Warminster: Aris and Phillips.

Brown, Chris (2007), 'Tragedy, "tragic choices" and contemporary international political theory'. *International Relations* 21.1.

Bull, Hedley (1995), *The Anarchical Society: A Study of Order in World Politics* (2nd edn). Houndmills: Macmillan Press.

Burian, Peter (1991), 'Introduction', in Aeschylus. trans. Peter Burian, *The Suppliants*. Princeton: Princeton University Press.

Calame, Claude. trans. Janice Orion. preface. Jean-Claude Coquet (1995), *The Craft of Poetic Speech in Ancient Greece*. Ithaca: Cornell University Press.

— (1999), 'Performative aspects of the choral voice in Greek tragedy: Civic identity in performance', in Simon Goldhill and Robin Osborne (eds), *Performance Culture and Athenian Democracy*. Cambridge: Cambridge University Press.

Camus, Albert (1967), 'Helen's exile', in Albert Camus. trans. Justin O'Brien, *The Myth of Sisyphus and Other Essays*. New York: Alfred A. Knopf.

— (1970), 'Lecture given in Athens on the future of tragedy', in Albert Camus. ed. and trans. Philip Thody, *Selected Essays and Notebooks*. Harmondsworth: Penguin.

Cartledge, Paul (1997), ' "Deep plays": Theatre as process in Athenian civic life', in P. E. Easterling (ed.), *The Cambridge Companion to Greek Tragedy*. Cambridge: Cambridge University Press.

— (2007), 'Democracy, origins of: Contribution to a debate', in Kurt A. Raaflaub, Josiah Ober and Robert W. Wallace (with Paul Cartledge and Cynthia Farrar), *Origins of Democracy in Ancient Greece*. Berkeley: University of California Press.

Castoriadis, Cornelius. trans. Kathleen Blamey (1987), *The Imaginary Institution of Society*. Cambridge: Polity Press.

— (1991), 'The 'end of philosophy'?', in Cornelius Castoriadis. (ed.) David Ames Curtis, *Philosophy, Politics, Autonomy*. New York: Oxford University Press.

— (1991), 'Power, politics, autonomy', in Cornelius Castoriadis. (ed.) David Ames Curtis, *Philosophy, Politics, Autonomy*. New York: Oxford University Press.

— (1996), 'The Athenian democracy: False and true questions, in Pierre Leveque and Pierre Vidal-Naquet. trans. and ed. David Ames Curtis, *Cleisthenes the Athenian: An Essay on the Representation of Space and Time in Greek Political Thought from the End of the Sixth Century to the Death of Plato*. New Jersey: Humanities Press.

— (1997), 'The Greek polis and the creation of democracy', in Cornelius Castoriadis. trans. and ed. David Ames Curtis, *The Castoriadis Reader*. Oxford: Basil Blackwell.

Chambers, Mortimer (1961), 'Aristotle's "forms of democracy"'. *Transactions and Proceedings of the American Philological Association* 92.

Chan, Stephen (1999), 'Typologies toward an unchained medley: Against the gentrification of discourse in international relations', in Vivienne Jabri and Eleanor O'Gorman (eds), *Women, Culture and International Relations*. Boulder: Lynne Rienner.

— (2003), 'A problem for IR: How shall we narrate the saga of the bestial man'. *Global Society* 17.4.

— (2003), 'A new triptych for international relations in the 21st century: Beyond waltz and beyond Lacan's Antigone, with a note on the Falun Gong of China'. *Global Society* 17.2.

— (2009), *The End of Certainty: Towards a New Internationalism*. London and New York: Zed Books.

Chayut, Michael (1999), 'Tragedy and science'. *History of European Ideas* 25.4.

Constantinou, Costas M. (1996), *On the Way to Diplomacy*. Minneapolis: University of
   Minnesota Press.
— (2004), *States of Political Discourse: Words, Regimes, Seditions*. London and New
   York: Routledge.
— (2006), 'The beautiful nation: Reflections on the aesthetics of Hellenism'. *Alternatives:
   Global, Local, Political* 31.1.
Crick, Bernard (1998), 'A meditation on democracy', in Takashi Inoguchi, Edward
   Newman and John Keane (eds), *The Changing Nature of Democracy*. Tokyo: United
   Nations University Press.
Csapo, Eric and William J. Slater (1994), *The Context of Ancient Drama*. Ann Arbor:
   The University of Michigan Press.
Curtis, David Ames (1991), 'Preface', in Cornelius Castoriadis. (ed.) David Ames Curtis,
   Philosophy, Politics, Autonomy. New York: Oxford University Press.
— (1996), 'Translator's foreword', in Pierre Leveque and Pierre Vidal-Naquet. trans. and
   ed. David Ames Curtis, *Cleisthenes the Athenian: An Essay on the Representation of
   Space and Time in Greek Political Thought from the End of the Sixth Century to the
   Death of Plato*. New Jersey: Humanities Press.
Curtis, Neal (2007), 'Tragedy and Politics'. *Philosophy and Social Criticism* 33.7.
Danchev, Alex (2008), 'Princes and players: From a play banned in Athens to Samuel
   Beckett in Sarajevo – Why theatre still matters'. *The Times Literary Supplement* 31
   December. http://entertainment.timesonline.co.uk/tol/arts_and_entertainment/
   the_tls/article5423443.ece.
Danchev, Alex and Debbie Lisle (2009), 'Introduction: Art, politics, purpose'. *Review of
   International Studies* 35.4.
Descamps, Christian (1996), 'Introduction', in Pierre Leveque and Pierre Vidal-Naquet.
   trans. and ed. David Ames Curtis, *Cleisthenes the Athenian: An Essay on the
   Representation of Space and Time in Greek Political Thought from the End of the Sixth
   Century to the Death of Plato*. New Jersey: Humanities Press.
Devetak, Richard (2005), 'Violence, order, and terror', in Alex Bellamy (ed.),
   International Society and its Critics. Oxford: Oxford University Press.
— (2008), 'Globalization's shadow: An introduction to the globalization of violence', in
   Richard Devetak and Christopher W. Hughes (eds), *The Globalization of Political
   Violence: Globalization's Shadow*. Abingdon: Routledge.
Dillion, Michael and Julian Reid (2001), 'Global liberal governance: Biopolitics, security
   and war'. *Millennium: Journal of International Studies* 30.1.
Docherty, Thomas (2006), *Aesthetic Democracy*. Stanford: Stanford University Press.
Doyle, Michael W. (1983), 'Kant, liberal legacies, and foreign affairs'. Parts 1 and 2.
   Philosophy and Public Affairs 12.3–4.
Dryzek, John S. (1999), 'Transnational democracy'. *The Journal of Political Philosophy* 7.1.
— (2000), *Deliberative Democracy and Beyond: Liberals, Critics, Contestations*. Oxford:
   Oxford University Press.

— (2006), *Deliberative Global Politics: Discourse and Democracy in a Divided World.* Cambridge: Polity.

duBois, Page (2004), 'Toppling the hero: Polyphony in the tragic city'. *New Literary History* 35.1.

Dunne, Tim (1998), *Inventing International Society: A History of the English School.* London: Macmillan.

Easterling, P. E. (1993), 'The end of an era? Tragedy in the early fourth century', in Alan H Sommerstein, Stephan Halliwell, Jeffrey Henderson and Bernhard Zimmermann (eds), *Tragedy, Comedy and the Polis: Papers from the Greek Drama Conference.* Bari: Levante Editori.

Ebbott, Mary (2005), 'Marginal figures', in Justina Gregory (ed.), *A Companion to Greek Tragedy.* Malden: Blackwell.

Else, Gerald F. (1972), *The Origin and Early Form of Greek Tragedy.* New York: W.W. Norton and Co.

Euben, J. Peter (1986), 'Introduction', in J. Peter Euben (ed.), *Greek Tragedy and Political Theory.* Berkeley: University of California Press.

— (1990), *The Tragedy of Political Theory: The Road Not Taken.* Princeton: Princeton University Press.

— (1993), 'Democracy ancient and modern'. *PS: Political Science and Politics* 26.3.

— (2001), 'The polis, globalization, and the politics of place', in Aryeh Botwinick and William E. Connolly (eds), *Democracy and Vision: Sheldon Wolin and the Vicissitudes of the Political.* Princeton and Oxford: Princeton University Press.

— (2007), 'The tragedy of tragedy'. *International Relations* 21.1.

Fairfield, Paul (2005), 'A modest phenomenology of democratic speech'. *The European Legacy* 10.4.

Farrar, Cynthia (1988), *The Origins of Democratic Thinking: The Invention of Politics in Classical Athens.* Cambridge: Cambridge University Press.

— (2007), 'Power to the people', in Kurt A. Raaflaub, Josiah Ober and Robert W. Wallace (with Paul Cartledge and Cynthia Farrar), *Origins of Democracy in Ancient Greece.* Berkeley: University of California Press.

Felski, Rita (2008), 'Introduction', in Rita Felski (ed.), *Rethinking Tragedy.* Baltimore: Johns Hopkins University Press.

Figes, Eva (1976), *Tragedy and Social Revolution.* London: John Calder.

Finley, M. I. (1963), *The Ancient Greeks.* Harmondsworth: Penguin.

Finney, Gail (2005), 'Modern theater and the tragic in Europe', in Rebecca Bushnell (ed.), *A Companion to Tragedy.* Malden: Blackwell.

Fiske, John (1987), *Television Culture.* London: Routledge.

Flickinger, Roy (1922), *The Greek Theater and its Drama.* Chicago: Chicago University Press.

Foa Dienstag, Joshua (2004), 'Tragedy, pessimism, Nietzsche'. *New Literary History* 35.1.

Foley, Helene (1995), 'Tragedy and democratic ideology: The case of Sophocles' Antigone', in Barbara Goff. ed. and intro., *History, Tragedy, Theory: Dialogues on Athenian Drama*. Austin: University of Texas Press.

Forrest, W. G. (1960), 'Themistokles and Argos'. *The Classical Quarterly* 10.2.

Forsdyke, Sara (2005), *Exile, Ostracism, and Democracy: The Politics of Expulsion in Ancient Greece*. Princeton: Princeton University Press.

Fritsch, Matthias (2002), 'Derrida's democracy to come'. *Constellations: An International Journal of Critical and Democratic Theory* 9.4.

Frost, Mervyn (2003), 'Tragedy, ethics and international relations'. *International Relations* 17.4.

— (2008), 'Tragedy, reconciliation and reconstruction'. *European Journal of Social Theory* 11.3.

Fukuyama, Francis (1993), *The End of History and the Last Man*. New York: Avon.

Gadamer, Hans-Georg. trans. and intro. P. Christopher Smith (1980), *Dialogue and Dialectic: Eight Hermeneutical Studies on Plato*. New Haven: Yale University Press.

Gambino, Giacomo (1996), 'Nietzsche and the Greeks: Identity, politics, and tragedy'. *Polity* 28.4.

Garvie, A. F. (1969), *Aeschylus' Supplices: Play and Trilogy*. Cambridge: Cambridge University Press.

— (2010), *The Plays of Aeschylus*. London: Bristol Classical Press.

Gellrich, Michelle (1995), 'Interpreting Greek tragedy: History, theory and the new philology', in Barbara Goff ed. and intro., *History, Tragedy, Theory: Dialogues on Athenian Drama*. Austin: University of Texas Press.

George, Jim (1994), *Discourses of Global Politics: A Critical (Re)Introduction to International Relations*. Boulder: Lynne Rienner.

Geuss, Raymond (1999), 'Introduction', in Nietzsche, Friedrich. Raymond Geuss and Ronald Speirs (eds) *The Birth of Tragedy and Other Writings*. Cambridge: Cambridge University Press.

Goff, Barbara (1995), 'Introduction: History, tragedy, theory', in Barbara Goff ed. and intro., *History, Tragedy, Theory: Dialogues on Athenian Drama*. Austin: University of Texas Press.

Goldhill, Simon (1990), 'The great Dionysia and civic ideology', in John J. Winkler and Froma I. Zeitlin (eds), *Nothing to Do with Dionysos? Athenian Drama in Its Social Context*. Princeton: Princeton University Press.

— (1996), *Reading Greek Tragedy*. Cambridge: Cambridge University Press.

— (1997), 'The audience in Athenian tragedy', in P. E. Easterling (ed.), *The Cambridge Companion to Greek Tragedy*. Cambridge: Cambridge University Press.

Gouldner, Alvin W. (1965), *Enter Plato: Classical Greece and the Origins of Social Theory*. London: Routledge and Kegan Paul.

Graham, Daniel W. (2006), *Explaining the Cosmos: The Ionian Tradition of Scientific Philosophy*. Princeton and Oxford: Princeton University Press.

Grenville, Kate (2009), 'The writer in a time of change: Learning from experience'. *Griffith Review* 26.

Griffin, Jasper (1998), 'The social function of attic tragedy'. *The Classical Quarterly* 48.1.

Groffman, Bernard (1993), 'Lessons of Athenian democracy: Editor's introduction'. *PS: Political Science and Politics* 26.3.

Grugel, Jean (ed.) (1999), *Democracy without Borders: Transnationalization and Conditionality in New Democracies*. London and New York: Routledge.

Hall, Edith (1989), *Inventing the Barbarian: Greek Self-Definition through Tragedy*. Oxford: Clarendon Press.

— (1997), 'The sociology of Athenian tragedy', in P. E. Easterling (ed.), *The Cambridge Companion to Greek Tragedy*. Cambridge: Cambridge University Press.

— (2004), 'Why Greek tragedy in the late twentieth century?', in Edith Hall, Fiona Macintosh and Amanda Wrigley (eds), *Dionysus since 69: Greek Tragedy at the Dawn of the Third Millennium*. Oxford: Oxford University Press.

Halliwell, Stephen (1996), 'Plato's repudiation of the tragic', in M. S. Silk (ed.), *Tragedy and the Tragic: Greek Theatre and Beyond*. Oxford: Clarendon Press.

Hamblet, Wendy C. (2003), 'The tragedy of Platonic ethics and the fall of Socrates'. *Ethics* 2.2.

Hamilton, Edith (1996), *Mythology: Timeless Tales of Gods and Heroes*. New York: A Mentor Book.

Hammond, N. G. L. (1986), *A History of Greece to 322 BC* (3rd edn). Oxford: Clarendon Press.

Hatab, Lawrence J. (1995), *A Nietzschean Defense of Democracy: An Experiment in Postmodern Politics*. Chicago and La Salle: Open Court.

— (2002), 'Prospects for a democratic Agon: Why we can still be Nietzscheans'. *Journal of Nietzsche Studies* 24.1.

Hayles, N. Katherine (1991), 'Introduction: Complex dynamics in literature and science', in N. Katherine Hayles (ed.), *Chaos and Order: Complex Dynamics in Literature and Science*. Chicago: The University of Chicago Press.

Held, David (1998), 'Democracy and globalization', in Daniele Archibugi, David Held and Martin Kohler (eds), *Re-imagining Political Community: Studies in Cosmopolitan Democracy*. Cambridge: Polity Press.

— (2006), *Models of Democracy* (3rd edn). Cambridge: Polity Press.

Herington, John (1986), *Aeschylus*. New Haven and London: Yale University Press.

Hirsh, Michael (2002), 'Bush and the world'. *Foreign Affairs* 81.5.

Holmes Beck, Robert (1975), *Aeschylus: Playwright Educator*. The Hague: Martinus Nijhoff.

Homer-Dixon, Thomas F. (1999), *Environment, Scarcity, and Violence*. Princeton: Princeton University Press.

Huntington, Samuel P. (1996), *The Clash of Civilizations and the Remaking of World Order*. New York: Simon and Schuster.

Ireland, S. (1986), *Aeschylus*. Oxford: Clarendon Press.

Irwin, T. H. (1983), 'Euripides and Socrates'. *Classical Philology* 78.3.

Janover, Michael (2003), 'Mythic form and political reflection in Athenian tragedy'. *Parallax* 9.4.

Jones, Peter V. (1984), *The World of Athens: An Introduction to Classical Athenian Culture*. Cambridge: Cambridge University Press.

Kagan, Donald (1961), 'The origin and purpose of ostracism'. *Hesperia* 30.4.

— (1991), *Pericles of Athens and the Birth of Democracy*. New York: The Free Press.

Kannicht, Richard (1988), *The Ancient Quarrel Between Philosophy and Poetry: Aspects of the Greek Conception of Literature*. Christchurch: University of Canterbury Press.

Kant, Immanuel. trans. J. H. Bernard (1932), *Perpetual Peace*. New York: Columbia University Press.

— (1951), *Critique of Judgment*. New York: Hafner Press.

Kanth, Rajani K. (1997), *Breaking with the Enlightenment: The Twilight of History and the Rediscovery of Utopia*. Atlantic Highlands: Humanities Press.

Kaplan, Robert D. (1994), 'The coming anarchy'. *The Atlantic Monthly* February.

Karagiannis, Nathalie (2006), 'The tragic and the political: A parallel reading of Kostas Papaioannou and Cornelius Castoriadis'. *Critical Horizons* 7.1.

Kaufmann, Walter (1948), 'Nietzsche's admiration for Socrates'. *Journal of the History of Ideas* 9.4.

— (1968), *Tragedy and Philosophy*. Garden City: Doubleday and Company.

Keane, John (2004), *Violence and Democracy*. Cambridge: Cambridge University Press.

— (2009), *The Life and Death of Democracy*. London: Pocket Books.

Kellen, H. M. (1912), 'The essence of tragedy'. *International Journal of Ethics* 22.

Knock, Thomas J. (1992), *To End All Wars: Woodrow Wilson and the Quest for a New World Order*. New York: Oxford University Press.

Kuhn, Helmet (1941), 'The true tragedy: On the relationship between Greek tragedy and Plato, I'. *Harvard Studies in Classical Philology* 52.

Labelle, Gilles (2001), 'Two refoundation projects of democracy in contemporary French philosophy: Cornelius Castoriadis and Jacques Ranciere'. *Philosophy and Social Criticism* 27.4.

Lape, Susan (2004), *Reproducing Athens: Menander's Comedy, Democratic Culture and the Hellenistic City*. Princeton: Princeton University Press.

Lebow, Richard Ned (2003), *The Tragic Vision of Politics: Ethics, Interests and Orders*. Cambridge: Cambridge University Press.

— (2005), 'Tragedy, politics and political science'. *International Relations* 19.3.

Lebow, Richard Ned and Toni Erskine (eds) (2012), *Tragedy and International Relations*. New York and Basingstoke: Palgrave Macmillan.

Ledbetter, Grace M. (2003), *Poetics Before Plato: Interpretation and Authority in Early Greek Theories of Poetry*. Princeton: Princeton University Press.

Lembke, Janet (1975), 'Introduction', in Aeschylus. trans. Janet Lembke, *The Suppliants*. New York and London: Oxford University Press.

Lindsay, James M. (2009), 'The case for a concert of democracies'. *Ethics and International Affairs* 23.1.

Locke, John (1995), *An Essay Concerning Human Understanding*. New York: Prometheus Books.

Lowes Dickinson, G. (1960), *The Greek View of Life*. London: Methuen and Co.

Lloyd, G. E. R. (1970), *Early Greek Science: Thales to Aristotle*. New York: W. W. Norton and Co.

MacIntyre, Alasdair (1985), *After Virtue: A Study in Moral Theory*. London: Duckworth Press.

Maffesoli, Michael. trans. Rita Felski, Allan Megill and Marilyn Gaddis Rose (2008), 'The return of the tragic in postmodern societies', in Rita Felski (ed.), *Rethinking Tragedy*. Baltimore: Johns Hopkins University Press.

Mansfield, Edward G. and Jack Snyder (1995), 'Democratization and war'. *Foreign Affairs* 74.3.

Marshall, C. W. (2007), 'Aeschylus and the foundation of Mee's Big Love'. *Theatre at University of British Columbia Companion Guide 24 January – 3 February 2007*. Telus Studio Theatre, Vancouver.

Mayall, James (2000), 'Democracy and international society'. *International Affairs* 76.1.

McCall, Jr. Marsh H. (1972), 'Introduction', in Marsh H. McCall, Jr. (ed.), *Aeschylus: A Collection of Critical Essays*. Englewood Cliffs: Prentice-Hall.

McKee, Alan (2001), 'A beginner's guide to textual analysis'. *Metro* 127/128.

Mee, Charles L. *Big Love*. The Re(making) Project. http://www.charlesmee.org/html/big_love.html.

— 'What I Like'. The (Re)Making Project. http://www.charlesmee.org/html/charlesMee.html.

— 'Notes toward a Manifesto 2002', in Big Love. *Theatre at University of British Columbia Companion Guide.*

— (2007), 'I like to take a Greek tragedy'. *Theatre Journal* 59.3.

Mee, Erin B. (2002), 'Shattered and fucked up and full of wreckage: The words and works of Charles L. Mee'. *The Drama Review* 46.3.

Meier, Christian. trans. David McLintock (1990), *The Greek Discovery of Politics*. Cambridge: Harvard University Press.

— trans. Andrew Webber (1993), *The Political Art of Greek Tragedy*. Cambridge: Polity Press.

Mendelsohn, Daniel (2008), 'The Greek way', in Daniel Mendelsohn (ed.), *How Beautiful it is and how Easily it can be Broken: Essays*. New York: Harper.

Menke, Christoph (2004), 'The presence of tragedy'. *Critical Horizons* 5.1.

Miller, J. D. B. and R. J. Vincent (eds) (1990), *Order and Violence: Hedley Bull and International Relations*. Oxford: Clarendon Press.

Monaghan, Paul (2005/2006), 'Managerialism meets Dionysos: Theatre and civic order'.
    Double Dialogues 3. http://www.doubledialogues.com/archive/issue_three/mona-
    ghan_two.htm.
Morgenthau, Hans J. revised. Kenneth W. Thompson (1985), *Politics among Nations:*
    The Struggle for Power and Peace. New York: McGraw-Hill.
Mouffe, Chantal (2000), *The Democratic Paradox*. London: Verso.
Moulton, Richard G. (1898), *The Ancient Classical Drama: A Study in Literary Evolution*.
    Oxford: Clarendon Press.
Nafisi, Azar (2003), *Reading Lolita in Tehran: A Memoir in Books*. Sydney: Hodder.
Nietzsche, Friedrich. trans. R. J. Hollingdale (1973), *Beyond Good and Evil*. London:
    Penguin.
— (1983), *Richard Wagner in Beyreuth*. Cambridge: Cambridge University Press.
Nietzsche, Friedrich. (eds) Raymond Geuss and Ronald Speirs (1999), *The Birth of*
    Tragedy and Other Writings. Cambridge: Cambridge University Press.
Nussbaum, Martha C. (1986), *The Fragility of Goodness: Luck and Ethics in Greek*
    Tragedy and Philosophy. Cambridge: Cambridge University Press.
— (1995), *Poetic Justice: The Literary Imagination and Public Life*. Boston: Beacon Press.
Ober, Josiah (1996), *The Athenian Revolution: Essays on Ancient Greek Democracy and*
    Political Culture. Princeton: Princeton University Press.
Ober, Josiah and Barry Strauss (1990), 'Drama, political rhetoric, and the discourse
    of Athenian democracy', in John J. Winkler and Froma I. Zeitlin (eds), *Nothing*
    to Do with Dionysos? Athenian Drama in Its Social Context. Princeton: Princeton
    University Press.
Odysseos, Louiza (2001), 'Laughing matters: Peace, democracy and the challenge of the
    comic narrative'. *Millennium: Journal of International Studies* 30.3.
O'Neil, J. L. (1981), 'The exile of Themistokles and democracy in the Peloponnese'. *The*
    Classical Quarterly 31.2.
Patsalidis, Savas (2006), 'Charles Mee's intertextual and intercultural inscriptions: The
    Suppliants vs Big Love', in Barbara Ozieblo and Maria Dolores Narbona-Carrion
    (eds), *Codifying the National Self: Spectators, Actors and the American Dramatic Text*.
    Brussels: PIE-Peter Lang.
Patton, Paul (2005), 'Deleuze and democracy'. *Contemporary Political Theory* 4.4.
— (2007), 'Derrida, politics and democracy to come'. *Philosophy Compass* 2.6.
Plato. trans. and intro. Francis Macdonald Cornford (1945), *The Republic of Plato*.
    London: Oxford University Press.
Podlecki, Anthony J. (1996), *The Political Background of Aeschylean Tragedy*. Ann
    Arbor: The University of Michigan Press.
Pollitt, J. J. (1972), *Art and Experience in Classical Greece*. Cambridge: Cambridge
    University Press.
Porter, James I. (2000), *The Invention of Dionysus: An Essay on the Birth of Tragedy*.
    Stanford: Stanford University Press.

Pritchard, David M. (ed.) (2009), *War, Culture and Democracy in Classical Athens*. Cambridge: Cambridge University Press.

Raaflaub, Kurt A. (1998), 'Contemporary perceptions of democracy in fifth-century Athens', in Loren J. Samons II. ed. and intro., *Athenian Democracy and Imperialism*. Boston: Houghton Mifflin.

— (2007), 'Introduction', in Kurt A. Raaflaub, Josiah Ober and Robert W. Wallace (with Paul Cartledge and Cynthia Farrar), *Origins of Democracy in Ancient Greece*. Berkeley: University of California Press.

— (2007), 'The breakthrough of demokratia in mid-fifth century Athens', in Kurt A. Raaflaub, Josiah Ober and Robert W. Wallace (with Paul Cartledge and Cynthia Farrar), *Origins of Democracy in Ancient Greece*. Berkeley: University of California Press.

Raphael, D. D. (1960), *The Paradox of Tragedy*. Bloomington: Indiana University Press.

Rehm, Rush (2002), 'Supplices, the satyr play: Charles Mee's Big Love'. *The American Journal of Philology* 123.1.

— (2002), 'Supplices, the satyr play: Charles Mee's Big Love'. *The American Journal of Philology* 123.1.

— (2003), *Radical Theatre: Greek Tragedy and the Modern World*. London: Duckworth.

Reid, Julian (2004), 'War, liberalism, and modernity: The biopolitical provocations of "Empire"'. *Cambridge Review of International Affairs* 17.1.

Reilly, Kara (2000), 'A collage reality (re)made: The postmodern dramaturgy of Charles L. Mee'. *American Drama* 14.2.

Rengger, Nicholas (2000), *International Relations, Political Theory and the Problem of Order: Beyond International Relations Theory?* London and New York: Routledge.

— (2005), 'Tragedy or scepticism? Defending the anti-Pelagian mind in world politics'. *International Relations* 19.3.

Ricoeur, Paul (1988), *Time and Narrative* (Volume 3). Chicago: Chicago University Press.

Ridgeway, William (1910), *The Origin of Tragedy*. Cambridge: Cambridge University Press.

Robinson, Eric W. (2004), 'Ancient Greek democracy: A brief introduction', in Eric W. Robinson (ed.), *Ancient Greek Democracy: Readings and Sources*. Malden: Blackwell.

Rocco, Christopher (1997), *Tragedy and Enlightenment: Athenian Political Thought and the Dilemmas of Modernity*. Berkeley: University of California Press.

Rodewald, Cosmo. ed. and intro. (1974), *Democracy: Ideas and Realities*. London: Dent.

Rojas, Christina. Foreword. Michael J. Shapiro (2002), *Civilization and Violence: Regimes of Representation in Nineteenth-Century Colombia*. Minneapolis: University of Minnesota Press.

Rosenmeyer, Thomas G. (1982), *The Art of Aeschylus*. Berkeley: University of California Press.

Rosenthal, Joel H. (1991), *Righteous Realists: Political Realism, Responsible Power, and American Culture in the Nuclear Age*. Baton Rouge: Louisiana State University Press.

Ross, Daniel (2004), *Violent Democracy*. Cambridge: Cambridge University Press.

Rubenstein, Richard (1978), *The Cunning of History*. New York: Harper.

Russett, Bruce (1993), *Grasping the Democratic Peace: Principles for a Post-Cold War World*. Princeton: Princeton University Press.

— (1998), 'A structure for peace: A democratic, interdependent, and institutionalized order', in Takashi Inoguchi, Edward Newman and John Keane (eds), *The Changing Nature of Democracy*. Tokyo: United Nations University Press,.

Said, Edward W. (2003), *Orientalism*. London: Penguin Books.

Schlesinger, Alfred Cary (1963), *Boundaries of Dionysus: Athenian Foundations for the Theory of Tragedy*. Cambridge: Harvard University Press.

Schmidt, Dennis J. (2001), *On Germans and Other Greeks: Tragedy and Ethical Life*. Bloomington and Indianapolis: Indiana University Press.

Schmitt, G. and T. Donnelly (2002), 'The Bush doctrine'. *Project Memorandum* 30 January. http://www.newamericancentury.org/defense-20020130.htm.

Schoolman, Morton (2001), *Reason and Horror: Critical Theory, Democracy, and Aesthetic Individuality*. New York: Routledge.

Schrager Lang, Amy and Cecelia Tichi (eds) (2006), *What Democracy Looks Like: A New Critical Realism for a Post-Seattle World*. New Brunswick: Rutgers University Press.

Schrift, Alan D. (2000), 'Nietzsche, Foucault, Deleuze, and the subject of radical democracy'. *Aneglaki: Journal of Theoretical Humanities* 5.2.

Schweller, Randall L. (2001), 'The problem of international order revisited'. *International Security* 26.1.

Scott, David (2008), 'Tragedy's time: Postemancipation futures past and present', in Rita Felski (ed.), *Rethinking Tragedy*. Baltimore: Johns Hopkins University Press.

Scott Burriss, Catherine (2002), 'Performance review: Big Love'. *Theatre Journal* 54.1.

Segal, Charles (1986), *Interpreting Greek Tragedy: Myth, Poetry, Text*. Ithaca and London: Cornell University Press.

Sewell, Richard (2007), *In the Theatre of Dionysos: Democracy and Tragedy in Ancient Athens*. Jefferson: McFarland and Co.

Shapiro, Michael J. (1989), 'Textualizing global politics', in James Der Derian and Michael Shapiro (eds), *International/Intertextual Relations: Postmodern Readings of World Politics*. Lexington: Lexington Books.

— (1997), *Violent Cartographies: Mapping Cultures of War*. Minneapolis: University of Minnesota Press.

— (2004), *Methods and Nations: Cultural Governance and the Indigenous Subject*. New York: Routledge.

Sharpe, Matthew (2002), 'Autonomy, reflexivity, tragedy: Notions of democracy in Camus and Castoriadis'. *Critical Horizons* 3.1.

Shien, Gi-Ming (1951), 'Being and nothingness in Greek and ancient philosophy'. *Philosophy East and West* 1.2.

Sidwell, Keith C. (2009), *Aristophanes the Democrat: The Politics of Satirical Comedy during the Peloponnesian War*. Cambridge: Cambridge University Press.

Signature Theatre (2008), 'Getting to know Mee'. *Signature Edition* July. http://signaturetheatre.org/0708/iphigenia_2.htm.

Silk, M. S. (ed.) (1996), *Tragedy and the Tragic: Greek Theatre and Beyond*. Oxford: Clarendon Press.

Silk, M. S. and J. P. Stern (1981), *Nietzsche on Tragedy*. Cambridge: Cambridge University Press.

Sinclair, R. K. (1988), *Democracy and Participation in Athens*. Cambridge: Cambridge University Press.

Sinclair, T. A. (1967), *A History of Greek Political Thought*. London: Routledge & Kegan Paul.

Singer, Max and Aaron Wildavsky (1993), *The Real World Order: Zones of Peace/Zones of Turmoil*. Chatham: Chatham House.

Slater, Niall W. (2002), *Spectator Politics: Metatheatre and Performance in Aristophanes*. Philadelphia: University of Pennsylvania Press.

Slaveva-Griffin, Svetla (2007), 'Philosophy and myth: A review of recent scholarship'. *The European Legacy* 12.2.

Slotkin, Richard (1973), *Regeneration Through Violence: The Mythology of the American Frontier, 1600–1860*. Middletown: Wesleyan University Press.

Smith, Douglas (2000), 'Introduction', in Friedrich Nietzsche. trans. and intro. Douglas Smith, *The Birth of Tragedy*. Oxford: Oxford University Press.

Snell, Bruno (1982), *The Discovery of the Mind in Greek Philosophy and Literature*. New York: Dover Publications.

Sommerstein, Alan H. (2010), *Aeaschylean Tragedy* (2nd edn). London: Duckworth.

Sourvinou-Inwood, Christiane (1989), 'Assumptions and the creation of meaning: Reading Sophocles' Antigone'. *Journal of Hellenic Studies* 109.

Sowerby, Robin (1995), *The Greeks: An Introduction to their Culture*. London and New York: Routledge.

Spatz, Louis (1982), *Aeschylus*. Boston: Twayne.

Spinks, Lee (2003), *Friedrich Nietzsche*. London: Routledge.

Steger, Manfred (2002), *Globalism: The New Market Ideology*. Lanham: Rowman and Littlefield.

Stein, Howard (2009), 'Theater as a humanizing force'. *Arion: A Journal of Humanities and the Classics* 16.3.

Steiner, George (1996), *The Death of Tragedy*. New Haven and London: Yale University Press.

— (2008), ' "Tragedy", Reconsidered', in Rita Felski (ed.), *Rethinking Tragedy*. Baltimore: Johns Hopkins University Press.

Stewart, Andrew (2008), *Classical Greece and the Birth of Western Art*. Cambridge: Cambridge University Press.

Stoessl, Franz (1952), 'Aeschylus as a political thinker'. *The American Journal of Philology* 73.2.

Suganami, Hidemi (1989), *The Domestic Analogy and World Order Proposals*. Cambridge: Cambridge University Press.

Taplin, Oliver (1999), 'Spreading the word through performance', in Simon Goldhill and Robin Osborne (eds), *Performance Culture and Athenian Democracy*. Cambridge: Cambridge University Press.

Tarnas, Richard (1991), *The Passion of the Western Mind: Understanding the Ideas That Have Shaped Our World*. New York: Ballantine Books.

— (1993), 'The 2500th anniversary of democracy: Lessons of Athenian democracy'. *PS: Political Science and Politics* 26.3.

Thomsen, Rudi (1972), *The Origin of Ostracism: A Synthesis*. Copenhagen: Gyldendal.

Thomson, George (1996), *Aeschylus and Athens: A Study in the Social Origins of Drama*. London: Lawrence and Wishart.

Thomson, Ruth (2006), '"Witnessing, weeping and outrage – Modern contexts and ancient woes in Euripides" the Trojan Women at the State Theatre Company of South Australia, November 2004'. *Didaskalia* 6.3, http://www.didaskalia.net/issues/vol6no3/thompson.html.

Thucydides. trans. Richard Crawley and intro. Lorna Harwick (1997), *The History of the Peloponnesian War*. Ware: Wordsworth Editions.

Tolbert Roberts, Jennifer (1994), *Athens on Trial: The Antidemocratic Tradition in Western Thought*. Princeton: Princeton University Press.

Tomasky, Michael (2008), 'It's all in the poetry – how Obama's vision and message of unity won over Iowa'. *The Guardian* 5 January, http://www.guardian.co.uk/world/2008/jan/05/barackobama.uselections2008.

Turner, Chad (2001), 'Perverted supplication and other inversions in Aeschylus' Danaid trilogy'. *The Classical Journal* 97.1.

Van Veeren, Elspeth (2009), 'Interrogating 24: Making sense of US counter-terrorism in the global war on terrorism'. *New Political Science* 31.3.

Vernant, Jean-Pierre (1981), 'Tension and ambiguities in Greek tragedy', in Jean-Pierre Vernant and Pierre Vidal-Naquet. trans. Janet Lloyd, *Tragedy and Myth in Ancient Greece*. Sussex: Harvester Press.

— (1981), 'The historical moment of tragedy in Greece: Some of the social and psychological conditions', in Jean-Pierre Vernant and Pierre Vidal-Naquet. trans. Janet Lloyd, *Tragedy and Myth in Ancient Greece*. Sussex: Harvester Press.

— (1992), 'Myth and tragedy', in Amelie Oksenberg Rorty (ed.), *Essays on Aristotle's Poetics*. Princeton: Princeton University Press.

— (2006), *Myth and Thought among the Greeks*. Cambridge: MIT Press.

Vickers, Michael (1997), *Pericles on Stage: Political Comedy in Aristophanes' Early Plays*. Austin: University of Texas Press.

Vidal-Naquet, Pierre (1996), 'Democracy: A Greek invention', in Pierre Leveque and Pierre Vidal-Naquet. trans. and ed. David Ames Curtis, *Cleisthenes the Athenian:*

An Essay on the Representation of Space and Time in Greek Political Thought from the End of the Sixth Century to the Death of Plato. New Jersey: Humanities Press.

Walker, R. B. J. (1988), *One World, Many Worlds: Struggles for a Just World Peace.* Boulder: Lynne Rienner.

Wasserstein, Bernard (2007), *Barbarism and Civilization: A History of Europe in our Time.* Oxford: Oxford University Press.

Weber, Cynthia (2001), *International Relations Theory: A Critical Introduction* (2nd edn). London: Routledge.

Weir Smyth, Herbert (1969), *Aeschylean Tragedy.* New York: Biblo and Tannen.

Wertenbaker, Timberlake (2004), 'The voices we hear', in Edith Hall, Fiona Macintosh and Amanda Wrigley (eds), *Dionysus since 69: Greek Tragedy at the Dawn of the Third Millennium.* Oxford: Oxford University Press.

Whitehead, Alfred North (1926), *Science and the Modern World.* New York: The Macmillan Company.

Widder, Nathan (2004), 'The relevance of Nietzsche to democratic theory: Micropolitics and the affirmation of difference'. *Contemporary Political Theory* 3.2.

Winkler, John J. and Froma I. Zeitlin (eds) (1990), *Nothing to Do with Dionysos? Athenian Drama in its Social Context.* Princeton: Princeton University Press.

— (1990), 'Introduction', in John J. Winkler and Froma I. Zeitlin (eds), *Nothing to Do with Dionysos? Athenian Drama in Its Social Context.* Princeton: Princeton University Press.

Winnington-Ingram, R. P. (1961), 'The Danaid trilogy of Aeschylus'. *The Journal of Hellenic Studies* 81.

Wolin, Sheldon (1993), 'Democracy: Electoral and Athenian'. *PS: Political Science and Politics* 26.3.

Woodruff, Paul (2008), *The Necessity of Theater: The Art of Watching and Being Watched.* Oxford: Oxford University Press.

Worcester, Kenton, Sally Avery Bermanzohn and Mark Ungar (2002), 'Introduction: Violence and politics', in Kenton Worcester, Sally Avery Bermanzohn and Mark Ungar (eds), *Violence and Politics: Globalization's Paradox.* New York and London: Routledge.

Young, Damon A. (2003), 'The democratic chorus: Culture, dialogue and polyphonic paideia'. *Democracy and Nature* 9.2.

— (2007), 'Sparta for our times'. *Meanjin* 66.2.

— (2008), *Distraction: A Philosopher's Guide to Being Free.* Melbourne: Melbourne University Press.

— (2008), 'On fiction and philosophy'. *Meanjin* 67.4.

Zelenak, Michael X. (1998), *Gender and Politics in Greek Tragedy.* New York: Peter Lang.

Index

www.ingramcontent.com/pod-product-compliance
Lightning Source LLC
Chambersburg PA
CBHW050441280326
41932CB00013BA/2193